URBAN RELIGION
AND THE
SECOND GREAT AWAKENING

URBAN RELIGION AND THE SECOND GREAT AWAKENING

Church and Society in Early National Baltimore

Terry D. Bilhartz

RUTHERFORD • MADISON • TEANECK
FAIRLEIGH DICKINSON UNIVERSITY PRESS
LONDON AND TORONTO: ASSOCIATED UNIVERSITY PRESSES

Associated University Presses
440 Forsgate Drive
Cranbury, NJ 08512

Associated University Presses
25 Sicilian Avenue
London WC1A 2QH, England

Associated University Presses
2133 Royal Windsor Drive
Unit 1
Mississauga, Ontario
Canada L5J 1K5

The paper used in this publication meets the requirements
of the American National Standard for Permanence of Paper
for Printed Library Materials Z39.48-1984.

Library of Congress Cataloging-in-Publication Data

Bilhartz, Terry D.
  Urban religion and the second great awakening.

  Bibliography: p.
  Includes index.
  1. Baltimore (Md.)—Church history. 2. Sociology,
Christian—Maryland—Baltimore. 3. Christian sects—
Maryland—Baltimore. I. Title.
BR560.B3B34 1986   277.52′6081   83-49455
ISBN 0-8386-3227-0 (alk. paper)

Printed in the United States of America

TO PATTY ANN

CONTENTS

Acknowledgments   9

Introduction: The Urban Challenge   11

Part One: The Churches Militant: Varieties of Structure,
      Method, and Belief
      1 Membership   19
      2 Leadership   28
      3 Clergy   38
      4 Discipline   52
      5 Worship   65

Part Two: The Militant Churches: The Effects of Religious Competition
      6 Revivalism   83
      7 Ecumenism   100
      8 Schism   117

Conclusion: The Baltimore Awakening in Perspective   134

APPENDIX A: Notes on Methodology   142
APPENDIX B: Vertical Categories: By Rank and Trade   146
APPENDIX C: Estimated Dates of Establishment of Houses of Worship   149
APPENDIX D: Clergy of Baltimore, 1790–1830   151

Tables   157

Notes   173

Select Bibliography   202

Index   232

ACKNOWLEDGMENTS

I began this project as a married but childless, young graduate student who was intrigued with the millennial and evangelical fervor of the early national period. Today I am a not-so-young father of two, assistant professor who remains fascinated with the color and excitement of the era of the Second Great Awakening. During my years of study, research, writing, and revising. I have become indebted to numerous scholars and institutions. I first wish to thank my mentor and friend Dewey Wallace of George Washington University for introducing me to this subject and for providing me with large doses of both guidance and encouragement. Likewise, I thank Professors Peter Hill, Howard Gillette, and James Horton, also of GWU, for their wise counsel and advice.

In the summer of 1980, I attended an NEH Seminar directed by Paul K. Conkin at Vanderbilt University. I emerged from this seminar with a clearer understanding of early national religion, a greater appreciation for precision in language, and a lengthy list of suggestions for transforming my dissertation into a publishable monograph. I am deeply and personally grateful to Professor Conkin for his invaluable comments on two separate drafts of this work. I also owe a debt of thanks to Karen Offen and Susan Bell of the Center for Research on Women at Stanford University for challenging me to consider the gender implications of the Second Great Awakening; to Naomi Lamoreaux, formerly of Johns Hopkins University, for introducing me to the SPSS procedures used in this study; to my graduate school companion Edward Angel for taking time from his research to encourage me in mine; to my colleague Randy Roberts of Sam Houston State University for his helpful editorial comments; and to my chairman Lee Olm for providing me with incentives to carry this project through to publication.

My appreciation also to the librarians and staffs at the following institutions for making their resources so readily available: The George Washington University Library; Wesley Theological Seminary Library; Enoch Pratt Free Library, Baltimore; Hall of Records, Annapolis; Maryland Historical Society, Baltimore; The University of Pennsylvania Library; The Library Company of Philadelphia; American Philosophical Society Library, Philadelphia; The Historical Society of Pennsylvania, Philadelphia; The Presbyterian Historical

Society, Philadelphia; St. Mark's Library, The General Theological Seminary, New York; The New York Public Library; Columbia University Library; The John Hay Library, Brown University; The Public Library of Providence; The Beinecke Rare Book and Manuscript Library, Yale University; American Antiquarian Society, Worchester; The Houghton Library, Harvard University; Massachusetts Historical Society, Boston; The Congregational Library, Boston; Boatwright Memorial Library, University of Richmond; University of Virginia Library; The University of North Carolina Library; William R. Perkins Library, Duke University; Vanderbilt University Library; and Green Library, Stanford University. I especially wish to thank Pablo A. Calvan of the Library of Congress, Rev. Edwin Schell of the Lovely Lane Museum, Baltimore; and F. Garner Ranney of the Maryland Diocesan Archives, Baltimore for providing assistance well beyond the normal call of duty. I also give a personal word of thanks to my great-aunt, Alice Ryan, and to Jim Morell for so generously providing me with lodging during my research trips to the Baltimore and Boston areas. Likewise, I thank the Philadelphia Center for Early American Studies and the American Philosophical Society for travel grants that helped subsidize the costs of research.

Finally, this work would never have been begun, much less completed, without the support and assistance of my wife, Patty Ann Bilhartz. From the very inception of the idea, Patty has been a part of this work. She has accompanied me on countless research trips, assisting me in library stacks and in nearby malls both by typing notecards and caring for our most precious commodities, Rocky and Teriann. Patty has typed and examined more drafts of this manuscript than either of us wish to recall, commenting on them in great detail with valuable criticism and expert editing. But, above all, Patty has been my companion on a wearisome and often lonely eight-year journey. We remain partners in all things.

INTRODUCTION
THE URBAN CHALLENGE

THE early national era was the formative age of American religion. In 1775 more colonists attended Congregational, Presbyterian, and Anglican churches than those of any other religious body. Within fifty years, however, these colonial giants stood in the shadows of the rapidly growing Methodist, Baptist, and Roman Catholic denominations. These changes were sudden, but indelible. To this day the religious profile of the nation, county by county, largely resembles the denominational complexion that emerged during these early decades of the republic.

What accounts for the dramatic alterations in the religious preferences of the American people? Immigration played a role, but only a minor role, for the most significant shifts in the church affiliation of Americans occurred during the Napoleonic years, when immigration slowed to a trickle. Land purchased from France and Spain brought thousands of Roman Catholics under United States jurisdiction, thus adjusting the denominational portrait of the country. But the transformation in the character of American religion was predominantly a consequence of the voluntary church system. In most states the revolution dethroned the ancient pattern of church establishment and placed all Christian denominations on equal footing before the law. No longer did the states dictate religious uniformity or provide church financial assistance. Generally, the various churches laid aside their exclusive claims on the kingdom, but to survive in the free religious marketplace, churches found it necessary to accentuate their distinctive attributes, and to persuade prospective converts why they should associate with a particular brand of Christianity. But while disestablishment bred religious diversity, it also raised the anxiety of countless Americans who believed that the future of the republic rested largely upon the ability of religious institutions to maintain a virtuous citizenry. Imbued with patriotism, early national churchmen, though natural competitors, stood shoulder to shoulder as comrades dedicated to the task of Christianizing American culture. Consequently, both church conflict and cooperation were major themes in early national religion.

By detailing the varied terrain of religious activity in early national Balti-

11

more, this study explores the development and consequences of the voluntary church system in one urban center during this critical era of ferment and change. As traditional church history, it underscores the great variations between denominations in membership, polity, clerical leadership, positions on social issues, doctrine, styles of worship, and methods of evangelism. As religious history in its broader sense, it attempts to identify the values and behavioral patterns that transcended denominational lines, and to connect the appearance of these forms of religiosity with the social pressures of the era that gave them birth. While not a microcosm of early national religion, this story of religious change in Baltimore sheds considerable light upon our understanding of the origins and consequences of the second great awakening, and upon how and why American denominations emerged as they did.

Selected by George Washington as America's city most likely to succeed, Baltimore during the early national period lived up to its high billing. While a community of 8,000 in 1782, by the first United States Census in 1790 Baltimore, with 13,503 inhabitants, was the fifth largest town in America. The population represented a diverse ethnic and national background. A strong majority was of English and Welsh extraction. Yet, with a thriving German-speaking community, a large urban black population, and a significant minority of Scotsmen alongside the smaller remnant of Irish and French, Baltimore even at 1790 had a definite cosmopolitan complexion.[1]

During the 1790s hundreds of Frenchmen and Africans fleeing the riot-torn island of Santo Domingo joined with the thousands of migrants from abroad and from nearby counties to settle in Baltimore. By the end of the decade the population soared to 26,514, and by 1810 reached 46,555. While the growth rate slowed after 1815, the second decade of the century brought a net gain of over 16,000 inhabitants. Now for the first time the majority of the citizenry was female—a demographic fact indicating the ascendancy of native over immigrant population. By the next census Baltimore was the third largest city in the United States, with a population of 80,990.[2]

Baltimore's rapid growth is particularly impressive when contrasted with its surrounding countryside. Between 1790 and 1830, while seven of the nineteen counties of Maryland suffered a net decrease in population, and while the state as a whole expanded less than 43%, Baltimore increased its 1790 population over 497%. This rate of increase was not equaled by any other urban community in America.[3]

The key to such phenomenal growth was Baltimore's economic dominance over its hinterland. Geographically, Baltimore had many advantages: an excellent harbor, nearby streams capable of providing power for flour, metal, and textile mills, and easily accessible water and land routes to Philadelphia and Virginia. Such a geography made Baltimore the natural outlet for goods of the Susquehanna River region. Northern Maryland and southern Pennsylvania farmers brought their grain to Baltimore mills for preparation and exportation. Paid in cash, farmers turned to Baltimore merchants and craftsmen to supply their needs. Millers hired smiths and carpenters to build and maintain their machinery. Shippers sought the work of mariners and shipbuilders. Increased housing starts demanded the skills of the construction trades. The growing working class supported scores of groceries and small retail stores. Even specialized luxury crafts such as piano or clock making flourished. In sum, city growth allowed a specialization of industry that in turn provided numerous opportunities for economic success.[4]

For some, rapid city growth brought escalating wealth; for others, it brought misery and poverty. Particularly noticeable among the dregs of society were the rising number of Baltimore blacks. Comprising about 12% of the population in 1790, the percentage of blacks increased to 22% in 1810 and to nearly 24% in 1830. Although after 1800 most city blacks were free rather than slave, without suffrage or the right of unrestricted assembly, and with few exceptions without property, even free blacks lived impoverished lives with no hope of advancement.[5] Alongside this serving class was a rising percentage of propertyless Caucasian artisans and laborers. In 1804 about four in ten white Baltimorean heads of households owned taxable property. A decade later less than three in ten owned property. Throughout this period it became increasingly difficult for new arrivals to work their way up from apprentices to journeymen to master craftsmen.[6]

Just as rapid growth brought to the economic sector both increased wealth and poverty, it presented Baltimore churches both opportunities and difficulties. On the positive side, the constant influx of new prospects made numerical church growth a relatively easy task. Also the wealth within the city provided the monetary resources necessary to build and sustain houses of worship and to acquire gifted clerics. While scores of churches scattered across Maryland were without ministerial aid, Baltimore churches multiplied, prospered, and assumed the principal leadership of their denomination. As the home of America's first Roman Catholic bishop, seminary, and cathedral, Baltimore was the locus of early American Catholicism.[7] Baltimore churches housed the organizational meetings that resulted in the Methodist Episcopal, Methodist Protestant, and United Brethren denominations, as well as the Protestant Episcopal Diocese of Maryland, the Presbytery of Baltimore, the Baltimore Baptist Association, and the General Synod of the Evangelical Lutheran Church.[8] Baltimore was also the site of the first New Jerusalem Swedenborgian Church in America, and the first Unitarian church south of the Mason Dixon line.[9] With such influential churches, Baltimore held a strong claim to being the religious capital of the young republic.

On the debit side, Baltimore's rapid expansion added burdens to urban congregations. Reaching the ever-widening array of ethnic and status groups, providing the basic necessities of life for the growing numbers of urban poor, and maintaining high standards of morality amidst a mobile and often rootless population were awesome tasks for city congregations. Moreover, with urban growth came secular diversions, which distracted even the godly from the tasks set before them. Theaters, taverns, prostitutes, unruly sailors, and Sabbath-breaking entrepreneurs were but a few of the corrupting influences that permeated the city environs. But for young, ambitious, white males—those whom churches needed most for their survival—the greatest temptation of all was the glitter of economic opportunity. To win over this crucial class, even while keeping the growing masses walking the straght and narrow, was indeed an ambitious challenge.

URBAN RELIGION
AND THE
SECOND GREAT AWAKENING

PART ONE
THE CHURCHES MILITANT: VARIETIES
OF STRUCTURE,
METHOD, AND BELIEF

1
MEMBERSHIP

HOW many attended church, and where did they attend? In 1790 eleven churches representing nine denominations worshiped in Baltimore.[1] The largest denomination was the Protestant Episcopal Church, which included approximately one-twelfth of the population. It is not surprising that the pre-revolutionary established church of Maryland held the highest percentage of nominal members. Such was of little consolation to Joseph Bend, the senior pastor of St. Paul's parish who, knowing all too well that Baltimore Episcopalians were more numerous at the graveyard than at worship, frequently bemoaned to his rural associates the need not so much to increase as to arouse a spiritually decrepit membership.[2] Behind the Episcopalians in 1790 were the Methodists, Roman Catholics, and German Lutherans, each comprising about 7% of the population. Slightly smaller, encompassing about one-twentieth of the populace, were the Presbyterians and German Reformed. Next in size were the Friends and the United Brethren, with about three and two percent respectively. Finally, the Baptists in 1790 were surprisingly small, with only a single congregation of well under a hundred individuals.[3]

These estimates suggest that in 1790 about four in nine Baltimoreans were at least nominal churchgoers. Comparing these figures with other locales or with the nation is difficult since most estimates rest upon "official" church membership and not the church-attending membership. Undoubtedly churchgoers outnumbered official members. Nevertheless, since only about 5% of Americans in 1790 were official members, it is probable that the proportion of Baltimore churchgoers easily surpassed the national average.[4] This might be attributed to the city's unique religious heritage. More likely, it was a function of the urban environment. The city's wealth sustained houses of worship at the very time that rural churches, suffering financially from the pains of disestablishment, fell into dilapidation. Furthermore, the specialization of labor within the urban economy provided growing numbers of Baltimoreans with the leisure to spend increased time in religious activities. In these ways the city shielded its congregations from the worst of the postrevolutionary religious depression. At any rate Baltimore, at least statistically, never experienced the extreme religious apathy that allegedly characterized the 1790s.

Between 1790 and 1810, changes in the ethnic composition of the city and mutations in the religious preferences of native Baltimoreans worked to the advantage of the Roman Catholics and Methodists. Roman Catholic congregations benefited from the immigration of Santo Domingo refugees. During the 1790s alone Catholic membership tripled, and by 1810 it was the city's largest denomination, with about 12% of the population.[5] Only the evangelical success of the Methodists challenged this rate of growth. In 1810 about one in ten Baltimoreans regularly attended Methodist houses. Meanwhile Episcopalians, Lutherans, and Baptists maintained their respective 1790 proportions. Also growing, but at a slower rate than the city, were the Presbyterians, Friends, German Reformed, and United Brethren. During this period one additional group, the Church of New Jerusalem (Swedenborgian), appeared in Baltimore, although it remained small, attracting less than one percent of the population.

Not until after 1810 did English Protestants make significant inroads into the city. This growth stemmed principally from the continued success of the Methodists. By 1830 about one in six were Methodist, one in thirteen Episcopal, and one in twenty Presbyterian. Meanwhile, Roman Catholics maintained their one-in-eight proportion. Growth among English Protestants and Catholics was needed to offset the dwindling percentage of German Protestant churchgoers. In 1830 the combined number of German Lutherans, Reformed, and United Brethren totaled no more than four percent of the city. Similarly, Friends, Baptists, and Swedenborgians, as well as Baltimore's newest body—the Unitarians—each attracted under one percent of the population. Overall, in 1830 about one in two Baltimoreans attended church. While this represents only a modest proportional increase from the 1790 proportion, the total number of churchgoers rose over 650%—a considerable accomplishment for America's most rapidly expanding community. Since less than one in four Americans in 1830 were official members, Baltimoreans probably still attended church more than the typical citizen.[6]

Naturally, not all segments of the community were equally likely to be churchgoers. First-generation German immigrants, determined to maintain their culture and language, viewed the church as the vital center of their community. The church was a sanctuary for their ethnicity. It was the primary public arena where Germans retreated to converse in their native tongue, introduce their children to potential marriage partners, and develop both business and personal support groups. As a result, few were delinquent in their religious obligations.[7] In contrast, the black community was on the whole institutionally neglected. Although the Methodists did evangelize actively among blacks, with no exclusive house of worship before 1802, and with no right to unsupervised assembly, blacks generally worshiped in only the galleries or back pews of the white congregations. Slaves in particular were expected to attend only the denomination of their masters, who tended to be Episcopalians or Presbyterians. Since the styles of piety of these denominations were not well suited to the tastes of the slave community, the religious needs of the enslaved often were met by informal fellowship within the black community. Consequently, while about five in nine whites attended church, only about three in eight blacks were church affiliated.[8]

An examination of some 3,000 Baltimore churchgoers suggests that occupational status as well as ethnic orientation influenced church attendance.[9] Low-status laborers attended church less than did the average urbanite. This finding is not surprising, for lower-class workers were spatially more mobile, had less leisure, and perhaps gained fewer financial benefits by church association. Moreover, churches recruited most rigorously for those most able to fill important positions of lay leadership and to contribute toward the financial needs of the congregation. Laborers, in short, were not the best catch for voluntary churches struggling for survival. For similar reasons certain upper-status occupations were also underrepresented among churchgoers. For instance, since most denominations frowned upon the bawdy behavior associated with city taverns, few tavern keepers or innkeepers were even nominally church affiliated.

While laborers and tavern keepers remained underchurched thoughout the era, the occupational and status groups most represented among churchgoers shifted during the period. Before 1815, skilled artisans were the most likely church prospects. Craftsmen in the clothing trades such as tailors, weavers, and cordwainers were particularly active. By 1830, however, workers in white-collar occupations overwhelmingly dominated local congregations. Lawyers, physicians, teachers, city officials, proprietors, and clerks were more likely to attend church than the typical Baltimoreans.

Church attendance, while significantly related to one's occupational status, was even more dramatically a function of gender. Throughout the national period women outnumbered men both in the pews and as communicants at the altars of Baltimore congregations. In 1790 about seven in ten women (as opposed to three in ten men) were nominal churchgoers. Over the ensuing forty years Protestant clerics, with the support of their predominantly female parishioners, engineered numerous campaigns designed to win back the men who had deserted the church fold. Yet, despite the innovative "new measures" of evangelism and energized efforts at recruitment, the female parishioners succeeded more in increasing their own numbers than in reenlisting their lost brethren. By 1830 the proportion of church-affiliated Baltimore males had risen only marginally to about four in ten, while the number of churchgoing women increased to about seven in eight. Hence by 1830, with more than seventy percent of the church attenders female, Baltimore congregations were well on their way to becoming "feminine" institutions.[10]

The broad trends outlined above did not affect all denominations, much less individual congregations, in identical ways. On the contrary, the occupational and gender analyses indicate a distinct profile for each denomination. As a rule, the proportion of female to male churchgoers was higher among the less revivalistic denominations. For instance, at Episcopal churches, female confirmands consistently outnumbered males by at least a three-to-one margin, while in revivalistic Methodist and Associate Reformed congregations, female members exceeded males by about a two-to-one ratio.[11] Among communicants, the gender disparity between revivalistic and nonrevivalistic denominations was even more apparent. Specifically, about eight in ten communicants in Baltimore Episcopal and German Reformed congregations were females, while seven in ten Presbyterian and only two in three Methodist communicants were women.[12]

Each denomination also had a distinct status profile. The religious body that deviated most significantly from the occupational tendencies of the combined sample of churchgoers was the Roman Catholic Church. This denomination more than any other in Baltimore embraced a considerable number of lower-class laborers. Around the turn of the century a majority of the heads of households drawn from St. Peter's Pro-Cathedral baptismal register were either not listed in the city directories—and therefore most likely poor laborers—or were specifically identified as unskilled workers. Meanwhile, only 17% were white-collar workers. While the percentage of unskilled gradually declined and the proportion of white-collar Catholics rose, this drift toward white-collar church participation was much slower for Catholics than Protestants. Throughout the period the Catholic Church in Baltimore remained skewed toward the lower classes, and was significantly underrepresented among city officials, professionals, and proprietors. Moreover, even within status ranks, Catholics generally owned less property than Protestants.

In contrast, Presbyterians clustered at the top of the social ladder. Around 1800 the First Presbyterian Church was the only congregation in the city with a majority of its male churchgoers employed in white-collar occupations. The mean tax assessment of these white-collar workers more than doubled the average assessment of non-Presbyterian white-collar employees. By 1815 over two-thirds of its membership fell within the upper-status occupations. In 1830 the congregation was underrepresented in every semi-skilled and artisan trade with the single exception of the shipping industry. While not quite so prestigious, Baltimore's Second Presbyterian and Associate Reformed Presbyterian congregations approached the occupational profile of First Church. Throughout the period Baltimore Presbyterians were far more likely to be wealthy professionals and proprietors than were members of any other large denomination. However, the few Presbyterian artisans actually owned less taxable property than non-Presbyterian artisans.

Unlike the Presbyterians, the upper-class orientation of Episcopalians developed more slowly. Initially, the Protestant Episcopal Church maintained its child-of-the-establishment posture with a membership that closely approximated a cross-section of the population. While keeping its share of unskilled laborers, by 1815 the denomination was underrepresented among artisans and over-proportioned among the white collared. This trend continued so that by 1830 a majority of Episcopal males worked in the highest-status occupations. One should note that these changes do not necessarily imply an upward mobility among the original families sampled, but more likely a loss of middle-class Episcopalians to other denominations.

If the Roman Catholic Church embraced the poor, and the Presbyterian and Episcopalian denominations increasingly served the social elites, the Methodist Episcopal Church remained the church of the middle class. At 1800 about one in two Caucasian Methodists were artisans, while about three in ten were white-collar workers. Despite a yearly turnover in membership of up to 10%, these proportions changed little throughout the period.[13] Thus, unlike most other groups, the Methodists did not experience a decline in their percentage of artisans after 1815; nor did they drift toward a white-collar orientation. This does not imply, however, that Methodists lacked wealth. On the contrary, in both 1804 and 1815 a greater percentage of Methodists was found within the wealthiest ten percent of the property holders than that of any other denomination. In short, the Methodist church, Baltimore's most consistently growing religious body, included a nucleus of wealthy professionals and city officials, while maintaining a dominant and remarkably resilient skilled-artisan profile.

Closely akin to the Methodists, both structurally and theologically, was the Old Otterbein Church, the mother church of the United Brethren denomination. Two-thirds of its males held skilled-artisan positions. Their above-average wealth, coupled with the extreme assessment of a handful of professionals, gave this German-speaking congregation the highest per capita wealth of all denominations. Unfornately, no baptismal records exist for the German Lutheran congregation. However, an analysis of those Lutherans who contributed to a building program in 1806 suggests that this congregation, while less wealthy than the United Brethren, shared its artisan-class orientation. Like other Germans in the city, many in this congregation were employed in construction and food trades. Members of the remaining German-speaking congregation, the German Reformed Church, apparently were less likely to be white-collar or artisan workers than their Wesleyan or Lutheran brethren. In both 1800 and 1815 the social complexion of this congregation approximated the lower-class pattern of the Roman Catholics. Largely owing to the rising proportion of lower-level white-collar employees, such as clerks and accountants, the church eventually lost its lower-class character. Yet, in 1830 the typical German Reformed male probably still ranked below other German churchgoers in status and wealth.

Neither complete baptismal records nor membership lists allow a confident analysis of the occupational status of Baltimore's smaller denominations. For example, the Baptist names came from lists of couples married by Pastor Lewis Richards of First Church and of members received into the Ebenezar Church between 1822 and 1830. Interpreting the occupational status of the newlyweds is particularly difficult. At the turn of the century over half of the husbands were not listed in any directory, either because of low status or because they moved from Baltimore. Of those listed, few held white-collar jobs, but their age may largely account for this. An examination of the husbands married in 1815 indicates a significant decrease in the percent not listed, and a similar increase in the proportion of white-collar workers. Perhaps this congregation indeed was shifting toward a white-collar orientation. The fact that ten of the seventeen members received in Ebenezar were white-collar workers supports the hypothesis that some Baptist congregations by the 1820s had lost a lower-class orientation.

The profile of Friends rests upon a list of males witnessing the marriage vows for the Baltimore Quarterly Meeting. Again the large percentage not found in city directories probably in part stems from non-Baltimoreans witnessing the event. Still, the evidence from those sampled suggests that Quakers were overrepresented among public officials, and in the clothing and leather trades. It is likely that the Friends—like the Methodists and United Brethren—were dominantly middle-class artisans. Similarly, while the sample is small, the analysis of the Swedenborgian males who signed the church constitution in 1799 and the few who appeared on the baptismal records during the 1810s indicates that most members of the New Jerusalem Church were low-propertied artisans. In dramatic contrast, the fathers of infants baptized at Baltimore's other non-Trinitarian congregation—the First Independent Unitarian Church—consisted overwhelmingly of merchants, physicians, and lawyers.

The clustering of occupational status is even more apparent at the congregational than the denominational level. Moreover, city growth exacerbated the tendency toward congregational homogeneity. In 1800 most denominations in Baltimore had only a single congregation. Even though each reflected the ascendency of a particular occupational class, each still included significant minorities from all levels of society. By 1830 a growing city supplied two or more congregations within the larger denominations. New churches that were located in formerly unchurched neighborhoods outside the central town seemingly drew away lower-class members from the original churches. This led to greater occupational diversity between churches of the same denominations, and to more socially homogeneous congregations.

The Episcopalians best illustrate this tendency. In 1800 only two Protestant Episcopal congregations served Baltimore—St. Paul's Church and Christ Church. Each was located in the inner city, within a quarter-mile radius of the courthouse. These congregations represented a general cross-section of the community. During the next decade the expansion of the city, coupled with internal vestry problems, created the need for two additional Protestant Episcopal houses of worship.[14] One of these newly established congregations, Trinity Church, was located beyond the inner ring of downtown churches and near Fells Point, the harbor area of Baltimore. Owing partly to its location, Trinity Church had greater appeal to the middle and lower social ranks than either the St. Paul's parish congregations, or the other newly established Protestant Episcopal congregation of St. Peter's. Even as Trinity Church attracted lower-class drifters, the proportion of white-collar workers among the other Protestant Episcopal congregations dramatically increased. By 1815 St. Paul's had undergone a rapid transformation in its social composition, shifting from a balanced cross-section of the community to a distinctly higher-class orientation. Once this transition was complete, the social complexion of

St. Paul's parish reached its equilibrium and remained constant throughout the remainder of the period.

This does not imply, however, that a congregation's status profile was simply a matter of church location. Rather, the data indicate that for both the wealthier inner city and the poorer peripheral congregations, the same denomination attracted the same status type in all parts of the city. For example, while the class composition of Trinity Protestant Episcopal near Fells Point was oriented more toward the lower class than the social complexion of either St. Paul's parish or St. Peter's, and in fact approximated the norm among the Methodists of Baltimore City Station, nevertheless, when compared with the Methodists of Fells Point, Trinity Church ranked considerably higher in status. Thus in any given neighborhood the white-collar workers were more likely to be Presbyterian or Episcopalian; the skilled artisans, Methodists or United Brethren; and the unskilled workers, Roman Catholic.

Church location also influenced the gender profile of the congregation. Churches in Fells Point had higher percentages of female churchgoers than did churches located within the central business districts. Perhaps this reflected a greater anxiety, or a stronger female bonding among women with husbands out at sea. More likely, it simply reflected the inability of churches in Fells Point to appeal to lower-class dock workers and sailors. Finally, while the location of the church affected the gender ratio of congregations, it did not override the influence of denomination upon church attendance. For instance, a smaller proportion of Methodist men worshiped at Fells Point than in the city station houses, but in both the inner city and harbor areas, a larger percentage of males attended revivalistic Methodist congregations than their neighboring, less revivalistic Episcopal houses of worship.

In summary, Baltimore churches throughout the early national era were unusually strong, because between four in nine to one in two urban dwellers at least nominally attended church. While the Methodists and Roman Catholics experienced the greatest growth, Episcopalians and Presbyterians remained large and influential. Ethnicity, gender, and status influenced church involvement. Generally, blacks and lower-class white households were least active, while the most active church attenders shifted during the period from middle-class artisans to white-collar families. Throughout the era women were far more likely to attend religious services than men, although the female majorities were less pronounced in the more revivalistic denominations. City growth, by allowing several congregations to serve the same denomination, tended to create more socially homogeneous congregations. The older, inner-city congregations were more affluent than the newer, peripherally located church houses. Yet in all neighborhoods significantly higher percentages of Presbyterians, Episcopalians, and Unitarians were white collared than in other denominations. Similarly, the membership in Methodist and Catholic congregations—the largest and most rapidly growing denominations—clustered around the artisan and laboring classes.

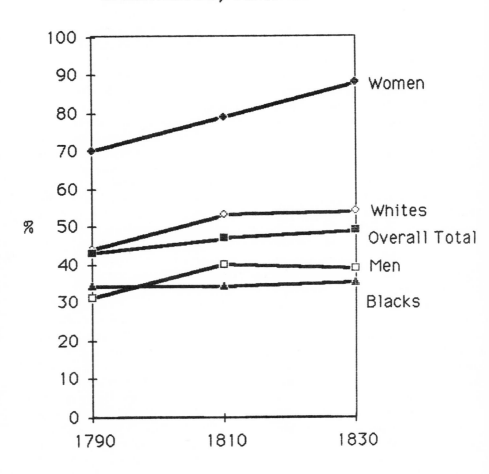

Graph 1
Percentage of Nominal Churchgoers
in Baltimore by Gender and Race

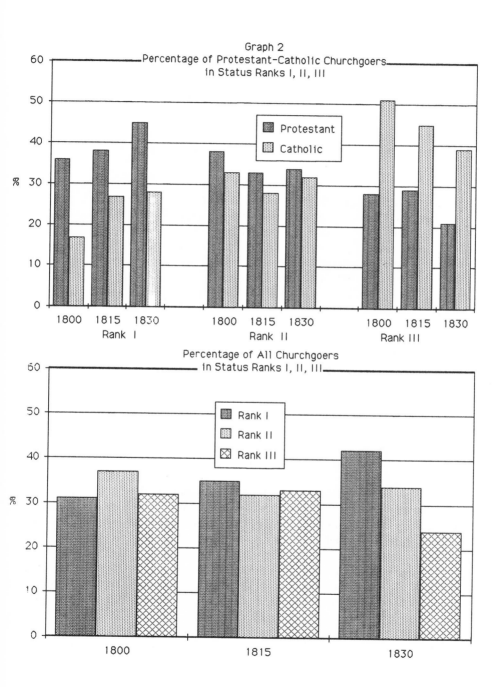

Graph 2
Percentage of Protestant-Catholic Churchgoers
in Status Ranks I, II, III

Percentage of All Churchgoers
in Status Ranks I, II, III

2
LEADERSHIP

SINCE Jesus awarded the keys of the kingdom to the Apostle Peter, Christians have squabbled over matters of church government. What was the constitution of the New Testament church? Does the Bible prescribe a particular ecclesiastic polity? Does the local community of believers have the right to establish for themselves the parameters of church activity, or does such authority lie in a higher ecclesiastical power such as a presbytery, prelate, or pope? During the early national era, Baltimore churchmen debated these questions with great intensity. Few other issues provoked such controversy. In this chapter I shall describe the fundamental differences in the constitutions of Baltimore's religious establishments, and speculate on reasons why polity issues were so important during this era. Finally, after presenting an analysis of the voters and office holders in the various Baltimore denominations, I shall conclude with the ironic observation that despite the great diversity of church constitutions, congregational decision-making across denominational lines was remarkably similar.

Baltimore housed a wide variety of church constitutions. At one extreme stood the Baptist, Independent Unitarian, and New Jerusalem congregations. Although doctrinally diverse, each of these bodies embraced a similar congregational church polity. With no bishop, synod, or pope to intervene in local affairs, the voting majority in each church formulated its own interpretation of scripture and imposed its own doctrinal and moral standards. Authority to select and ordain ministers, receive and expel members, and procure and release property resided solely in the decisions of the church electorate.[1]

Baltimore Friends also maintained a strong congregational consciousness. Their congregations placed the administration of all spiritual and temporal concerns in the hands of the Monthly Meeting, the basic structural unit and the unit of individual membership for the denomination. While the Monthly Meeting did yield to Quarterly and Yearly Meetings, these latter bodies were only quantitatively more authoritative since all Friends recognized in good standing by the Monthly Meeting could participate in the higher-level proceedings.[2]

Baltimore's Presbyterian, Associate Reformed, and German Reformed

28

bodies granted to voting members the authority to select or veto ministers and elect ruling elders. Together the minister and elders formed the committee, session, or consistory that received and disciplined members and administered the congregation's temporal concerns. Ultimate authority for the denominations, however, rested in the presbytery or classis. These legislative and judicial bodies—composed of the minister and representative elder from neighboring sister congregations—ordained ministerial candidates, settled disputes between local congregations, and transmitted area concerns via duly elected delegates to the higher denominational courts.[3]

Baltimore Lutherans shared a similar church polity. In both the German and English fellowships, the voting members elected their own trustees, elders, and deacons, and selected their own pastor from among Lutheran ministers. While each office carried specific independent responsibilities, the Church Council as the composite of all elected officials rendered the major decisions affecting the entire congregation. The Church Council also sent the pastor and several lay deputies to the annual synodical meeting of the Pennsylvania Ministerium. This association principally served as a ministerial licensing board, and an advisory council for congregations under its jurisdiction.[4]

Several Baltimore denominations advocated an episcopacy, although they differed considerably in their understanding of episcopal authority. Resembling the polity of the Church of England was the constitution of the Protestant Episcopal churches. These bodies accepted the Anglican argument that the Christian church always had been governed by three distinct orders—bishops, presbyters, and deacons—and that without a bishop as the successor of the apostles, the church was not present. However, rather than delegating complete power to the prelates, Protestant Episcopal polity divided authority among the bishops, ministers, and laity. Each congregation elected a vestry of lay officials who appointed (but did not ordain) its ministry, managed church property, and sent lay deputies and its ministers to the annual meetings of the Diocese of Maryland. This body of lay and clerical delegates examined candidates for the ministry, and judged the communicants and ministers accused of misconduct. The convention also elected a bishop, who presided over the diocese and fulfilled the episcopal functions of ordination and confirmation. The highest council of the Protestant Episcopal Church was the General Convention. This national arm of the denomination consisted of a house of bishops and a house of deputies comprised of an equal number of lay and ordained delegates. Together the bishops and deputies delivered the final word in matters of church doctrine and administration.[5]

Baltimore's Methodist Episcopal stations also inherited their basic organizational structure from the Church of England. But unlike the Protestant Episcopalians, Methodists viewed the bishop only as a superintendent within the order of presbyters, denied both the accuracy and necessity of a line of apostolic succession, and claimed that their episcopal polity was only the most humanely expedient—not the divinely decreed—form of church government. Yet if the Methodist bishop was without a sacrosanct garb, he none-theless held greater power than any other Protestant official. Acting alone, unchecked by any ministerial or lay council, the Methodist bishop defined the circuits that the itinerant ministers were to cover, assigned his preachers to fill these openings, and appointed presiding elders to aid him in super-intending the traveling connection. His other episcopal functions, however, were more restricted. For instance, he could only ordain ministerial candi-dates approved by the Annual Conferences, and bishops-elect duly chosen by the General Conference. These legislative conferences differed from the higher courts of most other Protestant denominations in that no lay delegates participated. Only in the Quarterly Conference—the governing board of the local station that managed church property and disciplined its membership—were Methodist laity included in the denomination's councils.[6]

Baltimore's other Wesleyan bodies, however, did allow some lay repre-sentation. Both the German-speaking United Brethren and the African Methodist Episcopal denominations sent both lay preachers and ordained itinerants to the annual and general conferences; otherwise these bodies shared the same organizational structure as the Methodist Episcopal Church. The Methodist Protestant Church, in contrast, not only opened its confer-ences to the laity, but also replaced the episcopate with annually elected con-ference presidents.[7]

The remaining congregations of Baltimore were Roman Catholic. Holding firmly to the doctrine of the papacy, they insisted that the Roman pontiff, as the successor of St. Peter and the Vicar of Christ, had been given divine authority to govern the universal church. Consequently, all ecclesiastical power rested with those in hierarchical communion with the pope. Any pastor or communicant who refused to submit to his jursdiction was heretical and schismatic. Although the Baltimore Diocesan Synod of 1791 placed Catholic property in the hands of elected trustees and not the Archbishop and his successors, the laity had no authority to interfere in any spiritual matter. Furthermore, Catholicism emphatically vested the right of appointing and dismissing pastors in the bishops.[8]

For Baltimore churchmen, polity differences were not inconsequential technicalities. Indeed, few issues provoked so much controversy. Using both the pulpit and press, Baltimore pastors prepared parishioners to understand the peculiarities of their church polity. Often young clergymen won their de-nominational laurels by articulating the classical arguments in favor of their brand of polity. James Kemp and J. P. K. Henshaw, two Baltimore Episcopa-lians who began their careers with scholarly publications defending episcopal authority, eventually were elected to the episcopacy.[9] Occasionally, the high-level argumentation deteriorated into name-calling brawls. In 1807 the Methodist George Bourne rebutted the stinging indictment of an anonymous Episcopalian who not only denied the validity of the Methodist episcopacy because it lacked a direct line of apostolic succession, but also insinuated that, owing to this deficiency, women married by Methodist ministers were begetting bastard children.[10] Equally as passionate were Protestant castigations of Roman Catholic polity as "dangerous" and "unAmerican."[11]

While contests over church government were not unique to this era, their intensity was partly a product of the political environment of postrevolutionary America. After the Maryland Constitution of 1776 disestablished the Anglican Church, church survival depended solely upon the ability of congregations to attract contributing members. The competition encouraged each church to emphasize its unique attributes. Advocating the superiority of a particular church polity was one way to separate one denomination from its rivals without denouncing all competitors as unChristian.[12] The debates over church polity also reflected a larger, culture-wide preoccupation with matters of governments. Confronted with the tasks of erecting and revising new governments, many Americans of the era understood the complexities of constitutional theory. Few generations have been so alert to political processes, or so committed to principles of republican government. In an age when all sources of authority were called into question, churches struggling to survive could ill afford to have their constitution fail to pass the test of scrutiny. Given the political climate, it is not surprising that the Roman Catholics, Episcopalians, and Methodists—those with the more authoritarian system of government and hence most prone to attacks by critics of republican bent— expended the greatest effort defending the legitimacy of their denominational polity.[13]

As the above summary suggests, polity differences between Baltimore congregations were both substantial and polemically exploitable. Some denominations allowed local congregations to select their own ministers and erect their own doctrinal and moral standards; others did not. But while the range of local authority varied, several common features blurred denominational differences. For instance, all incorporated congregations stood as equals before the law. Maryland law placed corporate responsibilities in the hands of male trustees. As the local congregation's legal overseers, the trustees had authority to sue, raise and disburse funds, and purchase and sell property. Law required that the selection process of trustees be specified in the act of incorporation. Although the eligible voters and candidates for trustees varied, most congregations followed the custom of the era, which limited the franchise to white male contributors (or pewholders) over twenty-one years of age.[14]

There were a few exceptions. The constitution of the First Independent Unitarian Church made special provisions for unmarried female pewholders. These females could vote in church elections, although their votes were cast by proxy.[15] First Baptist also granted women at least minimal political privileges. From its establishment, females, although not eligible to vote in church affairs, could instruct male members in their knowledge of the moral uprightness of the candidates for membership. In 1810 the church even approved a resolution allowing female members "to speak and vote at ... business meetings." However, the resolution added that "this privilege would continue until otherwise determined by the male members."[16] The only other religious groups with more generous policies toward female participation were the Friends, who granted full equality to their female members, and a small, quasi-religious group that called itself the "First Philosophical and Evangelical Association of Baltimore." This association was considered peculiar by the religious community in general for such unorthodox practices as the substitution of water for bread and wine in the Lord's Supper, the insistence on extemporaneous preaching and prayer, and the inclusion within its doctrinal statement of a secular creed that affirmed the importance of securing "personal liberty, private property," and guarding "against monopolies."[17] These exceptions only enhanced the well-established pattern among the more orthodox, which excluded females from the active politics of the local congregations.

A second group often excluded from the political life of Baltimore congregations was the black community, which represented up to 18% of the city's churchgoers. About one-third of the churchgoing blacks were slaves and, as slaves, disenfranchised from church political participation. Most of the remaining religiously affiliated blacks attended Roman Catholic, Episcopal, or Methodist churches.[18] These free blacks rarely participated in local congregational decision-making. With only one exception, Protestant Episcopal congregations restricted voting privileges to white male pewholders. Similarly, while Catholic bodies did not explicitly disenfranchise black communicants, their pewholding requirements indirectly excluded most blacks, as well as many whites, from the church electorate.

Methodists were more generous in allowing blacks the opportunity to participate in the affairs of the church. Some Methodist Episcopal blacks even held key leadership positions, such as deacons, elders, and local preachers. These leaders attained some degree of professional status among both blacks and whites, and frequently were the principal exhorters before blacks in city churches and before mixed audiences at summer camp meetings.[19] Still, the overall opportunity for black participation was unimpressive. To illustrate, the Methodist *Discipline* provided that "coloured preachers and official members shall have all the privileges which are usual to others in the district and quarterly conferences, where the usages of the country do not forbid it." When Maryland in 1806 prohibited black suffrage in state elections, Baltimore Methodists also disenfranchised blacks in church elections. Thus, despite the fact that blacks composed over one-third of the total Methodist Episcopal membership, at least after 1806 they were barred from all levels of church political participation.[20]

Frustrated at this second-class status, in 1816 approximately one-seventh of the Baltimore black membership broke off from the white-dominated mother denomination to join Richard Allen's and Daniel Coker's movement in establishing the African Methodist Episcopal denomination.[21] The local schismatics incorporated under the name "The African Methodist Bethel Church of Baltimore." They ratified a constitution that granted all temporal authority to five elected trustees, and limited eligibility for this office to free Africans who had been associated with the society for at least one year. The constitution also provided that all spiritual concerns be regulated by conventions of colored ministers and lay members, elected by the male members of the church. This schism among black Methodists created a bitter struggle between the Sharp Street Methodist Episcopal congregation and the independent Bethel African Methodist Episcopal Church. The new denomination never won over a majority of Baltimore's black Methodists, but by 1830 its two independent, self-governing, and self-supporting congregations did minister to nearly one thousand souls.[22]

Significant numbers of blacks participated actively in only one other Baltimore congregation, St. James African Protestant Episcopal Church. This body—unlike its African Methodist Episcopal predecessors—received endorsement from and remained in communion with its parent denomination. Organized in 1824 under the leadership of a recently ordained black Episcopal minister, William Levington, the congregation secured the financial aid of white benefactors, erected a house of worship, and in 1828 elected its first vestry. The constitution limited eligibility for the office of vestry to "free" blacks who contributed at least one dollar annually to the church's treasury.[23] This restriction excluded both slaves and free whites from the office. The franchise, however, included all contributing adult male members, both free and enslaved. This liberal election policy created quite a controversy, and forced the vestry to defend its position with a printed tract. Drawing upon scriptural authority, the vestry stood firm and concluded with the emphatic plea: "Can a wise man and a feeling heart, suppose that we, some of whom have felt the yoke of bondage, should draw a line of separation? No: let the day be darkened forever on which we should do it. Have we not all one father? Hath not one God created us? ... Shall we be partial in the house of God? ... No we remember them that are in bonds as bound with them ourselves."[24] This controversial defense of the political rights of slaves challenged established social mores, and made it more difficult for the trustees to secure financial assistance from white benefactors. Although remaining small and impoverished, St. James was the only Protestant Episcopal Church and the only one of three bodies in the city in which large numbers of black churchgoers actively participated in the life of the local church.

To summarize, in basing the franchise on race, sex, age, and wealth, churches imitated state election laws that excluded blacks, women, and the propertyless from the polls. Theoretically, local church government, at least in terms of the election of trustees, was neither more nor less restrictive than American politics in general. But owing to the substantial number of blacks in Baltimore, and the overwhelming female majority in the churches, the percentage of eligible voters was considerably less in church than in state elections. Consequently, in most congregations the task of electing church officials was exclusively a middle- to upper-class, adult, white-male affair. At best, no more than 15% of the city's churchgoers had an input in the selection of church officials.

But whom did the franchised minority select? What common characteristics, if any, did the elected church officials share? Most congregations gave precise guidelines as to whom should be selected. Bishop James Kemp provided a standard answer when he admonished Protestant Episcopalians to elect as vestrymen only the "most pious" churchmen.[25] Assessing the piety of church officials is neither practical nor possible. However, the fact that half of the trustees of Trinity Church in 1815 were not even active communicants indicates that at least occasionally church leaders fell short of the expected high standards.[26] Yet, if they were not universally the most pious, an examination of 269 church leaders suggests that they were among the wealthiest. Throughout the period church leadership among all Baltimore denominations was clearly an upper-class avocation.[27]

The decision-making leaders of the Protestant Episcopal congregations were the eight vestrymen, elected and reelected each year on Easter Monday. On an average each vestryman served about seven or eight terms. Of the eighty-six men who served as vestrymen in Baltimore's three principal Episcopal congregations between 1790 and 1830, seventy-one, or 83%, were white-collar workers. This percentage was considerably higher at the parish church, St. Paul's, where 93% were identified as white collar.[28] In terms of wealth, nearly nine in ten owned taxable property, each being assessed an average amount of £945 in 1804 and $2,692 in 1815. Hence the typical vestryman was twice as likely to be a white-collar employee and six times as wealthy as the typical white-male Episcopalian.

The distance between the average wealth of lay leaders and the average wealth of the typical members was clearly apparent in even the most prestigious First Presbyterian Church. Of the forty-one men elected as deacons, ruling elders, or committeemen, all were white-collar workers.[29] Furthermore, all of those serving around the year 1804 appeared on that year's tax assessment record, averaging £2,606 in taxable property. Among those serving between 1810 and 1818, 96% held property in Baltimore, averaging $5,887 in assessed value. These figures, when compared with the per capita assessment average of its prestigious membership, indicate that the typical church officer had ten times the wealth of the average white-male Presbyterian. Although no wealth requirement eliminated others from consideration, in practice the elected leadership at First Presbyterian was limited to the wealthiest 1% of the Baltimore community.[30]

Almost as impressive was the socioeconomic status of the ruling committee of Second Presbyterian Church. Of the thirty-eight officers serving this congregation between its incorporation in 1804 and 1830, 95% were white-collar workers.[31] Only one of those serving during the first two decades of the century was not located on at least one of the two examined tax-assessment returns. The per capita assessments for 1804 and 1815 were £1,437 and $4,750 respectively. These figures surpass the average assessment of church officials from any Baltimore congregation, with the single exception of First Presbyterian. Such findings reinforce the evidence presented in chapter one, which identifies Presbyterians as the economic elites of early national Baltimore.

Roman Catholic congregations often elected clergymen as church trustees. The laymen who were elected, however, were among the wealthiest 10% of the Catholic community.[32] These findings again underscore the socioeconomic elitism among the lay leadership of the major denominations.

In addition, the socioeconomic status of Methodist stewards approximated the rank and wealth of the trustees of the other denominations; namely, most were white-collar workers with substantial property holdings. In terms of per capita tax assessment, Methodist trustees ranked third among the four largest denominations, considerably below the average tax assessment of Presbyterian and Episcopal officers, but slightly above the assessed wealth of Catholic trustees. Yet, compared with their own white-male membership, Methodist stewards tended to own over six times as much personal property. Thus again, the pecuniary officers of the church were Methodism's most affluent men.[33]

Methodist organization also allowed other members to hold lesser positions of spiritual authority. These officers ranged from the local preachers to the class leaders. Many of the local preachers were ordained ex-itinerants who for health or financial reasons accepted secular employment in the city. Others were either ordained deacons or licensed lay exhorters. Together they assisted the appointed pastor in Sunday worship, and conducted evangelical religious services at the penitentiary, hospital, almshouse, and outlying rural-area churches.[34]

The class leaders were the sergeants in the hierarchy of Methodist leadership. As the virtual "subpastors" to the dozen persons assigned under their care, they directed the weekly class meetings by inquiring into the spiritual condition of each member. They also visited the sick and delinquent members, and attended the weekly Leader's Meeting, where they turned over the collections to the stewards and exercised discipline over the local membership.[35] While a few distinguished blacks led Negro classes, and on extremely rare occasions a white woman led a female class, most leaders of male, female, and black classes were white males. Limiting leadership to this minority created problems. For each class to have its own white-male leader required that one in five Methodist white men serve as class leaders. Rarely was this proportion found. Consequently, class leaders staggered meeting times to allow them to lead two or more classes. Generally, white-female classes met on weekday afternoons, white-male classes before Sunday morning worship, and black classes (which usually were not segregated by sex) immediately following Sunday worship.[36]

The social status of Methodist spiritual leaders varied directly with the rank of the office. Stewards and ordained local preachers, the higher positions of authority, drew from the higher ranks of society, while class leaders more closely approximated a cross section of the overall white Methodist membership. Specifically, nearly three in four stewards and local preachers with elder's orders pursued white-collar occupations. In contrast, only a slight plurality of the deacons and nonordained exhorters were white collared, while a similar plurality of class leaders were skilled artisans. Moreover, even class leaders were more likely from the upper-status levels, and less likely from the lower-status levels than the typical white member. In terms of wealth, this distance is even greater. For example, a comparison of the assessed wealth between white-collar class leaders and white-collar class members, and between skilled artisan-class leaders and skilled artisan-class members, indicates that within the same occupations class leaders tended to own more property than class members. In short, class leaders, even when not of higher occupational status, were the economic leaders within the profession.[37]

Why did the Methodist pastors who selected class leaders favor the wealthier members? And why did the franchised across all denominations select only the most prosperous male members to positions of leadership? Several answers seem plausible. First, only the well-to-do enjoyed the leisure time necessary to commit themselves to substantial charitable activity. Second, without state support, church finances depended entirely upon the voluntary contributions of its membership. Hence it was natural and wise for churches to cultivate a special relationship with the affluent by offering to them the positions of authority. Third, holding a church office carried with it a degree of respectability and prestige that could easily be transformed into pecuniary gains. Thus perhaps the more ambitious business types found added incentive to serve in church-leadership capacity. Fourth, the character and life-styles developed by the faithful practitioners of the religious norms may have inherently bred success in the business world. In short, perhaps talent, education, and piety—as understood by churchmen of the era—were naturally highest in white-collar categories and in the more affluent segments of society. Most likely, these components were complementary. In a culture that endorsed thrift and hard work, and believed that virtue should be rewarded, the selecting of the more financially secure as religious leaders did not appear as a discriminatory procedure. While scores of publications criticized the "undemocratic" structures of certain church governments, no Baltimore publication chastised the city's congregations for their failure to include any but the most "respectable" citizens in positions of authority.

To conclude, Baltimore's diverse religious heritage included congregations that embraced a wide variety of church constitutions. The competitive aspects of the voluntary church, coupled with an ardent concern for republican government, drove churchmen to accentuate their polity differences. Despite the frequent and occasionally heated disputes, incorporation laws required congregations to name male trustees as their legal overseers, and custom often restricted the church electorate to white-adult males of reasonable wealth. Consequently, only a small minority of churchgoers participated in even minimal congregational decision-making. Moreover, the profile of elected lay officials across all denominations was remarkably constant: church leadership was clearly an upper-class affair. Baltimore church life reflected a traditional conservative society in which the masses of nominal churchgoers deferred without complaint to the leadership of the most respectable classes. Class antagonism, if truly on the rise in early national Baltimore, was not readily visible in the decision-making processes in local congregations.

3
CLERGY

BETWEEN 1790 and 1830 some two hundred clergymen served Baltimore congregations. Called and ordained as priests, preachers, and pastors, they administered the sacraments, proclaimed the divine Word, and guarded the community's beliefs and practices. Who they were and what they accomplished were functions of both the denominations they served and their individual talents. But while diverse in religious orientation and social background, as "faithful shepherds" and "ambassadors of God" they shared the common joys, frustrations, and pressures of urban pastors serving churches during an age of rapid social change.

By denomination, half of Baltimore's clergymen were Methodists. This large proportion resulted from the Wesleyan itinerant system, which permitted the bishop to appoint its ministers. Each year between three and six itinerants served Baltimore City and Fells Point Methodist stations. Fifty-nine of the 102 appointed between 1790 and 1830 served only a single one-year appointment. Twenty remained only two years. Most of the nineteen who ministered in the area for three or more years served some time in both stations. Only three, Joseph Frye, James Hanson, and Beverly Waugh, stayed more than four years, and this was owing to their appointments as presiding elders of the Baltimore district.[1] Throughout the era there was no significant change in the itinerant system, nor in the average tenure of Methodist clergy.

The second largest group was that of Roman Catholic priests. About half of their number was associated with St. Mary's Seminary, America'a first Roman Catholic seminary. The remaining nineteen ministered at one of the four Catholic houses in the city. Like the Methodists, their service depended more upon episcopal appointment than congregational preference, although their bishops worked diligently to satisfy the desires of the local bodies. Priests remained an average of nine years at the parish churches, and fifteen years at the seminary. These averages fluctuated only mildly throughout the era.[2]

In contrast, the average stay among non-Methodist Protestant pastors shifted significantly during the early national period. Protestant preachers called to Baltimore pulpits before 1810 remained an average of eighteen years, while those coming after 1810 stayed an average of only nine years.[3] This shift toward shorter pastorates applied to both large and small congregations, although it was particularly pronounced among the city's smaller congregations. These tendencies were not coincidental, nor unique to Baltimore. Rather they signified the continued erosion of what Donald Scott has called the ideal of a permanent pastorate. Colonial ministers rarely moved from the church of their ordination. To do so appeared as an impious, selfish act that broke the sanctity of the ordination vow. Likewise, congregations removed pastors only for gross misconduct—never simply because they disliked their preaching. But with disestablishment and the emergence of the voluntary church system, congregations became less hesitant to dismiss unwanted preachers and seek more suitable replacements, even if this involved raiding other churches' ministers. Similarly, pastors no longer considered their calling an obligation to work hard and be content with their place. To labor where one could bear the most fruit became the new watchword for evangelical ministers. In short, the erosion of the ideal of the permanent pastorate created a more mobile Protestant ministry in which ambitious clerics worked their way up the ranks toward the better and more influential pulpits. Only at the top did they remain for extended periods. Hence it is not surprising that the larger and more prestigious congregations kept pastors longer than did the smaller churches.[4]

Loosening contractual obligations increased the flexibility both of ministers and of congregations. This allowed the more qualified greater opportunity to gravitate to better pulpits. But this gain did not come without cost. Under the new "star system," pastoral security depended largely on continued popularity, particularly among the economic elites who controlled local congregational decision-making. Moreover, by multiplying the frequency of ministerial selection, the likelihood of congregational friction and even schism also increased. On several occasions internal disagreements over congregational decisions to hire or fire pastors led to church schisms.

One of the more interesting battles occurred at First Presbyterian Church. In 1800, during an illness of Pastor Patrick Allison, church officers invited Archibald Alexander temporarily to fill the pulpit. While he pleased many, Alexander's refusal to give specific answers to certain theological questions disturbed a segment of the congregation. As a result two other candidates gained consideration. After Allison's death a January 1802 election gave the majority vote to Alexander. However, when he learned that a number of the wealthy and influential members vehemently opposed his election, Alexander declined the appointment.[5]

The election then focused on the remaining two candidates. One was the Irish-born John Glendy, whom President Thomas Jefferson, his personal friend, highly recommended. The second candidate was a young graduate of Columbia College, James Inglis, who before accepting a call to the ministry, studied law in the office of Alexander Hamilton. The major factor in the election was party politics: selecting between the candidate acclaimed by Thomas Jefferson and the candidate endorsed by Alexander Hamilton.

Inglis won by a narrow margin. Upset at the election results, the supporters of Glendy separated from the congregation and called Glendy as the pastor of the newly established Second Presbyterian Church.[6]

A similar schism resulted after the selection of an associate pastor of the Episcopal St. Paul's parish. In 1796 the vestry announced their intention of finding a suitable associate rector to serve with Pastor Bend. When they offered the position to John Ireland, one disappointed candidate, George Ralph, published a letter in the *Maryland Journal and Baltimore Advertiser* accusing Bend of assassinating his character in order to prevent him from finding employment in the community. This attack forced Bend to enter the controversy by denying the charge with a letter in the same newspaper. Attorney General Luther Martin eventually settled the issue in court when he ruled in favor of Bend and the St. Paul's vestry.[7]

However, this decision did not end the congregation's difficulties. Rumors insinuating an illicit relationship between Ireland and his sister-in-law provoked the vestry to seek Ireland's resignation.[8] At this point two additional candidates emerged as leading contenders for the vacancy: Elijah Rattoone, an ex-professor of languages at Columbia College, and George Dashiell, a young, evangelical, low churchman whom Bend privately castigated as having Methodistic tendencies.[9] Dashiell upset the selection process when he renounced the tradition of officially declaring his candidacy and refused to preach at St. Paul's unless personally granted an invitation by the vestry. To apply without invitation, Dashiell argued, prostituted the gospel and turned the ministry of preaching into a vain exhibition of talents.[10] Eventually Dashiell compromised and demonstrated his oratorical skills by preaching on several occasions at Christ Church. However, he prefaced his sermons with insistence that he was not a candidate for the office. Finally, in a close and controversial election, the vestry, on the third ballot by a five-to-three vote, selected the scholar Rattoone. Immediately the low-church party in the congregation rallied around Dashiell, withdrew from St. Paul's, established St. Peter's Church, and called the dynamic young evangelical as their pastor.[11]

Unfortunately, the controversy continued when the congregation soon charged Rattoone with drunkenness and asked him to resign. Initially, Rattoone proclaimed his innocence, and began soliciting witnesses to defend his character.[12] However, after losing the support of both the vestry and Pastor Bend, and after being advised by a physician that the health of his wife could not withstand the ordeal of a bitter trial, Rattoone voluntarily submitted his resignation.[13] Still insisting upon his innocence, Rattoone at the ensuing Protestant Episcopal Convention received permission to establish Trinity Church.[14] Thus, within a four-year period, the tensions and bitterness over the selection of associate pastors precipitated the establishment of two spin-off Episcopal houses of worship, and initiated controversies between the congregations that continued for nearly two decades.

Despite such unpleasant controversies, urban congregations generally benefited from the thawing of the ministerial market. The lure of the city drew numerous ministers to Baltimore churches. While scores of parishes across Maryland were either without ministers or lamenting the "frequent dissolution of the pastoral connection," Baltimore churches abounded with applicants for every pulpit vacancy. The reasons why pastors competed for Baltimore pastorates were numerous.

First, urban pastorates offered opportunities for service well beyond the normal bounds of the ministry. Illustrative of the power and prestige of the ministerial office was Joseph Bend of St. Paul's parish. During his twenty-one-year tenure in Baltimore, Bend was instrumental in the establishment of the Baltimore General Dispensary, the Baltimore Library Company, the Society for the Promotion of Ornamental Knowledge, and the St. Paul's Orphan Asylum. He also played an active role in the Maryland Society for Promoting the Abolition of Slavery and Relief of Free Negroes. Beyond participation in these educational and benevolent societies, Bend extended his civic influence to promote a vaccination campaign for the city, and to raise funds to be used as ransom money for the return of American sailors captured by the Barbary pirates. Through such active civic involvement, Bend's influence upon city life far exceeded the bounds of his parish or denomination.[15]

The honor roll of clerical civic leaders is lengthy: John Carroll of the Roman Catholic Church, Philip Otterbein of the United Brethren Church, James Kemp of the Protestant Episcopal Church, J. Daniel Kurtz of the German Lutheran Church, William Nevins of the Presbyterian Church, and Elisha Tyson of the Society of Friends. The response of the city at the time of these individuals' deaths provided ample testimony to their respective influence. For example, the *Baltimore Telegraph* reporter who described the entombment of Bishop Carroll was overwhelmed with the enormous crowds, drawn from all classes of society, who endured well-nigh intolerable cold to attend his funeral.[16] The mingling of blacks and whites, and Catholics and Protestants at such occasions suggested a civic influence of the eminent clergy that transcended the power of traditional religious suasion.

Second, positions of denominational leadership often fell to Baltimore pastors. Serving as editors of denominational journals, moderators of conventions, officers of denominational societies, and missionaries to vacant rural parishes, urban pastors carried more than their share of denominational responsibilities and correspondingly received an abundance of special recognition. That five Baltimore clerics were selected by their denominations for the episcopacy indicates that pastorates within the city were held in high esteem, and often were stepping stones to even more prestigious church positions.[17]

Third, the wealth of the city generally provided greater financial security to urban pastors than to their rural colleagues. Ministerial salaries—often paralleling the social structure of the congregation—were generally highest among the city's Episcopal, Presbyterian, and Independent Unitarian congregations. For example, William West, rector of St. Paul's Episcopal parish between 1779 and 1791, received an annual salary of £500. While church financial difficulties necessitated cutting his salary to £375, at his death in 1791 West held a considerable estate that included an impressive library of books and valuable paintings.[18] His successor, Joseph Bend, began at a salary of £300 per year, which gradually increased to £500. This income, coupled with the benefits of a handsome, newly built, four-unit parsonage, bath house, kitchen, and study, placed Bend's standard of living above the local median.[19] When St. Paul's parish opened Christ Church as a second house of worship, the vestry hired an associate pastor at Bend's current salary.[20] Similarly, in 1803 St. Peter's Protestant Episcopal Church—the third Episcopal house in the city—offered its rector a comparable annual salary of $1,600 plus housing.[21] In 1806 even the less affluent Trinity Church voted a salary of $1,500 to their selected pastor.[22] Wartime inflation brought salary increases, so that by 1814 the pastors of St. Paul's parish churches received $2,000 per year plus housing. Economic difficulties resulting from the Panic of 1819 forced St. Paul's to lower ministerial salaries to only $500 per year until the debt on a recently built church house was retired. Still, the annual income of clergymen serving Baltimore Episcopal congregations exceeded that of most other Episcopal parishes in the state.[23]

Ministers serving the prestigious First and Second Presbyterian houses of worship also were among the best-paid clergy in the state. In 1814 James Inglis of First Presbyterian received an annual salary of $3,000. Meanwhile John Glendy of Second Presbyerian served his congregation for $2,100 per year. The discrepancies in salary structure between these two competitive congregations stirred Glendy to threaten resignation if he was not rewarded with equal compensation. The trustees of Second Presbyterian immediately responded to Glendy's ultimatum by increasing the pew rent by 33% in order to meet the salary demands of their eminent pastor.[24]

Another prosperous congregation willing to make pecuniary sacrifices in order to attract the services of the particular minister they desired was the First Independent Unitarian Church. In 1817 William Hinkley wrote letters to Jared Sparks of Boston to convince this Harvard graduate to come to Baltimore. In addition to emphasizing the advantages of Baltimore's climate, and the expectations of Unitarian success in the southern city, Hinkley lured Sparks with the assertion "that as to the salary, $1,500 is the least sum that will be first offered, that in case the minister should marry, $2,000 with a dwelling will be given...." Hinkley then commented: "Perhaps the salary for a short time will be rather less than that of two or three ministers in Baltimore, but it cannot be long inferior to the best."[25] After further negotiation, Sparks accepted the pastorate in Baltimore at a salary of $2,000, with the agreement to raise the yearly income to $2,500 plus house rent if he married.[26]

Salaries in the $2,000 to $3,000 range, however, went only to pastors in the most prestigious city congregations. William Nevins, the successor to James Inglis at First Presbyterian clearly recognized the uniqueness of his lucrative position. In a diary entry dated 28 January 1830, Nevins declared:

How mercifully has God dealt with me! How entirely unencumbered am I with the care of providing for the earthly support of myself and my family! How many much more worthy ministers are straitened in their worldly circumstances, while I possess the greatest abundance! Oh that I may sympathize with my poorer brethren, and never harden my heart against them, but be always ready to communicate to them and in every way assist them.[27]

Such a private confessional vividly highlights both the precarious situation of most of the early-nineteenth-century clergy, and the affluence of the fortunate handful called to Baltimore's wealthiest congregations.

More common than the financial security provided such pastors as Nevins and Sparks was the adequate but modest funding provided other urban pastors. For example, Lewis Richards, who accepted the pastorate of First Baptist in 1787 for only $650 per year, saw his yearly income double during the thirty years of his ministry. After his retirement in 1817, the church voted to give Richards a pension of $600 per year for life. Meanwhile his successor, Edmund Reiss, received $1,200 annually.[28] A financial crisis in the congregation resulting from an overextension in the church's building program and the economic panic of 1819, provoked a ministerial shakeup. In 1821 Reiss resigned from the debt-laden First Baptist Church and established the Ebenezar Baptist Church. This schismatic congregation drained a considerable portion of the membership away from the troubled First Church. As a result, the newly selected pastor of First Church, John Finlay, taught school for his personal support for several years until the economic crisis passed. In 1824 the now-solvent congregation increased his salary to an attractive $1,500 per year.[29]

The financial uncertainties surrounding Finlay's beginning years at First Baptist were not unique. Several other clerics sought secular employment during times of congregational difficulties. John Healy of the Second Baptist Church worked as a silk dyer to meet his personal financial obligations. Although he advocated the principle of a "hired" ministry, Healy did not accept financial remuneration from his congregation for the first twenty years of his ministry.[30] John Hargrove, pastor of the New Jerusalem congregation, supplemented his meager salary by serving as the Registrar of the city for some twenty-four years.[31] Similarly, William Levington of St. James (African) Protestant Episcopal Church established a school for his support in order to render gratuitously his priestly services to the debt-ridden congregation.[32] In each case, however, after the congregation weathered the financial storm, it awarded its pastor a salary more commensurate with his talents.

Even more straitened were the Methodist itinerants. The General Conference of the church fixed a limit as to the maximum remuneration that the itinerant or bishop could receive above traveling expenses. Between 1784 and 1800 the limit was $64 per year, plus an additional $64 if the preacher had a wife, with $16 for each child under six years and $21 for each child between six and eleven. In 1800 this salary structure was raised to an $80-per-year base, with $16 allowed for each child under seven, and $24 for children between seven and fourteen. The maximum salary increased to a $100 base in 1816, and remained at this level until amended in 1836.[33] By holding both bishops and itinerants to a common maximum salary, dependent upon family needs and not talents, Methodism differed from all other Protestant denominations.

In practice, however, the maximum salary limit was immaterial, since there was no guarantee that local circuits or stations would meet even this meager fixed salary. On most circuits the preacher was fortunate if he collected half of his own allowance, while the assessment for family support was generally ignored.[34] In Baltimore, Methodist itinerants received better treatment. A Provisions Committee, appointed by the stewards, recommended the amount each minister needed to provide the necessities for his family. Generally, single pastors received $200 for table expenses and salary, plus living quarters. Married clergymen received between $425 and $500 for a family of four, and up to $1,000 for a family of nine.[35] Hence, while their income was below that of other city pastors, Methodist itinerants stationed in Baltimore at least received temporary financial security from the wealth of the city.

Apparently the city's wealth influenced episcopal appointments to Baltimore stations. Methodist historians studying this period suggest that no more than 25% of the itinerants were married. Methodism's preference for single pastors was a matter of financial arithmetic: two to five single itinerants could be supported for the same amount as one married preacher. Consequently, it is no wonder that this evangelically oriented denomination composed primarily of a middle to lower-class membership preferred their clergy to remain celibate. Still, two-thirds of the itinerants sent to Baltimore were married. Methodist bishops, knowing that urban stations could better provide the essentials of family support, appointed a greater share of the married itinerants to Baltimore churches.[36]

In sum, the financial status of the clergy of early national Baltimore varied according to the denomination and wealth of the congregation. While never among the economic elite of the city, the pastors of the major churches were at least financially comfortable. Even the less prosperous urban congregations usually provided greater financial support than the typical rural congregations of Maryland.

If urban congregations offered their pastors enlarged ministry opportunities, prestige, and financial security, they also placed high demands on ministerial excellence. To a greater degree than rural churches, city congregations expected an educated, industrious ministry. At St. Paul's Episcopal, eight of the nine rectors serving between 1790 and 1830 were doctors of divinity. Among all Episcopal pastors, eleven of nineteen (or 65%) held ministerial degrees. This percentage compared favorably with the 42% of Episcopal ministers in the Maryland diocese with similar credentials.[37] At First and Second Presbyterian, four of the five pastors received doctor of divinity degrees while serving in Baltimore. The fifth, John Breckenridge, received his doctorate shortly after leaving the city.[38] Jared Sparks, pastor at First Independent Unitarian, graduated from Harvard, and eventually returned to his alma mater as president.[39] J. Daniel Kurtz of Zion Lutheran Church held the distinction of being the first Lutheran minister in America to receive an honorary D.D. degree.[40] Baltimore Baptist congregations also attracted the more educated Baptist preachers in the state. Whereas most pastors in the Baltimore Baptist Association serving outside the city were farmer-preachers, with little or no formal education, both Lewis Richards, the patriarch of First Baptist, and his successor, Edmund Reiss, were college trained.[41]

Again Methodist itinerants were the exceptions. For three decades after the establishment of the Methodist Episcopal Church, the only Methodist clergyman to hold a doctoral degree was the unpopular Bishop Thomas Coke. Even the esteemed Bishop Francis Asbury lacked this distinction. The handful of itinerants with college education rotated, like all other traveling preachers, from rural circuits to a one-year urban appointment, and back again to the rural circuits.[42]

It was not that Methodism opposed an educated ministry. John Emory, an itinerant of Baltimore Station in 1823 and eventually a bishop in the church, strongly advocated that the traveling ministers become men of letters. His concern led him to prepare a reading list and study course for candidates for deacons' and elders' orders.[43] But most Methodists viewed education as a luxury that the circumstances of time did not permit. The first *Discipline* stated explicitly the priorities of the denomination: "Gaining knowledge is a good thing, but saving souls is better.... If you can do but one, let your studies alone. *We* would throw by all the libraries in the world, rather than be guilty of the loss of one soul."[44] Hence both in urban stations and rural circuits, Methodist preachers needed only a heartfelt religious calling and a commitment to submit voluntarily to the discipline of the church. But within other denominations, urban congregations expected a significantly more refined ministry.

Besides an educated ministry, Baltimore congregations also expected their money's worth in ministerial services. The job description of urban pastors was extensive—even without considering any additional civic or denominational responsibility. First, the pastor prepared and perhaps memorized two sermons per week. Second, he performed the traditional pastoral duties of baptizing, marrying, burying, comforting, counseling, visiting, instructing, and evangelizing. Moreover, as the principal overseer of the church, he devised a program of ministry, recruited, trained, and inspired lay leaders, sought financial benefactors, and guarded the church's budget. Fulfilling these obligations to the satisfaction of the sometimes critical parishioners and demanding lay officers was a herculean task. Many chafed under the burdensome work load and high expectations of the church's lay leadership. The subtle but constant pressures of the office drove even the talented and ambitious James Kemp to complain. In private correspondence to a rector serving outside the city, Kemp wrote: "I have no colleague and of course can not be spared a single day from the City. Since the Salaries here have been raised, our Vestry think themselves entitled to one of the first rate clergymen in the United States and it seems they can not please themselves."[45] Failure to satisfy the church's leadership brought stern admonition or even dismissal. Even bishops were not exempt. In 1806 the Baltimore Annual Conference chastised Methodist bishop Thomas Coke for skirting his clerical responsibilities.

> It is not our wish to debar any of our Bishops or preachers from entering into matrimonial or other engagements if they think it right: but if they do and thereby disable themselves from serving us in their respective relations, it is a right which we hold sacred and which we will not voluntarily give up that we will dismiss them from those relations and chose [sic] others to fill their place.[46]

In short, neither family problems nor involvement in denominational functions justified neglecting the traditional pastoral duties. Church needs were too great, and ministerial replacements too plentiful for churches to tolerate unindustrious pastors.

Urban congregations also expected their pastors to follow the traditions of the church. The advice an anonymous friend gave William Nevins, the newly selected pastor at First Presbyterian, signified the often unspoken demand for pastoral conformity. First he cautioned Nevins against deviating from tradition by failing to ascend to the pulpit by the east steps. "This contravention of established custom evinces on your part, a spirit of innovation and a virtual condemnation of the founders of our church, by a refusal to walk in their footsteps." Second, in regard to pulpit mannerisms, he advised against pounding the pulpit, since "it wears off the napping" and against the "unnatural elevation of your head while preaching." Continuing, Nevins's critic noted:

> That handkerchief, besides, gives you and us a great deal of trouble and uneasiness. I think you had better wipe your face and blow your nose at home, or let the sexton stand by to hold this part of your sermon. Duplicates of your slips of notes would be desirable, for Mr. Meredith's little son would not have the trouble of picking them up so often.

Finally, he concluded:

> Preach very short sermons, say fifteen minutes; for time must be given to all to remark upon the occurrences of the day and past week, the changes which fashion has brought about, the good and bad bargains made.... Now not more than ten minutes will be required for this part of divine service; five of course will be left for the preacher, during which he ought to be active and interesting, or else never complain of the people holding down their heads.... Five minutes are a very long time, sir, particularly if the week has been a busy one. Many of us are up late at balls, plays, cards, etc., and find a little slumber, induced by a well kept up monotony of sounds, greatly refreshing. The Sabbath is a day of rest to all, and this rest to which

your people have the right should not be invaded by any loud and harsh noises ... or by talking too seriously about sin, repentance, or damnation and the things of another life, with which, having a great deal to do here, we do not wish to concern ourselves. Those of my opinion constitute the great majority of your congregation. You are employed and are paid, sir by the majority who have the right to dictate to you and are determined to do so, ... and they expect to be treated according to custom with dainties and luxuries, leaving the loaves and fishes, the sackcloth and ashes to the more humble minority.[47]

In spite of the humor of the satire, most saw deviation from the expectations of the lay leadership as serious business. Even the popular William Wyatt, who was to remain at St. Paul's parish for fifty years, nearly lost his rectorship after only six years of service owing to a minor disagreement with the vestry. The controversy regarded whether or not an executed murderer would be interred in the church's graveyard. Despite the fact that while in prison the convict requested spiritual assistance, repented, professed Christianity, was baptized, and received communion, the conservative vestry refused to allow the body to be buried in the churchyard. In response to this action, Wyatt sent an ultimatum, asserting that should the vestry reverse his decision to permit burial, the parishioners could never again place value in any of his ministerial verdicts. Therefore the only remaining alternative would be for him to resign from his pastoral obligations. In spite of the ultimatum, the vestry upheld their decision. Only after Bishop Kemp stepped in as mediator between Wyatt and the vestry did the crisis pass.[48] While relatively insignificant, this incident was symptomatic of the pressures exerted on clergymen to refrain from controversy unless fully supported by the influential officers of their congregations.

Likewise, ministers risked their careers when they challenged the established denominational authorities. The well-published career of George Dashiell illustrated the dangers in developing a maverick reputation. Throughout his twelve-year tenure at St. Peter's, Dashiell was the outspoken leader of the low-church party of the Episcopal church, who favored congregational singing over instrumental music, extemporaneous to printed prayers, and heartfelt sermons intended to evoke spontaneous conversions.[49] More traditional Episcopal priests such as Joseph Bend and Bishop Kemp labeled Dashiell's church as "no more Episcopal than a Methodist conventicle" and his doctrines as "not unworthy of a camp meeting."[50] Thus the theological rift between Dashiell and the eminent clergymen of St. Paul's parish as well as Dashiell's effervescent personality made him unusually prone to snide and caustic remarks.

Dashiell's major problems emerged in the summer of 1815 with the circulation of a rumor charging him with improper conduct toward a parishioner by the name of Mrs. Worthington. The rumor alleged that Dashiell's improper advances toward Mrs. Worthington took place between February and April 1813. Supposedly, when Mr. Worthington learned of the episode in September 1813, he sought counsel from a friend, Francis Hollingsworth. Hollingsworth informed Worthington that he was not surprised at Dashiell's actions, since he believed Dashiell to be a "fallen man." Nevertheless, Hollingsworth said it would be pointless to inform St. Peter's vestry of the situation since the biased vestry would merely deny the charge in defense of Dashiell. Instead, Hollingsworth suggested that Worthington keep the incident secret for the sake of the family reputation. Following this advice, Worthington informed only his closest relatives of the incident.[51] The family secret remained submerged for two years before bubbling to the surface in the summer of 1815.

In response to the circulating rumor, on 28 August 1815 the vestry sent a letter to Mrs. Worthington asking for her testimony regarding the incident. Desiring to let the matter lie, Mr. Worthington prevented his wife from providing this information. Several days later a vestryman approached Worthington and informed him of the concern of the vestry to reach a decision in the matter, and presented him with a paper listing the rumored charges against Pastor Dashiell. Worthington asserted that the list was incomplete, but refused to give further cooperation. As a result, on 31 August, the vestry issued a circular clearing Dashiell of "the least imputation of guilt from the charges alleged against him," finding "his conduct to have been such as to remove (from the mind of any impartial person) even the suspicion of his motives being impure." The circular delcared that this decision rested upon the testimony of a Mrs. A. Lindenberger, who stated that she heard Mrs. Worthington confess she was mistaken in her assumption that Dashiell cherished improper affection for her, and that the reason the episode emerged in August 1815 was to prevent a marriage between Dashiell's son and a sister of Francis Hollingsworth.[52]

Angry at the decision, Worthington castigated the vestry for basing its verdict on improper evidence. He then suggested that the vestry meet with his wife and Dashiell. Although the vestry accepted this mediation, Dashiell refused, asserting that the case was already decided. One vestryman, admitting that the vestry made its decision too hastily, offered to Worthington a conciliatory, apologetic letter. Finding the letter unsatisfactory, Worthington prepared a publication defending his position. Shortly thereafter, Hollingsworth authored a second circular in which he denounced Dashiell's theology, conduct, and competence as a pastor. Hollingsworth's criticism of Dashiell carried further into a carping attack on the entire church:

> The fact is, that St. Peter's was a church of party.... What but this bewildering spirit could ... sanctify the folly of those, whose imprudence ... produced the lamentable consequences to which I allude? ... I am much afraid that Mr. Dashiell and some of this friends live upon the reciprocated flattery of each other; and I need hardly say that no cement is so strong as this to keep your would be religious folks together.[53]

The public denunciation of Dashiell's conduct created an uproar throughout the Maryland Diocese. In October official charges of "scandalous, immoral, and obscene conduct on several occasions" were presented to the Standing Committee of the Diocese. The committee then set 8 December 1815, as the date for the trial. Despite the fact that Dashiell was supported with letters from his vertrymen that defended his doctrine and character, Dashiell informed Bishop Claggett that he would not stand trial before this committee of his "avowed enemies." In addition, Dashiell renounced his connection with the church and asked for a certificate of removal in order to be admitted into the Virginia Diocese. When Dashiell failed to present a defense at his trial, the Standing Committee convicted him of "contumacy," disqualified him from conducting his ministerial functions, and excluded him from church membership.[54]

Although officially deposed from pastoral office, Dashiell remained at St. Peter's throughout the ensuing year. A number of members of the congregation petitioned the civil court to grant a mandamus

> to be directed to the vestry, commanding them to report the vacancy in the rectorship of St. Peter's Church to the bishop; enjoining and prohibiting them from permitting George Dashiell to occupy the parsonage house, and to officiate in any manner in the said church; and further commanding them to choose a minister.[55]

Although the court decided in favor of the vestry, the election on Easter Monday 1817 of a new vestry removed Dashiell's loyal supporters from office. The newly elected vestrymen immediately declared their adherence to the church, and elected John P. K. Henshaw as their rector. As a result, Dashiell and his followers separated from the congregation, and established the independent St. John's Evangelical Episcopal Church. Thus ended the prolonged controversy surrounding the alleged scandalous conduct of the Reverend George Dashiell.[56]

A second incident illustrating the dangers in confronting the ecclesiastical establishment involved the controversial Father F. C. Reuter. The controversy began shortly after a fund-raising campaign for the building of St. John's Roman Catholic Church. The church was built largely from subscriptions and proceeds of a lottery. At the settlement of the lottery, the wealthy subscribers of larger amounts of money were reimbursed. Poorer contributors of lesser amounts received no reimbursement. This action, along with the arrogant display of one wealthy trustee who insisted on having a shed built nearby for his horse and chair, to use when he visited the church, divided the congregation into factions. Although Bishop Carroll sympathized with the trustees, Reuter sided with the faction opposing that one wealthy member.[57] It was in the heat of this debate—at a time when Reuter was engaged in controversy both against a segment of his German brethren, and against the hierarchy of the church—that he was charged with illicit sexual conduct.

Gossip erupted into violence when Ignatus Shoemaker—the irate husband who claimed to have three witnesses who saw Reuter and Mrs. Shoemaker lying together in bed—physically assaulted Father Reuter. Allegedly, one witness claimed that Reuter told Mrs. Shoemaker that it was wrong for her to have a husband so old, and that it was better to have children by Reuter than none at all.

In order to clear his reputation, Reuter brought the case to court. After the judge instructed the jury to decide the case solely on whether the assault on Reuter by Shoemaker did occur, the jury decided the case in favor of Reuter. However, by awarding Reuter only one cent in damages, the jury expressed their sympathy for Shoemaker.[58] The result of the trial failed to settle the issue. When the laity of St. John's investigated the matter, the majority disavowed the charges against Reuter as being totally unfounded. Eventually, however, Bishop Carroll suspended Reuter for scandalous conduct, and forced him to leave the city.

Interestingly, both of the above religious scandals involved controversial clergymen in conflict with the dominant leaders of their respective denominations. While the evidence surrounding each case was clouded with bias, the innocence or guilt of the individual was of little significance. In both cases the scandal continued until the ministerial opponents successfully removed the accused from office. This identical cycle was repeated at other congregations. In 1818 the African Methodist Episcopal Church ousted the controversial Daniel Coker from the ministry.[59] Likewise it was shortly after a personal feud between Pastor James Inglis of First Presbyterian and a wealthy ex-trustee of his congregation that charges of drunkenness against Inglis precipitated his professional downfall.[60] The frequency of such scandals, particularly among the more controversial clergymen of the city, provided ample warning to incoming pastors of the danger of defying the established customs and leaders of the church.

Regardless of the frustrations of the ministry, few who put their hand to the plow ever turned back. Clergymen from all religious denominations accepted without question the notion that, come Judgment Day, they would be expected to account for their actions as the spiritual shepherds of their flocks. This central belief served as a constant reminder to be assiduous in their spiritual obligations.[61]

Emanating from such a belief was an abhorrence of idleness. For example, Pastor Bend lamented to a friend that his busy schedule prevented him the luxury of studying the Old Testament in its original Hebrew. Yet, without complaint, Bend asserted: "We must not be idle, my dear sir. 'The harvest truly is plenteous, but the laborers are few'; besides this, the greater our well meant exertions, the brighter will be the crown for which we ought to pant."[62] Echoing the same theme, Jared Sparks wrote: "I shudder ... almost at the thought of the burden I have taken upon me. I have more to do than you are aware.... But this is the place of my choice. So it was, and I do not regret it. If there is much to be borne, I can bear it; if there is much to be done, I shall not be idle. The cause is a noble one; God will give me strength."[63]

Similarly, William Nevins's diary exposed the motivational power flowing from the concern of a pastor for the eternal security of his flock. On 7 January 1830 Nevins wrote: "Last evening I spoke on the concern which Christians ought to feel for the salvation of souls. Oh that I might habitually feel it. How it would excite me to duty."[64] This intense concern produced occasional emotional trauma for Nevins. On 27 March 1830 he wrote:

> A memorable day! Last evening I heard of the death of my poor sister, Louisa Key; ... Oh if I were but assured that Jesus was with thee then, and that thou art with him.... Oh Louisa, I wish I had been more faithful to thee; I wish that I had prayed for thee more. I might have been a better brother to thee.... Oh Louisa, what could I do for thee now, now that nothing can be done for thee! I will be more faithful to thy sisters, and will say to them, what I know thou wouldst say, couldst thou speak to them from thy new home in eternity.[65]

Such heartfelt expressions signified the degree to which a theology that promised felicity to the faithful and judgment to the incredulous affected the actions of the conscientious divines.

In fine, typically the urban pastor was financially more secure than his rural colleague. His civic and denominational powers opened abundant avenues for professional advancement. But the spiritual benefits of the office drove him onward. Cognizant of his role as Christ's ambassador to the community, the urban pastor undertook his duties with the self-assurance of their eternal importance. While tempted to overmagnify his personal worth, the seriousness of his commitment to the profession provoked an unwavering diligence in his tasks. If fortunate to escape the burden of overwork, the slander of malicious rumors, and the exasperations of a stifling lay leadership, he remained at his charge for about a decade, only to retire, suffer a glorious death, and be interred with preferential treatment in the loveliest burial plot in the churchyard. Immediately after death, memories of his carnal nature were replaced with those of his saintly qualities. Eulogized as a man of "talent and piety—of ability and worth," possessing "a mind of no ordinary mould, and a heart of no common virtue,"[66] the deceased pastor finally achieved the deference never quite attainable this side of the grave. With a refurbished reputation, the ghost of the beloved saint remained to haunt his successor for years to come.

4

DISCIPLINE

BY interpreting the Bible, and disciplining parishioners, early Maryland churches helped define and enforce community standards of morality. Disestablishment may have severed the legal connection between church and state and disrupted the monopoly on moral stewardship previously held by the Anglican church; but throughout the early national era, nonestablished voluntary churches maintained their social roles as custodians of the culture.

Even after disestablishment, the government of Maryland retained a religious character, and to some extent churches maintained some legal benefits. For example, while the Maryland Constitution of 1776 declared all Christian denominations equal before the law, it stated that all citizens had a duty to worship God, and that all office holders must acknowledge a belief in Christianity. It was not until 1828 that non-Christians could hold public office. After 1776 the Maryland assembly renewed the old "sabbatarian" laws, and required that marriages be performed in the presence of a minister and in a house of worship. Land owned by the Church of England before 1776 remained the property of the Episcopal church. The new constitution even allowed the possibility of a state tax for the support of the church of the individual's choice. However, few non-Episcopalians supported the measure, and hence the attempts in 1780, 1783, and 1795 to legislate state church support failed. In short, as Thomas O'Brien Hanley has argued, the authors of the Maryland Constitution of 1776 intended to replace the confessional state with a Christian state that allowed equal opportunity to all religious denominations. The result was not a secularization, but a desectarianization of society.[1]

The Maryland pattern was not unique. Enlightenment thinkers and orthodox Christians from across the nation accepted the premise that the success of a republic depended upon the virtue of the people. Since church institutions best nourished a virtuous people, it followed that strong, vibrant churches were necessary for the health of the republic.[2] George Washington propagated this logic in his famous Farewell Address when he asserted that religion and morality were indispensable supports to political prosperity, and that morality could not exist without religion.[3] Four decades later this notion still circulated. In 1835 Alexis de Tocqueville, the French analyst of American society, wrote: "I do not know whether all Americans have a sincere faith in their religion ... but I am certain that they hold it to be indispensable to the maintenance of republican institutions. This opinion is not peculiar to a class of citizens or to a party, but it belongs to the whole nation and to every rank of society."[4]

Between the days of Washington and Tocqueville, city pastors constantly reminded Baltimoreans that religion was the cornerstone of the political republic. Remove the cornerstone and the edifice would crumble. Preachers delivered this message at public ceremonies, inter- and intradenominational gatherings, special occasion discourses, and typical Sunday worship services. To illustrate, during the dedication of the Washington Monument, James Kemp admonished the public hearers to "learn the important lesson ... that religion is the only base on which the happiness of a nation can stand secure."[5] At a fast-day discourse, James Inglis repeated a similar theme to his Presbyterian congregation. After urging all who love their country to repent, Inglis concluded: "As a Community cannot but suffer from the vices of the Individuals of whom it is composed, so, on the contrary, we have reason to conclude that the reformation of those individuals will essentially benefit the Community; and consequently, ... every person who renounces that which is evil, and cleaves to that which is good, lightens in a greater or less degree, the pressure of national iniquity."[6] Again, John Johns perpetuated the argument in a typical defense of evangelical missions: "We owe it to patriotism as well as to piety to keep this system. ... Should it cease, ... corruption and disorder [will] run riot over our country to the destruction of our civil and religious liberties. ... We must [go] onward for our country's sake as well as that of the church."[7] For such men the notion that the strength of the nation depended on the health of religious institutions was a self-evident truth.

Patriotism and the close alliance of national and religious loyalties only enhanced the natural propensity of churches to guard public morals. Christians of the era believed that rebellion against God's laws invited both personal ruin and national calamity. Christian love demanded that churches expose and cast out sin wherever it was found. Early national churches shared with their colonial predecessors a low tolerance for deviations from sanctioned behavior norms. However, in the religiously pluralistic society, the line between acceptable and unacceptable conduct was not always clear.

In one instance churches disputed even the numbering of the Ten Commandments. For example, an edition of the Roman Catholic *The Key of Paradise, Opening the Gate to Eternal Salvation*, reprinted and distributed in Baltimore in 1804, omitted the commandment "thou shalt have no graven images." This edition made ten commandments out of the remaining verses by dividing the ninth commandment (according to the Protestant count) into two parts.[8] Although a subsequent edition listed all the commandments in their traditional order, Protestant critics exploited the episode as proof that Catholicism was an unscriptural religion. Three decades later William Nevins of First Presbyterian was still harping against Catholic authorities for printing the Baltimore edition of 1804.[9]

Barring this exception, however, Baltimore churches generally upheld the specific commandments of the decalogue. Murder, stealing, cursing, and adultery, for instance, were easily identified as scriptural offenses. Particularly high among the "thou shalt nots" was improper behavior on Sunday. Few churchmen would have challenged Bishop Kemp's opinion regarding the "Christian Sabbath": "It was the design of the Almighty that there should be a complete pause in the operations of this world, an entire suspension of all its machinery, and that worship of God and the concerns of the soul should occupy that portion of time."[10] Ministers across denominational lines castigated any deviation from this standard—whether it were by the overly industrious merchant who opened a fruit shop on Sunday afternoon, or the delinquent child who rioted through the streets. Sunday was a day for worship and family religious instruction. To assist the Christian family in this pious task, denominations published scores of devotional guides, catechisms, and tracts. Clerics frequently warned that neglect of proper Sunday observances led to "superstition," "fanaticism," or "impiety" and thereby bred more serious offences.[11] Such rhetoric demonstrated more than simply the strong biblicism of the early national era. It also reflected the dual anxieties of city clerics who doubted both the ability of the church to compete against the marketplace for the allegiance of ambitious men, and the ability of the nation to maintain its Christian character even while embracing a pluralistic religious tradition.

On other moral issues, especially those not specifically addressed in Christian scripture, Baltimore's religious leadership expressed more divergent opinions. For instance, while the religious community in unity opposed such gambling as horse racing, cockfighting, and card playing, several Baltimore congregations—including St. Paul's, Christ, and Trinity Protestant Episcopal, First and Second Presbyterian, First Independent Unitarian, Second Baptist, St. John's Roman Catholic, and the Roman Catholic Cathedral—saw no moral difficulties in petitioning the Maryland General Assembly for permission to hold lotteries for fund-raising purposes. Only the Society of Friends, Methodists, and the congregation of First Baptist vocally condemned such practices as institutional vices.[12]

Denominations also placed varying emphases on questions concerning money and business. While all concurrently endorsed the virtues of hard work and thrift, and condemned the love of money as the root of all evil, only the Methodists and Friends frequently censured their members for "extravagant" and "luxurious" life-styles. Christian piety, at least as defined by Methodists, definitely excluded the wearing of expensive or fancy clothes.[13] Likewise, Friends' publications warned Quakers against the too "eager pursuit" of material possessions.[14] The following piece printed in a Methodist periodical also signified their contempt for overzealous capitalists:

Nothing is more easy than to grow rich. It is only to trust nobody—to befriend none—to get everything and save all we get—to stint ourselves and everybody belonging to us—to be the friend of no man, and have no man for our friend—to heap interest upon interest, cent upon cent—to be mean, miserable and despised, for some twenty or thirty years—and riches will come as sure as disease and disappointment.[15]

Baptists as well were apparently reluctant to embrace the ethics of aggressive businessmen. In 1808 the Baltimore Baptist Association resolved that it was not consistent with Christian character to receive more than legal interest for money lent. In addition, it resolved that Christians should not buy at the lowest rate and sell at the highest rate possible without regard to the value of the article of purchase. This latter point was quite controversial, for two years later the same association voted to rescind from the minutes that resolution dealing with "buying and selling."[16]

The most publicized area of controversy inevitably regarded matters dealing with entertainment. One humorous episode took place in July 1804 when the mayor of the city requested that a visiting delegation of Osage Indians perform a public exhibition of their national war dance. When a newspaper reporting the event noted that among the two thousand attenders were several ministers of the city, including George Dashiell of St. Peter's Protestant Episcopal, Dashiell responded with a letter in the *Federal Gazette* denying his presence and condemning those who did attend. Dashiell boldly asserted that "private Christians cannot innocently partake of such sports and amusements ... much less can a *minister* of the holy Jesus indulge in such silly vanities without tarnishing his sacred character and bring[ing] a blot upon his profession."[17] Using the paper as a pulpit, Dashiell continued: "No clergyman who possesses grace, or thinks anything of his character, would presume ... to frequent the theatre, which is now generally considered by pious people to be a regular battery against virtue and religion."[18] Perhaps Dashiell's condemnation of the Indian performers was in order, since the Episcopal convention specifically precluded its ministers from playing "cards, dice, tables" or engaging "in any vicious or unseemly diversion."

While Dashiell addressed this letter to "Reverend * * *," the context made it apparent that Dashiell's tirades were principally dircted against John Hargrove of the New Jerusalem Church. In response to this attack Hargrove wrote a public defense of both the war dance and the theater. In addition Hargrove used the occasion to attack Dashiell's "illiberal and bitter censures" as both unChristian and unpopular.[19]

The controversy raised by Dashiell and Hargrove provoked a series of public letters, which appeared in Baltimore newspapers throughout the months of August and September. One friend of Hargrove, justifying his letter as an attempt to "prevent the ridicule and mockery of the irreligious, the sneers of the infidel, and the satanic satisfaction of the bigoted enthusiast," blasted Dashiell's lack of charity and style of ministry.[20] Conversely, another condemned Hargrove by insisting that attending the theater and other like amusements was "inconsistent with a state of grace and contrary to the whole tenor of the Gospel."[21] Still another, after describing the controversial event in which the Indians "stripped themselves almost stark naked, painted their bodies ... and jumped about like a set of infuriated madmen" while "the blushing maiden there had an opportunity of gazing on man as he is, almost without disguise or covering," concluded by contrasting how differently the ministers of New York City treated the visiting Indians: instead of encouraging them to remain in "their state of savage ignorance and superstition," they presented them a Bible and instructed them in the doctrines of Christianity.[22] Generally, the letters attacking the intolerance of Dashiell came from members of the New Jerusalem Church or the high-church Episcopalian congregations of St. Paul's and Trinity, while those attacking the moral laxity of Hargrove were from Methodist or Quaker churches, or the low-church Episcopalian congregation of St. Peter's.

The crusade against theaters, rather than dying with this controversy, increasingly picked up momentum. In 1810 Roman Catholic bishops meeting in Baltimore issued a special warning against theaters, dances, and novels.[23] The following year the Protestant Episcopal Convention of the Diocese of Maryland voted to insert the phrase *frequenting of theatres* to the list of vices specifically condemned in Canon 22 of the church.[24] In early 1812, after a tragic fire in a theater in Richmond, Virginia, took several lives, Dashiell published a sermon with the hope of suppressing theatrical exhibitions, which he argued were "injurious to health, dangerous to life, baneful to morals, destructive to domestic happiness and female delicacy, and blasphemous against God."[25] Later that year Dashiell joined with Philip William Otterbein of the United Brethren church in petitioning the Maryland Assembly to enact a law prohibiting theatrical exhibitions in the state.[26] In short, by the second decade of the century, virtually all Baltimore congregations stood alongside the Methodists and Quakers in maintaining that attending the theater was outside of the standards of piety expressed in the scriptures.

Generally, the denominations holding the highest standards in matters of personal morality also took the hardest line against the evils of slavery. For example, Baltimore Friends avidly criticized the institution of slavery. Although the intensity of their struggle cooled after the legal end of slave importation in 1808, throughout this period Quaker individuals such as Elisha Tyson and Joseph Townsend continued the attack against the injustices of the peculiar institution.[27] Friendly allies of the Quakers in the battle against slavery were the Methodists, who, although toning down their initial policy of refusing communion to any slaveholder, continued to denounce the evils of slavery and refused to admit any slaveholder into the society without first requesting from him a deed of manumission.[28] Likewise, the Baptist congregations of Baltimore took a strong anti-slavery position. In 1789 the members of First Baptist sent a letter to the Philadelphia Baptist Association asking that body to use its influence to support the formation of such societies as the recently formed Abolition Society of Baltimore.[29] Second Baptist Church also showed its disapproval of slavery when at a specially called meeting in 1802, the congregation resolved that "if any person make application for fellowship who holds slaves to exhort them and endeavor to show them the evil thereof."[30] Similarly, shortly after its establishment, Third Baptist voted that no slaveholder could become a member of the congregation.

Denominational opposition to slaveholding, the theater, Sabbath-breaking, or any other disapproved behavior meant little without efforts by churches to enforce their standards upon their membership and, to some extent, upon the community at large. Occasionally this involved appealing to local, state, or federal government for laws intended to raise moral standards. One illustration of such activity was the previously mentioned anti-theater petition sent to the Maryland Assembly by Baltimore Episcopalian and United Brethren ministers. In addition, in 1807 a committee of the Protestant Episcopal Diocese of Maryland, which included Joseph Bend and William Dorsey of St. Paul's parish, sent a memorial to the state legislature in which they opposed the practice of granting divorces on insufficient grounds. At this time the Episcopal church granted divorces only when the wife was guilty of adultery. Accompanying this memorial was a second petition, seeking a new and stronger law against gaming.[31] Similarly, on several occasions the Baltimore Annual Conference of the Methodist Episcopal Church petitioned the state legislature for laws of gradual emancipation of slaves.[32]

Even more active in lobbying for reform measures were the Society of Friends. In early 1802, after a meeting between Baltimore Friends and several chiefs of the Wyandot nation, the Indian Committee of the Baltimore Yearly Meeting sent a memorial to the United States Congress stating that unless Congress resolved or greatly restrained alcohol sales, all efforts at improving the distressed condition of American Indians were futile. Following up on this petition, several local Friends traveled to Washington to present their concern personally to congressional leaders. The outcome of this action was the passage of a law empowering the President to prevent or restrain the vending and distributing of spirituous liquors among any Indian tribe.[33] While not always so successful, Baltimore Friends frequently sent memorials to the Maryland Assembly in an effort to strengthen state laws intended to protect free blacks from illegal enslavement, and to prevent slaves from being kept in bondage beyond the date of their legal manumission.[34] Moreover, during times of national crises, Friends sent letters to governmental officials urging them to pursue peaceful measures that would not propel the United States into the calamity of war.[35]

On two occasions a few Baltimore church leaders became involved directly in presidential politics. In 1808 a Methodist printed a tract urging all Christians not to vote for the "deistic" James Madison.[36] Then in 1828 the circulation of pamphlets that both asserted and denied the friendship of John Quincy Adams with the Roman Catholic Church created a mild controversy.[37] But these episodes were rare. As a rule, Baltimore churches and church leaders refrained from involvement in partisan politics. William Nevins of First Presbyterian more nearly captured the prevailing sentiment of the period when he told his congregation that "religion and politics do not mix."[38]

Generally, voluntary churches preferred persuasion over legislation as the way to control community conduct. The persuasive powers of the local church were extensive. First, the congregations' near monopoly of city burial grounds gave churches some leverage in influencing public morals. In an effort to crack down on sexual misconduct, Baltimore Methodists prohibited the burial in their graveyards of any deceased illegitimate infant.[39] Similarly, Protestant Episcopal churches disallowed the burial of any adult killed in the anathematized custom of dueling.[40] Churches also maintained discipline by wielding the powers of censure and excommunication. No religious body tolerated flagrant or habitual wrongdoing. Episcopal congregations elected church wardens to present members guilty of disorderly conduct before ecclesiastical courts. Roman Catholic bishops excommunicated delinquent Baltimore Catholics. Similarly, ruling elders sat in judgment over erring Presbyterians, while the voting membership of each congregation expelled unrepentant Baptists, Unitarians, and Swedenborgians. But extant church records suggest that the most aggressive enforcers of church discipline were the Methodists and Friends.

On an average, Methodists of Baltimore City Station censured or excommunicated about two members per month. While occasionally the charges dealt with doctrinal impurities, far more typically they pertained to matters of profanity, drunkenness, adultery, lying, neglect of church attendance, and nonpayment of debts.[41] Even prominent members suffered disciplinary action. To illustrate, Baltimore Methodists dismissed Mayberry Parks, a wealthy fish inspector, from his lay leadership responsibilities after he deceivingly led the incoming governor of the state to believe that he would be unable to feed his family if he lost his appointment as fish inspector.[42] This nineteenth-century version of "income tax fudging" was sufficient offense to evoke censure upon even this well-respected and financially influential lay leader.

The peculiarities of Quaker discipline prompted Friends to place an even tighter control upon their own membership. Besides the common list of disciplinary offenses, the Society of Friends expelled members for printing articles without the consent of the Meeting for Sufferings, reading plays, dancing, visiting fortune tellers, observing holy days, accepting civil offices, selling liquor, holding slaves, taking oaths, accruing debts, supporting war, moving without obtaining proper certificates, and marrying outside the faith.[43] Notwithstanding a dwindling membership, Baltimore Quakers chose to decline numerically rather than mitigate these high standards. As a result, being a Quaker in early national Baltimore meant far more than belonging to a religious organization. It was a commitment to a life-style that was easily distinguishable from the norms of even a religiously oriented society.

The campaign for public morality did not stop with the discipline of adult churchgoers. Experience taught churchmen that breaking bad habits was more difficult than inculcating virtuous ones. Churchmen intent on nurturing a morally upright citizenry relied heavily upon the biblical injunction: "Train up your child in the way he should go and when he is old, he will not depart from it."[44] To help fulfill this promise, churches supported numerous educational programs for the young.

Among the first Baltimore churches to sponsor schools were the German Reformed, German Lutheran, and Society of Friends congregations. The German groups erected church schools in order to ensure that their children learned the German language.[45] Friends established schools because their discipline advocated universal education under religious direction. Specifically, the Baltimore Yearly Meeting advised all Monthly Meetings not only to provide funds for the education of the poor of the society, but also to provide Quaker schools in which the children would be free from "the corruptive customs and harmful example of mixed and undisciplined schools."[46] The pressure from the Yearly Meeting did not guarantee the success of Monthly Meeting schools, but it did move the lower meetings to reach for the goal of universal childhood education. In 1784, 1794, 1800, 1815, and 1821 the Baltimore Monthly Meeting opened Quaker schools. Unfortunately, owing to financial difficulties, none survived longer than four years.[47]

Beginning around the turn of the century several additional churches considered sponsoring schools for the children of the city. The impetus for this sudden concern was the disconcerting demographic changes of the 1790s. Aided by the arrival of thousands of refugees from Santo Domingo, Baltimore's population nearly doubled during the decade. The result was a rapid rise in the number of "spiritual orphans" who were deficient in both the knowledge of religion and the reading skills necessary to obtain scriptural truths idependently of parental guidance. As arbiters of the community's conscience, Baltimore churchmen responded to the crisis. Within a decade six charity schools opened. Four of the six operated under the supervision of religious institutions.[48]

The first charity school in the city was an interdenominational venture begun in 1798 by the Baltimore Female Humane Association. When the school was incorporated in 1801, its legal supervision fell to nine male trustees. This group included two Methodist, two Episcopal, and one Presbyterian laymen, plus four clergymen from the Roman Catholic, United Brethren, Lutheran, and Methodist denominations.[49] The success of the school inspired both individual congregations and civic associations to attempt similar enterprises. In 1801 female members of St. Paul's parish opened a school for indigent girls.[50] This same year Baltimore Methodists established a charity school for boys. Next the St. Peter's Protestant Episcopal Church opened a school for all needy children within its congregation. Shortly thereafter, two civic organizations followed the churches' lead in sponsoring schools for the city's indigent children.[51]

Whether supported by interdenominational, denominational, or civic associations, the charity schools shared the common goal of preparing the younger generation for responsible citizenship. The schools taught all children the rudiments of reading, writing, and arithmetic. In addition, girls received special instruction in needlework, and boys in agricultural and mechanical industry. To protect the students from corrupting influences, the schools secured foster families for children found in "morally depraved homes." Besides providing weekday instruction within a Christian environment, the charity schools required the students to attend Sunday worship with their parents or guardians. Finally, when the students reached sixteen years of age, the schools assisted them in finding suitable employment.

Some churchmen believed that providing higher learning as well as the fundamentals of education was a responsibility of the church. In response to this obligation, Baltimore Roman Catholics and Methodists established local schools of higher education. Father F. C. Nagot and his companions instituted St. Mary's Seminary in 1791 as a branch of the Seminary of St. Sulpice of Paris, France. Its purpose was to prepare priests for ministry in America. Alongside the seminary, St. Mary's Academy opened in 1799, and a year later it was promoted to the status of a college. Initially, the academy taught only Spaniards, since Bishop Carroll preferred American students to attend Georgetown College in Washington, D.C. But when most of the Spanish students left the city in 1803, Carroll opened the college to Americans. That the college admitted all males without distinction of creed created quite a controversy among local Protestants, who were offended that some Protestant parents would send their children to the "den of Satan" to receive further education. In spite of the controversy, the college flourished, becoming by 1806 a university of 106 students.[52]

In contrast, Methodist attempts at establishing institutions of higher learning in and around Baltimore consistently met with bitter frustration. As early as the 1784 Christmas Conference that gave birth to American Methodism, the denomination discussed plans to erect a college where "learning and religion go hand and hand."[53] In December 1787, after constructing a schoolhouse at Abingdon, Maryland—a small town twenty-five miles outside of Baltimore on the road to Philadelphia—Cokesbury College opened to twenty-five students. While offering instruction in English, Latin, Greek, Logic, Rhetoric, History, Geography, Natural Philosophy, and Astronomy, the stated purpose of the college was: "To answer the Design of Christian Education, by forming the Minds of the Youth, through divine Aid, to Wisdom and Holiness, by instilling into their Minds the Principles of true Religion, speculative, experimental and practical, and training them in the ancient way, that they may be rational, scriptural Christians." To meet these ends, rigid rules governed every hour of the student's day. They rose at five, with public prayer at six and breakfast at seven. Morning studies were from eight to twelve noon, followed by dinner and three hours of supervised recreation. Studies resumed from three to six P.M., after which came supper, public prayer at seven, and evening recreation. Students observed a strict nine o'clock bedtime.[54]

In spite of its religious designs, John Wesley, the founder of Methodism, never embraced the college. In a letter to Bishop Asbury, Wesley quipped: "I study to be little, you study to be great. I creep, you strut along. I found a school, you a college! Nay, and call it after your own names."[55] Moreover, the college gave Asbury more headaches than simply this caustic chiding from Wesley. Between 1785 and 1795, Asbury's correspondence was punctuated with complaints regarding the financial burden imposed on him by the school.[56] Then, on 7 December 1795 a fire totally destroyed the building and library of Cokesbury College. Upon hearing the news Asbury retorted: "Would any man give me £10,000 per year to do and suffer again what I have done for that house, I would not do it. The Lord called not Mr. Whitefield nor the Methodists to build colleges. I wished only for schools—Doctor Coke wanted a college."[57]

While Asbury had learned his lesson, apparently Thomas Coke had not. After learning of the tragedy, Coke returned to Baltimore and raised $4,500 from seventeen prominent individuals for the rebuilding of the college. When the denomination decided to move the school to Baltimore and make it an academy rather than a college, the local Methodists enthusiastically gave their support, collecting $3,000 cash in a house-to-house pleading campaign, and an additional $3,500 in Methodist subscriptions. With seventeen of Coke's friends underwriting the balance, the Methodists purchased a large dance hall adjacent to Light Street Church. As a result, within several months after the tragic fire, some two hundred students were again pursuing academic education under Methodist auspices.[58] Ironically, on 4 December 1796—three days before the anniversary of the burning at Abingdon—a second fire erupted in an adjoining house, bringing both Light Street Church and the relocated academy to the ground. In his typical resolute manner, Asbury simply concluded that "God loveth the people of Baltimore, and he will keep them poor, to make them pure."[59]

Although local residents rebuilt Light Street Church, Methodists gave no further consideration to establishing a Methodist institution of higher learning for nearly two decades. Finally, in 1816 a stock company of prominent Baltimore Methodists organized an academy named Asbury College.[60] At the suggestion of the aging Bishop Asbury, they called Samuel K. Jennings, a graduate of Rutgers College, as president of the institution. An admirable selection, President Jenning's reputation as a distinguished educator, physician, and local preacher brought immediate respectability to the school.[61]

In November 1817 the male members of the society voted to purchase from the stockholders of the academy all claims to the school for the amount of their initial investment of $8,500, and to erect a new house near Eutaw Street Church for the immediate accommodation of the academy. To help defray these expenses, they agreed to sell a valuable church lot.[62] Thus, with rapidity and enthusiasm, Baltimore City Station plunged once again into the business of higher education.

Temporarily, the vision of Bishop Coke to establish a Methodist college in

Baltimore was restored. Boosted by a written and financial endorsement in 1818 by the Baltimore Annual Conference—the first such official action by a Methodist conference since the burning of the academy in 1796—Asbury College initially flourished, with a student body of 170 students.[63] However, in spite of its popularity, the school soon plummeted into financial crisis. By the early summer of 1819 the rising debt resulting from the high expenses of boarding and educating youth in the city, compounded by a withering economy, forced the trustees of Baltimore City Station to propose drastic measures. When the male members of the society rejected the alternative of selling additional lots, they began a subscription campaign, asking all Baltimore Methodists to give a penny a week toward the sinking of the debt.[64] Eventually, the willingness of the religious community to carry the burden of this benevolent venture gave way to the fiscal realities of the day. In early 1820 Asbury College closed. The failure of the institution brought back bleak memories. Disillusioned and embittered by the most recent experience, in March 1820 the Baltimore Annual Conference rejected two separate recommendations to establish a centrally located seminary, and a boarding school for the children of Methodist preachers.[65] With this defeat, Bishop Coke's vision was replaced once again with Bishop Asbury's inner conviction that the Lord never intended Methodists to build colleges.

The expenses and limitations of classroom instruction demanded that churches find other, more general ways of educating city residents in public virtue. Printing and circulating free or inexpensive reading material was one such way. In any age the media exert an influence upon public conduct. In this era the principal medium was the printing press, and Baltimore churchmen used it to their fullest advantage. If the classroom reached its thousands, the printing press reached its tens of thousands.[66]

Between 1790 and 1830 Baltimore presses printed about one thousand separate religious titles. In some years more than 30% of the volumes published in Baltimore concerned religious subjects.[67] Numerous volumes were specifically printed for a particular pastor, prominent layman, or congregation. Some churches, including local Episcopal, Methodist, and Quaker fellowships, organized special committees to raise funds for the printing and circulation of religious materials. Given the impressive size of the religious market, it is likely that individual churchmen across all denominations actively supported such efforts.

While many titles were strictly theological works, hundreds were inspirational or devotional guides to Christian living. Frequently published were a number of Christian classics, ranging from François de Sales's *Devout Life* to John Milton's *Paradise Lost*. Also appearing were scores of lesser known guides such as William Percy's *True Christian's Character* and Hannah More's *Practical Piety*. Mason Locke Weems's writings also fell within this genre. While this Maryland Episcopal rector was best remembered for his biography of George Washington, which originated the cherry tree myth, his religious tragedies *God's Revenge Against Murder*, *God's Revenge Against Adultery*, and *God's Revenge Against Gambling* provided his readers with ample warnings of the consequences of sinful behavior.[68]

Churches also promoted the works of their spiritual fathers. On several occasions Baltimore Methodists had the writings of John Wesley and John Fletcher reprinted for circulation in the city. Similarly, Swedenborgians peddled the writings of Emanuel Swedenborg, while Lutherans propagated those of Martin Luther.[69] Even more popular than the theological commentaries of religious giants were the spiritual biographies of faithful Christians both great and small. Friends and Methodists in particular printed tracts that eulogized the piety of deceased ministers and laity. The principal purpose of the biographies was not to memorialize the dead. Instead it was to illumine that way of life expected of all conscientious Christians and citizens.[70]

Eulogies of George Washington illustrate the multiple uses of the religious biographies. Shortly after Washington's death in December 1799, the United States Congress designated 22 February 1800 as the day for the nation to pay final respects to the beloved hero. On this date the various congregations of Baltimore met in their respective houses of worship to commemorate the life of the deceased general. Seven discourses delivered on this occasion soon were circulated in the city. The theme of each message was identical: George Washington, providentially trained to save his country from bondage, was unexcelled in genius, virtue, and religion. While his greatness could not be duplicated, his noble example should be emulated.[71]

In developing this theme, two Episcopal ministers, Joseph Bend and James Kemp, compared Washington and Moses. Just as Moses delivered the Israelites from bondage in response to God's call, Washington, Bend and Kemp asserted, in obedience to the providentially directed Continental Congress, took charge of the American army, and with divine assistance broke "the iron rod of a cruel despot."[72] Continuing the analogy, Kemp observed: "Moses was only forty days absent ... when they made the golden calf. And had Washington been withdrawn from us at one particular crisis, this house may have perhaps been a temple of Reason, instead of a Christian Church.[73] Likewise, the Presbyterian Patrick Allison, after noting the similarities between Judah mourning for Josiah and America mourning for Washington, concluded: "Render his name precious ... till the end of time. Let the remembrance of his public and private virtues excite others to go and do likewise."[74]

Methodist Thomas Morrell, in depicting the general's life, noted virtues in Washington's character not mentioned in the other pastoral discourses. Interestingly, Morrell's eulogized Washington epitomized the dutiful Methodist. Morrell asserted that Washington fought for "freedom, not money"; that "no excess nor luxury was permitted at his table"; that he never used "contemptuous language"; that he gave "gifts to charity schools"; that "his will freed all negroes"; and that with reverence for God he attended public worship and read his Bible. Finally, Morrell concluded that while others may have been as wise, unambitious, and pious, "none have all these qualities concentrated as

Washington." Consequently, above all other men Washington should be the example for Americans to imitate.[75]

No less sublime were the praises expressed by Bishop John Carroll of the Roman Catholic Church. After initially asserting that Washington "stands supereminent and unrivaled in the annals of mankind," Carroll traced Washington's career, emphasizing how the finger of God directed his actions from youth to death. Then after quoting passages from the Book of Wisdom that prophetically described Washington's virtues, Carroll summarized: "While he lived we seemed to stand on loftier ground, for breathing the same air, inhabiting the same country, and enjoying the same constitution and laws, as the sublime and magnanimous Washington.... May these United States flourish ... as long as respect, honour, and veneration shall gather round the name of Washington."[76] Such exaltations were indeed remarkable, coming from the bishop of a church that anathematized the religious denomination to which Washington belonged.

The biographies of Washington dramatize the efforts of Baltimore preachers to imbue the public citizenry with a passion for virtue. The eulogies also reflect the ever-present link between religious and national loyalties. Early national churches accepted without hesitation their role as guardians of public morality, and were willing to use whatever means were at their disposal to meet these ends. Occasionally they appealed to state authorities for legal support to enforce their moral standards. But generally this support was neither requested nor needed. By disciplining their membership and indoctrinating the masses with a sense of public virtue through classroom instruction and a media blitz, churches voluntarily evoked from many the desired behavior patterns.

In discipline as in doctrine, churches did not always agree. Some held stricter standards than others. As a rule, Methodists, and to an even greater degree Friends, were the most likely to condemn questionable activity as immoral and outside the bounds of Christian conduct. Unlike some churches, these groups spoke unequivocally against institutional evils such as public lotteries and slavery, and personal vices such as theater-attending, extravagant living, and the too-eager pursuit of money. But in many areas churchmen across all denominations agreed. The Bible was the ultimate standard of conduct, and knowledge of the basic ethical standards in scripture was considered essential for the well-being of both church and society. In the end the extent to which churches disciplined their members and educated the masses was the degree to which they influenced general standards of conduct and fulfilled their patriotic and evangelical mission of spreading Christian virtue across the land.

5
WORSHIP

WORSHIP—literally "worth-ship" or declaring the worth of God—is the total response of the creature to the Creator; it is the giving to God the glory due his Name.[1] In popular usage, however, the definition of worship has been chiseled into meaning simply the public gathering, usually on Sundays, for a religious service of instruction and praise. Even in this narrowly constructed meaning, the practice of worship is significant, since it reflects if not shapes the moods and interests of society. Particularly in an age before secular enterprises replaced the church as the center of social and intellectual stimulation, the repeated experience of Sunday worship no doubt had a profound influence on the faithful churchgoer's perception of the world and his or her relationship to it.

In early national Baltimore, as in any pluralistic community, patterns of worship varied widely. Some "liturgically oriented" churches emphasized a strict order of worship. Others rejected outward forms and stressed the freedom of man in responding to the direction of the spirit. Still others, fearing the dangers in both extremes, retreated into safety and accepted in worship only what they thought specifically was commanded in scripture.[2] Yet no matter how liturgical, spiritualistic, or Word-oriented, most congregations recognized the propriety of at least four components of public worship: song, prayer, teaching or preaching, and at least on special occasions, the Eucharist or Lord's Supper. How each congregation incorporated these elements into a religious service, while remaining true to its doctrines and avoiding the extremes of cold-heartedness or extravagance, is the focus of this chapter.

The worship services in Friends' meetinghouses were exceptional. Of the four components of worship mentioned above, Quakers treated three as voluntary and prohibited the fourth. Believing that the spirit of Christ resided within all mankind as an "inner light" that illuminated truth to those who sought aid, Quakers met for public worship in silence, and awaited the guidance of the Inner Light. When anyone—regardless of age, sex, or race—felt moved, they stood and offered under the direction of the spirit a hymn, prayer, or sermon; but no words were required. If no one felt moved, the Friends remained for the period allowed for worship and then quietly left.

Since Friends saw communion with the divine as internal, they never celebrated the sacrament of the Lord's Supper.[3]

With the exception of the Friends, Baltimore churches acknowledged congregational singing as a scriptural and thus necessary ingredient in public worship. The preface of a Roman Catholic hymnal published in Baltimore in 1807 stated that next to the "eucharistical sacrifice," singing praises was "the noblest employment of a Christian."[4] This sentiment was widespread. To assist in this aspect of public worship, scores of psalters, hymnals, and musical guides were purchased by city congregations. Between 1799 and 1819, Baltimore presses alone printed at least sixty-eight separate musical volumes useful for public worship.[5]

Beyond this consensus the harmony ended. At one extreme, Baltimore's most conservative congregations, such as the Church of the Covenanters, sang only the lyrics of biblical psalms in metered English verse without any musical accompaniment.[6] Similarly, the Methodists, United Brethren, and at least some Baptist congregations rejected musical accompaniment in worship. These churches, however, were willing to sing contemporary hymns and gospel choruses alongside the scriptural psalms.[7]

And sing they did. Methodist services were notorious for their hearty, fervent singing. While critics labeled such activity an embarrassment to Christianity, the Methodists boasted that with only the aid of a tuning fork they fulfilled the scriptural injunction to make a "joyful noise unto the Lord." The lyrics of the popular chorus sung at worship illustrated their disregard of public criticism.

> The Pharisees and Formalists, They stand and are amazed.
> They wonder what's the matter, With the shouting Methodists.
> But if they would repent, And believe in the Lord,
> They also would go shouting, And praising of their God.[8]

In 1818, a Methodist songbook, *Social and Camp Meeting Songs for the Pious*, underwent two editions—the first edition having sold out within a nine-month period. So central to Methodism was the hearty congregational singing that Thomas Bond, when he wrote a defense of Methodist polity, included fervent singing as a distinctive characteristic of the denomination.[9]

Most other bodies, including the Episcopalians, Roman Catholics, Lutherans, German Reformed, and Unitarians, accepted instrumental accompaniment (i.e., organ music) as a legitimate aid to public worship. But preachers of congregations with organs still felt obliged occasionally to justify instrumental music by espousing its spiritual benefits. In one sermon, Joseph Bend of St. Paul's Church asserted:

> Wisely managed and employed, it [instrumental music] contributes to awaken our attention in the house of God. It enlivens and renders more fruitful our devotion. It helps to remove ... those accidental distractions ... and flatness to which we are all too liable; ... It exhilarates our spirits; it

renders more active our better propensities and more extensive and strong our chain of Christian love.[10]

Despite such praise, the use of the organ in public worship only gradually won acceptance. While St. Paul's parish installed Baltimore's first church organ as early at 1753, by the end of the eighteenth century only two additional churches, St. Peter's Roman Catholic and Zion Lutheran, had joined St. Paul's.[11] In 1802 Christ Protestant Episcopal purchased an organ for $1,000, and two years later, for a similar price, St. Paul's replaced its dilapidated antique with a new model.[12] Then in 1808 St. Patrick's Roman Catholic congregation purchased an organ, and the following year the German Reformed Church invested $3,000 to become the sixth Baltimore congregation to procure an organ.[13]

Apparently expense was not the only obstacle to the purchase of an organ. Church doctrines and patterns of worship were also important. It was no coincidence that while none of the above churches, with the exception of St. Paul's, were among the most prominent congregations of the city—in fact, the membership of the Catholic congregations was overwhelmingly of lower-class orientation[14]—all six congregations placed emphasis upon a liturgical order of worship. Thus the denominations that perceived public worship as principally a liturgical drama found great utility in instrumental accompaniment as an aid to worship.

The use of the organ in maintaining both the unity and dignity of the service was apparent in the typical order of worship used by J. Daniel Kurtz at Zion Lutheran. After an organ prelude the service proper began with a formal processional led by the pastor and the church council. Then followed a musical piece by the choir, a congregational hymn, a confessional prayer closing with the triple Kyrie, a second hymn, and the proper collect from the hymnbook. Next the congregation read the gospel lesson, recited the creed, and sang another hymn. During the singing of this hymn, Pastor Kurtz left the altar for the pulpit, where he remained for the reciting of the Lord's Prayer and the general discourse. After the sermon came a general prayer and a closing hymn, followed by the benediction, an organ postlude, and the processional.[15] A similar concern for formalized corporate participation encouraged Episcopal, German Reformed, and Roman Catholic congregations to embrace the organ. In contrast, the "evangelical" denominations, which viewed worship as a more individualized, spontaneous response to the Word, found the organ less necessary, and thus remained more likely to label it as either an unscriptural addition or an unnecessary luxury. Before the 1820s the only Protestant Episcopal house in Baltimore without an organ was St. Peter's, a church noted for its "evangelical" or low-church inclinations.[16]

The growing popularity of instrumental music within the larger Episcopalian, Catholic, Lutheran, and German Reformed congregations, as well as the growing affluence of the city and its churchgoers, encouraged even Baltimore's Calvinistic congregations to become more receptive to organ purchases. But change also wrought controversy. For example, First Presbyterian had always followed the Presbyterian custom of having a precentor read line by line the words of the hymn as the congregation sang *a cappella*. In 1811, however, after a dispute over the purchase of an organ caused several prominent Scottish members to bolt in disgust from the congregation, the church became the first Presbyterian house in the city and one of the first in the nation to include organ accompaniment in a service of worship.[17] Shortly thereafter, the Associate Reformed Church purchased an organ. Later in the decade Trinity Episcopal and the First Independent Unitarian congregations installed organs. Then in 1820 the newly completed Roman Catholic Cathedral brought to Baltimore a $6,000 pipe organ, which at that time was the largest such instrument in the United States.[18] Thus, by the third decade of the century, no fewer than eleven Baltimore congregations incorporated organ music as part of their worship experience. By this time churchmen no longer viewed the organ as simply a useful accessory for liturgically oriented congregations. Now it sat alongside stained-glass windows as an ecclesiastical status symbol that not only aided in worship but also served to lure prospective members into the fold of that particular congregation.

In order to receive the greatest benefit from their organs, churches hired trained musicians as organists. The salary of the organists rose with the prestige of the organ and the wealth of the congregation. In 1795 the schoolmaster of the Zion Lutheran school also doubled as the church organist.[19] Similarly, in 1796 the organist at St. Peter's Roman Catholic congregation served for an annual salary of only $50.[20] In contrast, in 1814 the organist at Christ Church received $200 annually, while in 1817 the First Independent Unitarian Church organist, Thomas Carr—the man remembered today for arranging Francis Scott Key's "The Star Spangled Banner" to a contemporary bar tune—was offered an impressive salary of $450 per year.[21]

In addition to hiring organists, churches organized choirs and ensembles, trained soloists, and opened classes for the musical instruction of children. These innovations served as a dignified way of removing the webs of apathy from the service of worship by cultivating the Methodist enthusiasm for music without acquiring its vulgarities. For example, shortly after arriving at the nearly defunct Second Presbyterian Church, John Breckenridge, in an effort to invigorate the congregation and choir, established both a school to teach "the rudiments of sacred music to youth" and a musical society for vocal practice during the week.[22] Another believer in the transforming power of musical instruction was the talented organist at St. Paul's, John Cole. Between 1799 and 1818, Cole published eight volumes of musical works—five of which underwent multiple editions. In his textbook *The Rudiments of Music* Cole asserted:

> Let but a taste of this delightful science become once encouraged and cultivated and we may expect to see our churches well filled, our congregations induced to join their voices with the choirs, all vying with each other in

taste and performance! An elegant and rational amusement will then be presented to the *youth of both sexes*. They will imperceptibly acquire habits of regularly attending public worship. They will be the more strongly attached to it from ... a consciousness that the service of the church is, in part, sustained by their presence, by their laudable exertions, and by their polished attainments. Then shall we 'sing unto the Lord a new song.'[23]

The "delightful science" to which Cole referred was simply the elemental knowledge of musical notes and rhythm along with such practical advice as singing within one's range and keeping gestures "manly and decent." Such instruction, Cole argued, would not only aid in congregational singing, but would vivify the service through the inspiration of a plentiful and harmonious choir.[24] Cole at least achieved the latter. To join the choirs at St. Paul's parish required an audition, acceptance by a three-fourth's majority of the choir membership, and a commitment to attend all religious services and to four hours of rehearsal each week. Despite the standards, the choirs included over fifty members.

The city's largest congregations, with their organs, organists, and choir-masters, offered musical opportunities not available to parishioners in rural churches. At least one pastor, John M. Duncan of the Associate Reformed Church, recognized the dangers of making a church's music program too professional. While supportive of instrumental music and childhood musical instruction, Duncan warned that an overemphasis on musical perfection could obstruct a meaningful worship experience. In the introduction to a book of hymns published by his church, Duncan lamented that "many unduly affected by love of music, have gone most extravagant lengths, and with improvement for their objective, have 'shut the mouths of God's people from praising his Name.'" He felt musical appreciation must encourage, not deter, all the congregation to praise God in song. That Duncan felt obliged to caution against simply enjoying and not participating in congregational music demonstrated the degree to which this Calvinistic congregation had wandered from its earlier custom of *a cappella* congregational singing.[25]

A second common element in worship was prayer. Just as congregations differed over what and how to sing, they disagreed as to the proper forms of public prayer. The controversy over written versus extemporaneous prayer separated denominations, and even congregations within a given denomination. As a rule the more "evangelical" bodies preferred extemporaneous prayer. For instance, despite the fact that John Wesley prepared especially for American Methodists an order of worship that included prescribed prayers, Baltimore Methodists never used the ritual. Methodists viewed ministers who read prayers as lacking in spirituality. This same sentiment also pervaded Baltimore's Baptist and United Brethren congregations.[26]

The city's Reformed churches were less inflamed over the issue. Following in the tradition set forward in the 1644 Directory of Worship, all Reformed services included a lengthy pastoral prayer of ten to twenty minutes which concluded with the well-known Lord's Prayer.[27] The clergy could either read a previously drafted prayer or offer one extemporaneously from the pulpit. Since the ability to pray extemporaneously exemplified a spiritual gift, a sign of ministerial maturity, most parishioners preferred the free style. This encouragement provoked at least one Baltimore pastor, James Inglis of First Presbyterian, to switch from written to extemporaneous prayer during his ministerial stay in Baltimore.[28]

Among Baltimore's Episcopal houses, the issue reeked with intensity. On the one side were the high-church clergymen of St. Paul's parish, who favored reading the beautiful, printed prayers of the Book of Common Prayer over prayers that "savour ... the folly, the vanity, or the spiritual pride of the individual."[29] In contrast, the pastors of the low-church St. Peter's Protestant Episcopal congregation opposed "formalists," who neglected "the great doctrines of the church" by advocating "with a zeal disproportioned to the importance of the subject, an undeviating adherence to all prescribed forms and ceremonies."[30] This debate over the form of public prayer was symptomatic of the theological rift between the two branches of the Protestant Episcopal church. Generally, the high-church advocates—laboring for "the laudable purpose of establishing and perpetuating uniformity of worship and discipline"—emphasized a strict allegiance to a set order of worship.[31] Conversely, the low-church evangelicals—concerned more with inner experience than outward show—favored a less-structured order, which allowed greater flexibility to meet the particular circumstances of the day.

Despite the inter- and intradenominational differences, most services included prayers of adoration, confessions, thanksgiving, supplication, and intercession.[32] Churches remembered the nation, the president, and the civil magistrates in their prayers. For example, the Roman Catholic mass offered in the city often included the following prayer for the commonwealth:

> Save O Lord the Commonwealth. Let the people's rights prevail.
> Let Columbia trust in thee to whom she owes her liberty.
> Voice of praise let us raise. Great Jehovah praise to thee.
> We are free thanks to thee. Father of our liberty.[33]

The liturgies of the Episcopal, Lutheran, and New Jerusalem churches included similar prayers for the nation. Although the extemporaneously uttered prayers were rarely recorded, the fact that Jesse Lee advised the Methodists that their time would be better spent praying for government leaders than abusing them, suggested that the evangelicals also recognized a duty to uplift the nation and its leaders in public prayer.[34]

A third element of public worship was holy communion. Except for the Roman Catholics, who believed the celebration of the eucharist was central to all experiences of worship, Baltimore congregations observed holy communion only infrequently. The First German Reformed Church offered the sacred rite only twice yearly. First Presbyterian served communion twice a year until 1815 when Pastor Inglis established a new tradition of four annual observances.[35] Methodist congregations followed this quarterly pattern, while the German Lutheran congregation celebrated the Eucharist just three times yearly.[36] Apparently no Protestant bodies observed the sacrament more often than did the Episcopal houses and Second Baptist Church, which generally designated one Sunday of each month as a communion Sunday.[37]

Baltimore churchmen insisted that the infrequency of communion did not imply any downgrading of the sacrament. During the early national period most congregations placed a strong emphasis on the proper preparation for the supper. For example, the consistory regulations of First German Reformed required all members to visit the pastor of the congregation on the day preceding communion Sunday to be examined in regard to their spiritual condition.[38] Likewise, the Synod of the German and English Lutheran churches instructed ministers not to admit slaves to the supper unless they were baptized, properly indoctrinated, and known to be of Christian character.[39] While not requiring strict examinations, Episcopal clergymen urged their parishioners to follow *The New Week's Preparation*, a devotional guide and confessional that was intended to prepare the communicant for the holy sacrament.[40] John P. K. Henshaw of St. Peter's, believing this guide to be deficient in theological instruction, published his own communion guide especially for the members of his congregation. Asserting that a "due preparation ... has ever been esteemed in the Christian church as the most exalted act of devotion, and the most estimable of all means of grace," Henshaw warned of the danger of neglecting the Lord's Supper, and challenged his reader anxiously to "seek to Know whether he *does indeed believe*."[41] In addition, Pastor William Nevins of First Presbyterian underscored the importance of communion when he broke with the tradition of his congregation by denying communion to the baptized but unconverted children of full members.[42] Even the United Brethren congregation, known for its open communion table, required that nonmembers be examined by the vestry before receiving the sacraments.[43] In short, while holy communion among Protestant bodies during this period was infrequently observed, there were stringent requirements for attending the Lord's Table.

In comparison with European churches, American denominations generally were not so sacramentally oriented. In most Baltimore houses, the pulpit, not the altar, was the center of worship. The sermon—significant to the "liturgical" and paramount to the "evangelical"—was perceived, at least by all Protestants, as the heart of the religious service. In the final analysis, congregations judged ministers successful or incompetent by their pulpit talents.

Preachers were not judged by the same standards. What Methodist congregations expected from their preachers was hardly congruous with the expectations of parishioners from a high-church Protestant Episcopal congregation. In some ways, Methodist itinerants had distinct advantages over other preachers. Appointed to a station of churches rather than to a single congregation, and with a tenure of no more than two years, Methodist preachers easily avoided repeating themselves. Then too, the lower educational background of the Methodist membership removed the need for an elaborate, sophisticated apology. Instead, they demanded only the simple gospel message.[44] Yet, in one sense Methodist preachers had to meet a higher standard. Unlike Presbyterians, Episcopalians, Lutherans, and Unitarians, Methodists considered it inappropriate if not unspiritual to predraft a text of the sermon. For example, in an address before the Baltimore Annual Conference of 1807, George Roberts candidly expressed this attitude with the comment: "I do not deem a reader of sermons deserving the name of a preacher of the Gospel." Such a custom, it was argued, dampened "the ardour of devotion" and prevented the preacher from placing sufficient dependence on the spirit for guidance.[45]

This did not mean that Methodists ascended to the pulpit unprepared. Extemporaneous preaching could be mastered only through spiritual diligence and perseverance. To assist aspiring young preachers in learning the trade, the eminent evangelist John Summerfield penned the following advice:

> Be not anxious to say all that might be said. . . . Prepare a skeleton of your leading ideas, branching them off into their secondary relation; this you may have before you. Digest well the subject, but be not careful to choose your words previous to your delivery. Follow out the idea in such language as may offer [itself] at the moment. Don't be discouraged if you fall down a hundred times, for though you fall, you shall rise again.[46]

Typically, Methodist itinerants preached extemporaneously for fifty to sixty minutes.[47] Assuming an additional hour for music, prayer, and lay testimony, an average Methodist Sunday morning service of worship lasted about two hours. That the Baltimore City Station lay leaders felt obliged to pass a resolution limiting services to no longer than two hours suggests that Methodist preachers occasionally abused even the liberally appropriated one-hour sermon slot.[48]

While the total service was of no shorter duration, the Episcopal congregations that followed closely the order of worship contained in their Book of Common Prayer, designated no longer than fifteen to twenty minutes for the pastor's sermon.[49] Other denominations that strictly followed a set order— including the Roman Catholic, Lutheran, and New Jerusalem churches—also expected relatively short sermons. At St. Peter's Protestant Episcopal, however, where portions of the liturgy were omitted, sermons generally ran considerably longer. Rather than preaching extemporaneously from a skeletal outline, most Episcopal clergy—with the exception of the evangelical George Dashiell of St. Peter's and John Johns of Christ Church—wrote out their sermons in full, and then either read them from the pulpit or recited them from memory.[50]

Both in terms of length and manner of delivery, Presbyterian sermons usually fell somewhere between the characteristic discourses of Methodists and Episcopalians. An average Presbyterian sermon, excluding the pastoral prayer, was about thirty minutes long.[51] While insistent upon a well-organized, eloquently composed message, Baltimore Presbyterians generally disapproved of the custom of reading manuscript sermons. Hence most Presbyterian pastors either memorized the message, or purposely departed from the manuscript version before them and added extemporaneous expressions during the height of the sermon.[52] John Glendy and William Nevins chose the former course, while John Inglis selected the latter. Among the eminent Presbyterian pastors of the city, apparently only John Breckenridge preferred the Methodist custom of preaching extemporaneously from short notes.[53]

Besides the different methods of delivery, contemporary accounts by Baltimore sermon critics revealed a diversity in the oratorical techniques used by the popular preachers. At one extreme the Methodist Henry Slicer won repute for his effective interplay of soft, whisperlike tones punctuated by thundering cries that "well nigh start you from your seat." A critic applauded John M. Duncan of the Associate Reformed Church for his "commanding tone" and frequent gestures, which were described as "exceedingly forcible." Such reviews described charismatic preachers willing and able to use drama as a means of arousing the congregation to action. In contrast, the same critic characterized the Unitarian George Burnap as "always dignified" and the English Lutheran John Morris as a "plain, common sense speaker" who "talks rather than declaims." For such men the effectiveness of a sermon depended more upon its rhetoric and logic than its dramatic presentation.

This critic placed Episcopal ministers in both categories. While noting the "calm earnestness" and "pleasantly modulated" tones of William Wyatt of St. Paul's—a church known for its high-church propensities—he observed the "steady even current" and "graceful and impressive" gesticulations of John Johns of the doctrinally moderate Christ Church. Similarly, he described the "earnest zeal" and "exhibitions of love and compassion" of John P. K. Henshaw of the city's low-church St. Peter's Episcopal. Although subjective and not without bias, these accounts suggest an observably different oratory demeanor between the spirited Methodist, Presbyterian, and low-church Episcopalian preachers, and the more refined Lutheran, Unitarian, and high-church Episcopal ministers.[54]

Paralleling the diversity of preaching techniques were certain variations in the form and content of Baltimore sermons. An analysis of these variations exposes distinguishing characteristics reappearing in the typical Episcopal, Presbyterian, and Methodist sermons. Unfortunately, the lack of extant sermons from ministers of Baltimore's smaller Protestant bodies prevents their inclusion in this analysis.

The discourses of Episcopal ministers were often the more easily identifiable, since many were unashamedly sectarian in nature. Generally Episcopal ministers offered at least one sermon per year on the nature of the Episcopacy. The purposes of these sermons were to attack the "errors" of Presbyterian and Methodist church polity and to assert the uniqueness of their denomination's direct line of episcopal succession, which they dated back to the apostle John.[55] Other popular topics for Episcopalians included discourses on confirmation, and the beauty and benefits of the Book of Common Prayer.[56]

Since not everyone favored sectarian sermons, other messages defended the right of the Episcopal clergy to emphasize the unique attributes of their denomination. In one defense William Wyatt of St. Paul's parish asserted:

> In Politics, it is honourable to be bold, proselyting and inflexible. In Science, each man has his favorite theory, and nomenclature; and he glows with the zeal of a partisan.... But the moment that he enters the precincts of religious discussion, every principle must be reversed. Here to distinguish between tenets, is deemed rash; to imagine that any association, self-styled Christian, can be in errour, is uncharitable: to be attached to any particular mode of rendering divine homage to the Deity, is bigotry.[57]

While similar sectarian emphases periodically appeared among Methodists and Presbyterians, generally the practice better characterized Episcopal divines.

In addition, Episcopal sermons were frequently distinguishable by their topical orientation. Although Presbyterians often divided discourses into two parts—the topic being introduced in the morning service and completed in the evening service of the same day[58]—Episcopal ministers more likely prepared sermon series, with large topics discussed each week for a period of several months. Joseph Bend of St. Paul's preached each week for a month on the parable of the "Rich man and Lazarus," for two months on the Lord's Prayer, for three months on apologetical arguments in favor of Christianity, and for four or more months on topics such as the Ten Commandments and the attributes of God. Similarly, Bend's successor, James Kemp, preached a four-month series on the Articles of the Church, and another lengthy series on the book of Acts.[59] This practice of treating subjects in depth over an extended period of time contrasted sharply with that of the extemporaneous Methodists, whose every sermon was a separate entity.

Episcopal sermons often emphasized the virtue of moderation. Although emphatically denying that any common ground existed between things of the world and true religion,[60] ministers like Joseph Bend and James Kemp made it clear that the pious life was a balanced life that avoided the pitfalls inherent in all extremes. While condemning both idleness and an overly zealous interest in temporal concerns as evils, Bend admonished his parishioners to "seek a competency of worldly goods and enjoy the pleasures of life in moderation, without neglecting the duty which we owe to heaven."[61] Likewise, Kemp reminded his constituents not to avoid riches but pride, not industry but covetousness, not power but oppression, and not "the moderate enjoyment of all bounties of Providence that ... their abuse to intemperance and prodigality."[62]

Both Bend and Kemp valued moderation, even in the godly activities deemed essential to the Christian life. In a sermon on prayer, after castigating inattention and cold-heartedness in public worship, Bend also cautioned against falling into the "extravagance of enthusiasm."[63] In another message

Bend tempered his endorsement of "meditation, prayer, retirement, devout reading, abstinence, and other duties of a similar nature" by asserting that even these virtues can be destructive to the godly life if carried to the point of interfering with the other duties of man. Bend warned:

> He who indiscreetly spends in religious exercises so large a portion of his time, as to break in upon ... honest industry, runs a risk of falling into poverty, of involving his family in distress, on neglecting the education of his children, and of becoming ... a petitioner of the bounty of another.[64]

Kemp also crusaded against the dangers of religious extravagance when he asserted:

> Those who instead of purifying their hearts, controlling their passions, and cultivating true godliness, are continually expecting visionary attestations of divine favour, will find they have been pursuing a shadow and neglecting the substance.... They who cherish frenzied agitations for the divine impulses of the Holy Spirit which only operates by inspiring holy purposes ... prepare for themselves insupportable consternation in the last great day.[65]

In a funeral discourse, Kemp underscored the same theme by encouraging his parishioners to follow the pious example of the deceased member who was constant at the Lord's Table, and kept religion as the focus of his life without becoming a "fanatick."[66] In sum, while detesting the religious enthusiast who neglected his familiar and social responsibilities, Episcopalians eulogized the self-controlled, industrious, pious citizen who was an asset to both the church and society.

If an underlying intention of Episcopal sermons was to venerate the "moderate" and castigate the "fanatick," then conversely, a purpose of Methodist sermons was to accentuate the "true convert" and expose the ominous nature of the religious formalist. The sermons of the renouned Methodist John Summerfield often exhibited just such a juxtaposition. On one occasion he declared:

> A formalist may confess, but he only feels sin as an offense against society, or his own character; but the true convert is so convinced that sin is against God, that he cries "against thee only".... The formalist confesses, but says much to excuse—that God acts too hard: the true penitent ... feels no such thing as a little sin—he feels that he is doomed to eternal death, and thus feeling, cries, "it is just, the sentence should take place.[67]

In another message on the nature of true conversion, he proclaimed:

> It [conversion] does not consist in a name of Christianity, in an attachment to this or the other persuasion.... Nor does it consist in the ... changing from erroneous views ... to orthodox creeds.... Nor does it consist in a reformation of life.... Conversion is more than all this—it is no less than

an entire change from the love of sin to the love of holiness, from the power of Satan to God.[68]

The above extracts illustrate two common traits appearing in Methodist sermons: first, the emphasis on feeling as well as understanding; and second, the dualism that create the gulf between the lukewarm formalist and the converted sinner. Again, while not entirely unique, such emphases characterized Methodist messages.

Akin to Methodist tirades against formalism were the frequent Presbyterian cautions against "practical atheism" or "counterfeit Christianity"—that is, "believing that there is a God yet thinking and feeling and living just as if there was none."[69] Apparently this concern was strong at First Presbyterian, for its pastors, James Inglis and William Nevins, referred to the topic in eight of the sixty-four sermons included in their two published volumes.[70] These sermons combated "unbelief in the household of faith" by warning the communicants that "the nominal friends of Christ have as little of the true and saving faith as his undisguised enemies" and that "undisguised infidelity and unproductive faith ... are equally foreign to ... eternal life."[71] Also like Methodist sermons, most Presbyterian messages first directed the congregation into a self-examination of their spiritual condition, and then concluded with an invitation to respond to the demands of the gospel. In order to correct popular misconceptions regarding the tenets of Calvinism, Baltimore Presbyterians frequently reminded their congregations that *anyone* willing to take up the cross of Christ would be received by the Savior and inherit eternal life.[72]

To summarize, both the form and substance of Sunday discourses varied with the denomination. Generally, Episcopal sermons were in length relatively short, in form segmented into prolonged series, in delivery memorized or read, in style, graceful, in content occasionally sectarian, and in emphasis, directed against the pitfalls of religious extremism. In contrast, Methodist sermons were characteristically long, extemporaneous "outpourings of a full heart," calculated to awaken sinners and arouse "lukewarm formalists" to greater spiritual diligence. Presbyterian sermons were carefully composed, argumentative discourses of medium length designed to motivate the congregation to respond to the gospel call.

In spite of these variations, Protestant sermons did reflect a few common features. First, all the preachers found their text in scripture. Even the most sectarian addresses were not exempt from this requisite. Preachers also added an abundance of supportive biblical references. About seven in ten texts came from the New Testament, the most popular books being the Gospels, Acts, Romans, 1 and 2 Corinthians, and Galatians. Isaiah, Psalms, and Proverbs were the more frequently cited Old Testament books.[73]

Second, preachers during this era delivered practical rather than theological or speculative discourses. Even the Presbyterian ministers, who often appealed to the doctrine of predestination, wanted more often to refute practical misconceptions of the doctrine than to speculate about the mysteries of the divine decrees. For example, the central thesis of James Inglis's published sermon "The Sovereignty of God" was to emphasize that God's predetermining counsel "does not exonerate us from the obligation to personal diligence, activity and obedience."[74] Similarly, William Nevins laboriously reminded his congregation that Christ "came into the world, not to answer curious but useful questions, not to demonstrate theorems but to solve the one grand problem, 'How shall man be made just with God?'"[75] To this statement Baltimore sermon writers across denominations could add a loud "amen."[76]

Third, Baltimore preachers acknowledged that "the life and soul of Christianity" was contained in the doctrine of the atonement.[77] As illustrated in the words of James Inglis, religion, when torn from this doctrine, resembled "a superstructure resting on no solid groundwork—a beautiful statue ... pleasing ... to the eye, but incapable of influencing, affecting, or even reaching the heart."[78] Moreover, Methodists, Episcopalians, and Presbyterians alike expounded Anselm's "objective" version of the doctrine when they asserted that the sacrifice of Christ was necessary in order to satisfy the justice of the Father.[79] Together they renounced Abelard's "subjective" theory of the atonement. According to Abelard, the death of Christ was merely an exemplary act of self-denial intended to spur mankind toward a greater devotion to a loving God. Since this notion did not require man to recognize his sinful condition and "God's infinite love for holiness and detestation for sin," it fell alongside the denial of the divinity of Christ as one of the two damnable heresies castigated consistently from these Baltimore pulpits.[80]

A fourth common thread running throughout sermons of these congregations was an emphasis on the trinity of death, judgment, and eternity. Preachers alluded to this awful trilogy in order to arouse the parishioners to self-examination and spiritual decision. One common motif used to produce this effect was a contrast of the uncertainties of life with the certainties of death, judgment, and eternal reward or punishment, and then the question: "Are you prepared to die?"[81] Ministers endlessly stressed the need for forgiveness and told of a coming judgment—a time when a righteous judge would know every action, word, and thought.[82] Then they painted the blissful beatitudes of heaven against the eternal fires of hell, and stressed the two alternatives open to mankind—pardon or punishment.[83] Variations of these themes appeared in scores of early Baltimore sermons. Moreover, a purpose of all funeral orations was to remind the living that death and judgment were near.[84] Interestingly, few preachers felt compelled to argue that judgment and reward or judgment and punishment awaited mankind at the day of resurrection. Apparently the Bible-believing Methodists, Episcopalians, and Presbyterians alike accepted these events as either self-evident truths or mysteries of scripture that needed no vindication.[85]

Fifth, in sermons as in prayers, preachers reinforced a link between religious and national loyalties. Believing that God's providential judgments interfered in the immediate affairs of individuals, cities, and nations, ministers told Baltimore congregations that local calamities and national crises were acts of Providence "designed to reclaim them from the evil of their ways."[86] Hence in response to emergencies—which included such crises as yellow fever epidemics and the threat of war or armed invasion—Baltimore preachers called special days of humiliation, prayer, and fasting, and sounded loud jeremiads in an effort to stay the awful hand of judgment.[87] Typically, these sermons began with a text such as:: "If my people which are called by my name, shall humble themselves, and pray, and seek my face, and turn from their wicked ways; then will I hear from heaven, and will forgive their sin, and will heal their land."[88] Following a short exposition of the text, the ministers delineated the specific evils infecting society. This list generally included such offenses as doing business on Sunday, inattention in public worship, dueling, debauchery, drunkenness, ingratitude, dishonesty, and taking advantage of the ignorant and poor. At this point they made reference to former times when "our pious forefathers were exceedingly jealous for the Lord God of hosts."[89] After contrasting the pious past with the promiscuous present, they urged a public repentance: "If you love your children—Repent: If you love your church—Repent: If you love your country—Repent: If you love the Saviour of the World—Repent: If you would escape the righteous judgments of Almighty God—Repent."[90] Finally such discourses ended with a patriotic call. Whether exhibited in the orthodox Presbyterian James Inglis's comment that "true patriotism is a Christian virtue" or in the unorthodox Swedenborgian John Hargrove's more extreme assertion that "no man can be a good Christian except he be a real Patriot," Baltimore preachers encouraged an unquestionable allegiance to the young republic.[91]

The diversity of sermon style and content from denomination to denomination was great enough so that an aware observer could enter a house of worship without knowledge of the religious commitment of the preacher, and leave after hearing the discourse with a strong suspicion as to his denominational affiliation. Yet if the same observer was then to hear sermons of the other clergymen in the city, he or she would most likely note that each discourse was biblically based, practical, theologically similar in the soteriological essentials, and concerned with the present condition of the nation and the future condition of the individual soul. Exceptions, particularly among Unitarians and Swedenborgians, of course would be found. Still, most preachers of this era would have harmoniously endorsed the statement made by Frederick Beasley on the occasion of his inaugural discourse at St. Paul's Church: "Henceforth, I would make it the first desire ... that you may be saved. To the accomplishment of this grand object, all my pleadings with you from this sacred place shall be invariably directed."[92] With salvation as a common goal, preachers were in their own way "truly evangelical," often differing less in what they said than in how they said it.

In conclusion, worship in most early national Baltimore churches was serious business. With a theology that emphasized the sinful state of man, the necessity of satisfying the justice of God through the atoning sacrifice of an obedient Savior, the nearness of death, judgment and everlasting felicity or torment, and the ever-present possibility of divine retribution for personal or national sins—the act of worshiping the Author of this theology could not be taken lightly. Reflecting this sober mood were the controversies surrounding such seemingly inconsequential matters as incorporating organ music into worship, praying extemporaneously, or reading sermons, the injunctions against coming to the Lord's Table with an unprepared heart, and the incessant warnings from the pulpits to be prepared for judgment. If such a religious atmosphere fostered sectarian loyalty, subordinated the love of God to his justice, and diluted the religion of Christ with nationalism, the Sunday services, by their stress upon the accountability of man and the righteousness of God, at least cushioned the community from the evils of economic exploitation and common criminality. If the call to personal holiness was not universally heeded, it was not due to a lack of effort of Baltimore clergy.

PART TWO
THE MILITANT CHURCHES: THE EFFECTS OF RELIGIOUS COMPETITION

6
REVIVALISM

IN June 1800 several Presbyterian and Methodist preachers held a four-day sacramental meeting near Red River, Kentucky. The meeting brought unexpected and extraordinary results. Hundreds of attenders trembled under the terror of divine judgment, screamed for mercy, and experienced an emotional ecstasy of assurance of their forgiveness. A second meeting near Gasper River produced similar manifestations. Then in 1801 followed the largest and most spectacular meeting at Cane Ridge. These early camp meetings inaugurated and symbolized a new era of religious intensity—an era filled with fervent singing and preaching, acrobatic exercises, rising millennial expectations, "new measures" of evangelicalism, and an abundance of reform associations, utopian communes, and exotic cults.

Labeling this age of religious ferment the "second great awakening," historians have noted how the religious upheavals affected the cultural life of the new nation.[1] Too often, however, the emotional revivalism of the turn of the century has been considered a rural or backcountry affair, with the urban manifestations of the awakening erupting a generation later with the arrival of the famed professional evangelist Charles Finney.[2] In this chapter I shall discuss the origins, locations, and impact of revivalism within the environs of Baltimore. This story will demonstate that two decades before Finney's "second birth," urban revivalism, engineered by the same "new measures" that Finney ultimately would claim as his own, was commonplace in America's fastest-growing community.

Revivalism begs definition, particularly since the word carries multiple connotations. Etymologically, revivalism means simply reviving or restoring the church from indifference and declension. This involves inspiring the faithful to greater diligence, and bringing the unchurched into the congregational fold. In the nineteenth century the word *revival* also implied the wooing of individuals toward spiritual regeneration or conversion—that process by which sinful man through God's grace obtains the inheritance of eternal salvation. But revivals meant more than the preparation of mankind for eternity and more and better church members. All churchmen, including those opposed to the activities of revivalists, acknowledged these responsibilities as fundamental obligations of Christians. Instead, revivalists were those evangelicals who insisted upon a special kind of conversion—an instantaneous experience of faith, preceded by a strong sense of personal guilt, and followed by a joyful assurance of forgiveness. Experiences apart from this norm were suspect. Moreover, since they viewed this conscious, instantaneous event as the prerequisite of the Christian life, revivalists were willing to use innovative measures calculated to provoke this type of religious experience. Unlike many, revivalists unhesitantly appealed to emotion as well as to reason, and tolerated emotional responses to the preaching of the Word.[3]

The number of Baltimoreans involved in revivals depends upon the meaning of the term. All churchmen throughout the era were evangelical in the sense that they acknowledged that propagating the gospel message was a basic Christian obligation. Likewise, most agreed on the soteriological essentials, believing that God through the atoning death of Christ granted pardon and life to the regenerate, but punished the unconverted with eternal damnation. These common doctrinal positions preconditioned the city for a mass revival. But not all churchmen placed equal emphasis upon a conversion telescoped in time to a single datable experience. Neither did all embrace those "new measures" of evangelical activity which consistently evoked extremes of emotional behavior. At least before 1815 revivalistic enterprises in Baltimore, in this restricted sense, were principally a Methodist affair.

Methodists were not alone in noting the lack of spiritual vitality in the city during the early decades of the national period. Although the proportion of churchgoers to the population was greater in Baltimore than in the nation at large, urban pastors still complained about religious apathy. Particularly depressed was Joseph Bend of St. Paul's parish. In 1796 Bend wrote: "This is, I believe, an unprecedented instance of negligence and lukewarmness in the Church of Maryland."[4] Two years later he complained: "I consider religion in this state to be in a confirmed declension; nor do I know when to fix a period in my own days at which the prospects will begin to brighten."[5] Again in 1799 he lamented that in Baltimore "religion gains no ground" and "morality has evidently declined."[6]

Only slightly more encouraging was *Observations on the Present State of Religion in Maryland*, published in 1795 by the Episcopal minister William Duke. Duke acknowledged that religion as a whole had marginally improved since 1775 as a result of the spirited, although sometimes overly zealous, activities of the Methodists. But Duke quickly added that religious vitality was deficient in many areas. He attributed the overall state of declension to divisiveness within the Christian community, the failure of the clergy to discern the difference between the gospel and simple morality, and the increased affluence of the citizenry, which unfortunately produced indolence and an unholy spirit of materialism.[7] At least for Duke, economic prosperity was not a friend to religion.

These complaints reappeared in sermons and journals of other religious leaders. In 1809 Stephen Grellet, a traveling Quaker minister, expressed concern for the spiritual health of Baltimore Friends when he wrote that "the spirit of the world has taken deep root among many, estranging them from the Love of God."[8] Another minister visiting Baltimore's First Presbyterian observed that "the congregation was large, wealthy, fashionable, strong in all the elements of material and social strength, but waiting for power on high."[9] Lutherans, German Reformed, and Roman Catholic leaders also noted the lack of vigor displayed by their parishioners.

Other evidence validates these estimates of low-level church involvement during the early years of the republic. Between 1775 and 1789, only about one in eight titles published in Baltimore dealt with religious subjects. This proportion jumped temporarily to one in four between 1790 and 1794, but it dropped again during the remaining years of the decade to one in seven. Between 1800 and 1815 the proportion of religious publications rose from about one in five to one in four. After 1815 the proportion averaged better than one in three titles.[10] Moreover, shifts in membership sizes indicate the problems suffered by non-Methodist Protestant bodies. In 1790 approximately 4,200 or 70% of the city's churchgoers attended non-Methodist Protestant congregations. Twenty years later the 12,000 non-Methodist Protestants represented only about 55% of the city's churchgoers. These figures denote a decline in the percentage of non-Methodist Protestant nominal members from 31% to 26% of Baltimore's population.[11]

While most Protestant bodies experienced difficulties, Baltimore Methodists enjoyed revival—in terms of both numeric growth and emotional vigor. The first unusual season of evangelical success occurred in 1789. From February to August of that year Methodists held services almost every night. Occasionally the services lasted until past two in the morning. The exhausted Baltimore preachers called in recruits from Annapolis and other nearby stations to assist in the work. Ezekiel Cooper's *A Brief Account of the Work in Baltimore* described the revival scenes with such phrases as "heart-rending cries," "throbbing lamentations," "gushing-tears," "writhing agitations," and "convulsive throes of the human frame." Within a nine-month period the church added an estimated four to five hundred persons to the rolls.[12]

Throughout the national period Baltimore Methodists experienced similar "special seasons" of grace. The revival times were emotional and sporadic, but they brought impressive results. In 1790 about one in five Baltimore Protestants was a Methodist. By 1810 the ratio had climbed to nearly one in three and by 1830 to nearly one in two. For many years the rate of Methodist growth within the city exceeded that of the denomination as a whole. Whereas nationally the Methodist Episcopal Church expanded an impressive 293% between 1800 and 1820, in Baltimore the percentage increase was 350%, notwithstanding the fact that hundreds of Baltimore blacks left the denomination for the schismatic African Methodist Episcopal Church.[13]

Historians often attribute the extraordinary success of American Methodism to the denomination's itinerant system, which enabled circuit-riding preachers to reach a westwardly mobile population with a gospel of "free grace."[14] While the itinerant system and Arminian theology were important, particularly in the less-settled regions, Methodist revival in Baltimore had little to do with the system of traveling ministers, and its free-grace doctrine was only technically different from the soteriologically centered doctrines preached by most Protestant bodies. Even Bishop Asbury, an outspoken foe of Calvinism, admitted that the "difference between us lay not so much in doctrines and forms of worship as in experience and practice."[15] Baltimore Methodists of the era achieved revival principally because they labored so diligently to promote it. Whereas others desired an enlarged and invigorated congregation but were unwilling to risk disrupting either the dignity of religion or the status profile of the church to reach these ends, Methodists made evangelism their top priority and unhesitatingly pursued all means available to achieve this goal.

After 1800 a proven revival machine was the camp meeting, and Baltimore Methodists were quick to embrace it as a "new measure" of evangelism. Too often students of the camp meeting have overlooked its utility for urban congregations, labeling it instead with the descriptive noun *frontier*. For example, the classic study on this subject is Charles Johnson's *The Frontier Camp Meeting*. In the preface Johnson candidly states his intent "to portray the ever evolving revival institution against the backdrop of the raw backwoods society that originated and enthusiastically supported it."[16] A more recent widely acclaimed monograph is Dickson Bruce, Jr.'s *And They All Sang Hallelujah*. Like Johnson, Bruce interprets camp-meeting religion in terms of its frontier conditions. He perceptively argues that:

> Life on the Southern frontier was not easy for the plain folk and their religion was addressed to its hardships. Created on the frontier, camp meeting religion consisted of forms and expressions which had developed as immediate answers to the practical problems posed by sparse population and general infidelity. The final product was not based upon book learning and theological speculation but upon practices and beliefs that successfully jibed with the thinking and feelings of the frontier settlers.[17]

While applicable to frontier society, the analyses of Johnson and Bruce fail to provide a complete understanding of the camp meetings organized by Baltimore Methodists. For their meetings the descriptive label *frontier* is misleading with regard to the location of the meeting sites, and the residence of its participants and leaders.

First, camp meetings of southern Pennsylvania, Maryland, and northern Virginia were not limited to "frontier" areas. Methodist organizers purposely selected camp sites within an easy day's journey of the major communities of Baltimore, Frederick, Carlisle, and Lynchburg. Since Baltimore was by far the largest of these communities, more meetings took place near this city than in any other area of the region. Between 1828 and 1830, the Methodist Protestant Church alone sponsored at least seven meetings within this radius.[18] Occasionally they rescheduled their dates so as to avoid direct competition with nearby meetings of the Methodist Episcopal denomination.[19] By the 1820s Baltimoreans could select from a number of dates and locations the meetings most convenient for their personal schedules. Furthermore, the pre-meeting publicity announced the location sites in terms of their distance from Baltimore. The typical newspaper announcement read: "to be held at Holly Run, near Sweetser's bridge, Anne Arundel County, 5 miles from city of Baltimore," or "in neighborhood of Savage Factory and All Saint's Church, nearly equi-distant from Baltimore and Washington, about 1 mile from Washington Road."[20] In sum, even while acknowledging that the frontier is as much a process as a location, religious events purposely held at camp sites just five miles from America's third largest city or at a point conveniently situated near the turnpike, and equidistant from Baltimore and the nation's capital, can hardly be depicted as frontier gatherings.

Second, the participants of these meetings probably included more urban-ites than raw backwoodsmen. Typically, the meetings opened on Thursday or Friday evening, and concluded on Monday morning. Often the attendance on Sunday was five to ten times as great as the attendance on the other days of the meeting.[21] This swelling of the crowds on Sunday resulted from a con-siderable migration of urbanites leaving their shops on Saturday afternoon, and traveling a half-day's journey to the campsite for a weekend of intensive spiritual rejuvenation. Opponents of the meeting noticed this movement and warned of the dangers of holding camp meetings too close to cities. One such critic, signed "Scrutator," wrote to the *Wesleyan Repository* the following comment:

Hundreds and perhaps thousands of the spectators who attend on these occasions day after day, *losing their time, spending their money, and acquir-ing or indulging in habits of dissipation*, would be much better employed in pursuing their respective occupations at home, for the support of their families.[22]

This skeptical capitalist concluded by suggesting that the typical camp meet-ing produced a waste of $25,000 in expense and loss of labor. Despite his advice, camp meetings thrived near urban centers.

The leaders as well as participants in camp revivals were often urban resi-dents. The frequency and duration of the camp meetings made it impossible for the overladen traveling itinerants to carry the entire preaching responsibil-ity for the services. On most occasions local preachers and lay exhorters filled the makeshift pulpits. Since a large number of lay preachers and retired or located ex-itinerants lived in the city, the principal leaders of nearby meetings were generally residents of Baltimore. Seven of the thirteen preachers direct-ing an 1828 Eastern Shore meeting held more than thirty miles away were Baltimoreans.[23]

The most successful meetings of Maryland in terms of attendance, religious intensity, and professions of faith were those held within the vicinity of Balti-more. The one most endearingly remembered by both preachers and members of the Methodist Episcopal Baltimore Annual Conference was a 24–26 September 1803 revival at a site off Reister's Town road some fifteen miles northwest of Baltimore. The leaders included Samuel Coate, an itinerant stationed in the city, and Nicholas Snethen, a close companion of Bishop Asbury who twenty-five years later became known as the father of the schismatic Methodist Protestant denomination. With others they arrived three days early to clear a grove of three-to-four acres and to erect the preacher's stand. On Saturday the 24th, the participants began arriving, stationing their tents, wagons, carts, and stages in a circle surrounding the central platform. Owing to the coolness of the weather, and "partly to a prejudice they had taken against camp meetings," the number actually lodging on the site was only two to three hundred. However, the number attending on the weekdays was one thousand to fifteen hundred—a number that swelled on Sunday to about five thousand.[24]

The schedule for this three-day meeting was typical of most camp revivals. At 8 A.M. a trumpeter called the people to general prayer. By ten o'clock they began the morning service. After lunch was an afternoon service, followed by the climactic campfire service at night. At each service two or three exhorters followed the principal speaker. It was during these times of exhortations that "many fell down slain with the sword of the spirit, and groaned like men dying in the field of battle, while rivers of tears ran down their cheeks."[25] Nicholas Snethen reported that while "several converts hailed the beam of the Sabbath morning," it was not until noon on Sunday that "the work became visible, and general." The intensity continued into the evening service, which lasted until three o'clock in the morning. But the Monday departing service was the most meaningful to Snethen:

> O Happy Day! O day of mercy and salvation, never to be forgotten! Twice I fell prostrate upon the stand, beneath the overwhelming power of saving grace. The day is canonized ... as the happy Monday, the blessed 26th of September, 1803. The number converted cannot be ascertained, but all will agree that there were one hundred or upwards who were subjects of an extraordinary work, either of conviction, conversion, or sanctification.[26]

Extracts from the private correspondence of Fanny Lewis, a young female participant from Baltimore, captured even more vividly the ecstatic excitement of the meeting.

> I hasten to give you some account of our glorious camp meeting: but alas! all description fails. It would take an Addison or a Pope to give you even an idea of the lovely grove, particularly in the night, when the moon glimmered through the trees, and all was love and harmony.... There was scarce any intermission day or night. It looked awful and solemn to see a number of fires burning before the tents, and the trees and lanterns and candles suspended to them. No sound was heard except Glory to God in the highest! or mercy! mercy! Such a night, my father, I never saw or felt before.... On Monday morning there was such a gust of the power of God

that it appeared to me the very gates of hell would give way.... We call it the happy Monday! Yes it was a happy, happy Monday! a day long to be remembered and a night never to be forgotten.... I can but lament my inability to give you an account of it; but it was better felt than expressed. Sometimes you would see more than one hundred hands raise in triumphant praise with united voices, giving glory to God for more than one hour together, with every mark of unfeigned humility and reverence. The time between services was not taken up with "what shall we eat or what shall we drink"; but in weeping with those that wept and rejoicing with those that rejoiced, and that had found the pearl of great price. The preachers all seemed as men filled with new wine. Some standing crying, others prostrate on the ground, as insensible to every earthly object; while the Master of assemblies was speaking to the hearts of poor sinners, who stood trembling under a sense of the power and presence of a sin-avenging God.[27]

Fanny Lewis's account of "Happy Monday" was mild in comparison with other reports of meetings held near Baltimore. Henry Smith described an October 1806 meeting that produced 579 conversions and 118 experiences of "sanctification." The physical exercises accompanying these religious experiences were acrobatical. Smith recalled:

Oh, what a power while hundreds were prostrate upon the earth before the Lord.... To see the people running, yes running from every Direction to the stand weeping, shouting, and shouting for Joy, Pray[er] was then made—and every Brother fell upon the neck of his brother and wept and the Sisters did likewise.[28]

Methodist itinerant French Evans noted similar scenes when he described the 1826 Rattlesnake Springs meeting. Calling it "one of the best ever held in this part of the country," Evans concluded his report with a statistical summary and a parting observation: "It is supposed 250 persons were the subject of converting grace—several of sanctification—besides many hundreds under conviction.... There were still many mourners unwilling to leave the place until Jesus should appear."[29]

But camp meetings did more than win converts and sanctify saints. The meetings also inspired the devout to new levels of commitment so that when they returned to the city, protracted town meetings spontaneously erupted. Significant Baltimore revivals immediately followed successful camp meetings in 1817, 1818, 1825, and 1829.[30] In several ways these town meetings held logistic advantages over the camp meetings. While indoor church services lacked the atmosphere of the meetings held in the romantic forest groves, it made the success of the meeting less dependent on the weather. Also, since the participants could continue their normal economic functions during the day, the protracted town meetings were not limited as to length. Moreover, by providing services within the immediate neighborhood of a nonchurched populace, town revivals were more self-perpetuating than those gatherings which required participants to make special efforts to attend. Preachers were particularly exuberant when the curious, who attended the meetings simply because it was the current talk of the town, became "convicted and converted before leaving the house."[31]

Besides the camp meetings and protracted town meetings, Methodist conventions held in Baltimore churches often sparked seasons of intense evangelical activity. During these periods Baltimore Methodists opened their pulpits—sometimes two or three times daily—to the eminent itinerants visiting the city.[32] The most spectucular convention revival took place during the week of the General Convention of 1800. Between 11 and 18 May some two hundred Baltimoreans were converted and added to Methodist classes. Henry Boehm, writing more than a half century later, recalled this week as the "greatest revival that has ever occurred during the session of any General Conference."[33] Its success apparently spoiled Methodist leaders in future years. During the session of the 1804 General Conference, the preachers blamed the lack of religious stir in the city upon the experimental plan of permitting church members to observe the proceedings of the conference from the galleries. As a result, future debates took place behind closed doors.[34] Disagreements among preachers hereafter were kept in-house so as not to quench the spirit of revival. In short, Methodists expected revival to be the norm and, when it was not present, they took appropriate actions to combat the unnatural state of declension.

Another technique used by Methodists to provoke revival was the calling of days of fasting, prayer, and humiliation. The Baltimore Annual Conference of 1810, after noting an unprecedented low increase in membership for the previous year, asserted that "vital and practical piety" was declining, and "the spirit of backsliding and declension" prevailed. In seeking "for the causes of this unfortunate state of things," the Conference identified "the neglect of private and family devotion," "the use of spirituous liquors," "the love of dress, the love of unprofitable company," and "the inordinate love of money" as the sources of the evil. After bringing these "secret things" to light, the Conference declared the first Fridays in June and November as days of fasting and prayer, in which all societies were to unite in supplications to the Almighty "to spare thy people and give not thine heritage to reproach."[35]

Baltimore preachers called local congregations to observe similar days of prayer and fasting. Occasionally such days served as catalysts for general revival. In September 1817, for instance, John Davis of Fells Point Station proposed that the members of his charge follow his example of fasting and prayer every Friday. Those keeping the fast met together each week for an hour of prayer. Around the first of the year, a number became convicted and sought information as to what they should do to be saved. Davis held nightly meetings to assist the anxious, and to allow the occasion for public testimony for those relieved. For six weeks the church house was filled nightly, and as a result five hundred whites and one hundred blacks joined Methodist classes.[36] News of the events in Fells Point triggered a similar response at Baltimore City Station. The Leader's Meeting of 17 January 1818 resolved to encourage its members to "observe each Friday in every week as a day of fasting and prayer ... for the purpose of imploring almighty God to revive his work." Soon they established nightly services at the Old Town house to accommodate the revived spiritual interest. Within four weeks Baltimore City Station added between three and four hundred whites to its rolls.[37]

Methodists differed from most other denominations in whom as well as in how they evangelized. Their preachers prided themselves on bringing the gospel to the poor of all races. The status profile of Baltimore Methodists indicates some success in this area. More so than other Protestant bodies, Methodist membership reflected a general cross-section of the community. Although there was a tendency between 1815 and 1830 toward white-collar domination, the pattern was less pronounced among Baltimore Methodists than other city congregations. The Methodist discipline, which condemned extravagant life-styles and slave holding and made austerity a Christian virtue, no doubt popularized the church among the lower classes. Likewise, its "democratic" free-grace doctrine and emotional religiosity particularly were well suited for those generally labeled as the "less respectable masses." But again, Methodism's evangelical success among the poor was principally the result of calculated preparation and perspiration. Methodist lay and local preachers held weekly services at the alms house, Powhatten Factory, and penitentiary. They organized missions in Fells Point for sailors, and brought to Baltimore the first organized Sunday School. They opened their pulpits at least occasionally to ordained black preachers, and purchased the first two church houses in Baltimore used exclusively for black worship.[38]

Even the location and architecture of Methodist churches reflected their concern for evangelical outreach. To a greater degree than other denominations, Methodists built meeting houses in all sections of the city. In 1820 approximately 85% of the city's population lived within a half-mile radius of a Methodist church.[39] That only one in five churchgoers at this time lived farther than a half mile from their church home suggests that convenient church location was an important requisite for significant church growth.[40] Methodists could erect numerous meeting houses since the ones they built were simple—without bells, towers, or organs—and inexpensive. Their most expensive house built during this period cost $13,720, about half the price of the least expensive white Episcopal meeting house.[41] Whereas the average cost per seat in Baltimore Methodist houses was $15, among the city's Presbyterian, Lutheran, and Baptist houses the average cost ranged from $20 to $35, among Roman Catholic and Episcopal from $35 to $50, and in the Unitarian Church over $65 per seat.[42] Among Baltimore denominations, only the Friends built meeting houses as inexpensively as the Methodists.

Two additional factors enabled Methodists to fill city maps with church houses. First, the Methodist *Discipline*, which based ministerial salaries upon need and not talent, enabled local congregations to save money for church building by keeping ministerial salaries low. And second, since Baltimore Methodist trustees were responsible for all houses within the city as opposed to a single house of worship, there was less intradenominational rivalry between Methodist congregations. Consequently, within Methodism there were fewer pressures to build elaborate church houses, or to oppose the construction of an additional house, which would drain members from existing congregations.

In sum, evangelism was Methodism's top priority. All church functions—whether building projects or financial campaigns—were subordinate to this goal. Methodists expected revival, and to promote it they preached at camp, town, and convention meetings, in worship houses, public places, and forest groves, before bishops, artisans, and slaves. They sang and shouted, prayed and praised, and while others complained of declension, they counted their converts by the thousands. During the early decades of the national era, Baltimore revival was principally a Methodist affair.

On rare occasions isolated sparks of religious enthusiasm flickered within non-Methodist congregations. In 1800, for instance, the Methodist itinerant Freeborn Garretson described a visit to Philip Otterbein's United Brethren Church. He reported:

> There was such a noise among them, that many of the Christian people were immeasurably frightened, and as there was no opportunity for them to escape at the door, many of them went out the window.... The noise had alarmed hundreds of people who were not at the meeting, and they came running to see what was what was the matter, till the house was surrounded by the wondering multitude.[43]

This church was in essence a German Methodist congregation, since in doctrine, piety, and priority it followed closely the Wesleyan model. Baltimore Baptists during the period were surprisingly few, and their extant records unfortunately scarce. Yet evidence does suggest a small-scale revival at First Church in 1802, and at First and Second Church in 1816 and 1818. During these years the numbers received into the congregations more than double the annual averages of new members.[44] Before 1815 the only other Baltimore congregation noted for its revivalistic efforts was St. Peter's Protestant Episcopal. Methodists applauded George Dashiell, the congregation's first rector, for his avid encouragement of extemporaneous prayer and hearty singing of "Methodist tunes." While considerably more reserved, Dashiell's successor J. P. K. Henshaw continued the tradition. A Baltimore Methodist reporting on the winter revival of 1817–18 contrasted Methodist excitement with the lack of enthusiasm in other city congregations. The one exception he noted was St. Peter's, where several had been converted under Henshaw's preaching.[45]

That revivalistic activity aided church growth was uncontested. Yet at least before the 1810s many Baltimore churches not only rejected its method but labeled it as the enemy of Christianity. The natural opponents of Wesleyan "enthusiasm" were high-church Episcopalians like Joseph Bend and James Kemp. Bend lamented that Methodists "cannot think it compatible with Christian duty to give up ranting, noise, and other follies which disgrace their profession ... to promote the cause of the gospel, in the same rational and dignified way in which the clergy of almost all other churches proceed."[46] Even more condemning of Methodist services was the public attack by an anonymous member of the New Jerusalem Church, who wrote: "I have seldom seen a preacher of respectability join in these night revellings, it is generally conducted by the ignorant understrappers, who know of nothing but jumping, hallooing, and squeezing, and the freedom they take on such occasions with the young female converts...."[47] In essence, critics asserted that revivalism accentuated the emotional instability of the masses, and separated religious experience from the disciplined Christian life.

Revivalists conceded neither point. Methodists typically countered such attacks by stressing that "it was not the noise that produced the effects, but the effects of the power which produced the noise."[48] Moreover, Methodists reminded opponents that they enforced strict standards of conduct across their membership. Yet, while never willing to quench the spirit, by the second decade of the century Methodist leaders made greater efforts to control the emotional excesses of their camp and town meetings. In 1811 the Baltimore Conference disavowed any endorsement of a camp meeting unless it was officially under the "direction and approbation of the Presiding Elder."[49] Six years later it drew up a "list of Rules for the Government" of all Methodist sponsored meetings.[50] Baltimore City Station apparently strictly enforced these rules, for in October 1817, the Quarterly Conference censured a Samuel Krebs for attending an unendorsed camp meeting.[51] To ensure orderly services, Baltimore City Station congregations on 15 March 1820, passed a series of resolutions regulating behavior at worship. These regulations required all to enter the church peaceably and quietly, to seat themselves, and to remain until the congregation was dismissed. Each congregation appointed a committee with authority to prevent persons from unruly entrance or making unnecessary departure during worship, to prevent persons from standing in the aisles if seating was available, and to instruct the overflow crowd gathered outside the doors of the building to leave the premises.[52]

Methodist reporters describing camp and town revivals eventually learned to emphasize the respectable and deemphasize the emotional exercises of the meetings. In an article narrating the extensive Methodist town revival of 1817–18, Stephen Roszel observed: "It is a little remarkable that here has been less extravagance in the work, and less opposition to it from those without than I ever knew in any revival."[53] In another report, he wrote: "It is not uncommon for the altar to be crowded with ... young, middle aged, and old ... and many very respectable citizens."[54] In reporting the 1825 revival Samuel Merwin noted: "But one or two things have marked the work so far, and that is we have very little, if any extravagance, or what I should call extravagance. Our meetings have concluded at a reasonable hour: the people have retired in order and with solemnity." Merwin also gave notice to the respectable individuals converted in Methodist gatherings when he commented: "All classes and ages have been embraced in the work, but by far the greatest proportion have been persons of good moral standards."[55]

Apparently by the 1820s, Methodists had worked to improve their image so as to make revivalism acceptable to the "respectable" as well as lower classes. In so doing, however, they also sacrificed a portion of their distinctively evangelical posture, which had separated them from the other denominations of the era.

As the Methodists toned down their fervor, Baltimore Presbyterians loosened their belt of religious sophistication. Although Presbyterian preachers always had delivered evangelical messages, no unusual seasons of religious renewal occurred before the 1810s. But during the decade following the war, several periods of intensive evangelical activity disrupted the status quo of Presbyterian congregations. While they never embraced the camp meeting, Presbyterians called fast days and prayer concerts for worldwide revival, organized church missions and Sunday Schools, invited Methodists to give testimonies from their pulpits, and introduced camp-meeting choruses into their worship services. Their acceptance of these "new measures" of evangelism laid the foundation for decades of more general city-wide revival.

First Presbyterian experienced a growth spurt in 1817, as did the Associate Reformed congregation in 1818 and 1819.[56] Yet the significant story of revivalism among Baltimore Presbyterians begins with the origins of the Third Presbyterian Church. In October 1819, Nicholas Patterson, a licentiate of the Presbytery of Philadelphia, visited his uncle in Baltimore who was a member of Second Presbyterian. Upon noticing that no evangelical church house existed west of Eutaw Street, Patterson and his uncle publicized their desire to establish one. Soon they received permission to occupy a schoolhouse on Franklin Street for preaching services on Sunday mornings. They opened the house to evangelicals of all denominations. While not legally incorporated, the congregation established a Sunday School, a Missionary Mite Society, and began raising funds for erecting a new house of worship. Aiding in this effort, Patterson left Baltimore on a fund-raising preaching tour of the northeast. There he met the New England evangelist Asahel Nettleton, embraced his new methods of revival, and resolved to become a traveling evangelist should he find a candidate to replace him in Baltimore. In May 1822, with the new house complete, his Baltimore congregation incorporated as the Third Presbyterian Church and called his friend W. C. Walton as pastor—thereby freeing Patterson to pursue his career as an evangelist.[57]

Walton, like Patterson and Nettleton, believed that "if we made use of the proper means, we might have a revival."[58] After a year of patient anticipation, Walton decided that the time for revival was now. Determined to arouse the spiritually inert, Walton in June 1823 delivered a sermon in which he explained his views, and urged all communicants to meet daily together in twos or threes to pray for revival. He also established a Monday-night meeting for young people, began visiting his members house to house to inquire into the state of their souls, and initiated a Friday-evening meeting to teach professors of the faith how to lead others into self-examination, humble confession, and prayer for an outpouring of the spirit.

Walton's efforts brought results. By early July the young people's Monday-night services became anxious meetings and provoked several conversions. In October the church received sixteen converts on a Sunday set aside as a day of fasting, prayer, and thanksgiving. Three days later thirty more individuals professed conversion. To further satisfy the aroused spiritual thirst, the congregation organized a Saturday-night prayer meeting, open to evangelicals of all denominations to pray for general revival. By early February 1824 the small congregation had added sixty-three members, with eighty to ninety more still seeking eternal assurance.[59]

The revival at Third Church won the attention of other Presbyterian congregations. After arriving at First Presbyterian in 1820, William Nevins increasingly recognized the need of preaching more direct, plain, and pungent messages. Also influencing Nevins's evolution in thought was the evangelical success of his close personal friend and spiritual adviser, John Summerfield—the Methodist evangelist whose leadership sparked the extensive Methodist revival of 1825.[60] During this time Nevins made the difficult decision to break with the custom of the congregation by denying baptism to children of parents who had not made a profession of faith. While expecting this decision to cause conflict and possibly even lead to his dismissal, Nevins was pleasantly surprised to find that instead it brought about a greater seriousness within the membership regarding their religious obligations.[61]

Meanwhile, the coming of John Breckenridge to Second Presbyterian in 1826 as an associate pastor aroused the spiritual vitality of this congregation. For years Second Presbyterian had been on the decline owing to the poor health of the aged Pastor Glendy and to the personal conflicts between him and the leaders of the church regarding his salary.[62] Finding the church virtually without male participants, Breckenridge tried to reinvigorate religious interest by calling upon Methodist laymen to help him initiate a weekly prayer meeting. This small gathering became a potent band of thirty to forty men when it was joined by Nevins and his circle of committed First Presbyterian laymen.[63]

The growing spiritual awareness, enhanced by the increased male participation and the renewed sense of mission of the pastors, finally broke open at First Church on Sunday, 7 March 1827. Preaching on the text "Now is the accepted time ... of salvation," Nevins brought home the urgency of responding to the gospel call. That afternoon, students anxious about their salvation besieged the Sunday School teachers at First Presbyterian with questions. In response, Nevins invited all those interested in spiritual counseling to his home on Monday evening. Within a few weeks these Monday-night meetings were crowded with seventy to eighty inquirers.[64]

The excitement at First Church triggered a similar response among Breckenridge's congregation. Suddenly, the number attending the weekly joint meetings of the two congregations swelled beyond the limits of the small lecture rooms, requiring the rental of a public hall to accommodate the crowd. Pastor Morrison of the Bethel African Methodist Episcopal Church added to the success of these meetings with his spirited singing and exhorting. The presence of this black Methodist ministering to the wealthy Presbyterians dramatized both the "leveling" and ecumenical spirit of the revival. During this period upward of one hundred new converts joined the rolls of both First and Second Presbyterian Churches.[65]

The revivals altered Presbyterianism in Baltimore. Several Sunday Schools, prayer meetings, tract and visitation societies, and city missions emanated from this season of evangelical activity. One of the missions later became the Fourth Presbyterian Church. Another mission, established at Crook's Factory, hired a young George W. Musgrave as its overseer. Two years later Third Presbyterian selected him as their new pastor, a position he was to maintain for several decades.[66] More significantly, the Presbyterian revivals of 1823 and 1827 modified the expression of the faith. The revival movement reinforced Walton's evangelical tendencies to such an extent that it separated him from many of the stalwarts of his church. In a tract entitled *Narrative of a Revival of Religion in the Third Presbyterian Church in Baltimore, with Remarks on Subjects Connected with Revivals in General*, Walton publicized his newly discovered ideas, giving specific details as to how a church could be revived. Walton boldly asserted that if all professors of religion were truly evangelical, then

> the cause of Christ would not languish as it does, churches would be built where they are wanted; and those that have been built would be paid for.... Revivals would be common and perhaps continue without intermission, the Millennium would soon commence; and the Kingdoms of this world would soon become the kingdoms of our God and of our Christ.[67]

With the same confident spirit, he concluded:

> There is a connexion between the faithful discharge of duty, and the blessing of God. When therefore we do not enjoy revival, we should freely acknowledge that the church is to blame; and take it for granted that something more ought to be done than we are doing.[68]

While "Old School" Presbyterians assailed such talk as misguided and dangerously close to the Methodistic heresy of Arminianism, for Walton the use of the "new measures" was not only the key to the opening of the millennial age, but also the solution to the churches' temporal problems occasioned by the desertion of financially contributing males.

Nevins also underwent an intellectual metamorphosis as a result of his ministerial experiences of 1826–27. The editor and publisher of Nevins's papers noted that "about the year 1826 there was a decided increase in solemnity and directness of appeal of his sermons."[69] Although Nevins attempted to abstain from the controversy within Presbyterianism over the use of "new measures," he increasingly accepted the practices of aggressive religion.[70] Such an attitude, exhibited by the pastor of the most distinguished congregation in Baltimore, did much to remove revivalism from the confines of "fanatical Methodists" and make it more palatable to the dignified populace of the city. In this way Nevins's impact in Baltimore is comparable with Charles Finney's influence in the urban communities of the northeast.

Besides altering the religious mood of Presbyterian preachers, the revivals left an imprint upon the city at large. Most observable was the building of additional church houses. Between 1817 and 1830 Baltimoreans erected twenty-two houses of worship. In 1830 there was one church house for every 1,091 Baltimoreans. This proportion was down from the 1:1,788 and 1:1,957 ratios of 1810 and 1820 respectively, and also under the contemporary 1:1,769 and 1:2,410 ratios of New York and Philadelphia.[71] Also, more churchgoers filled the pews. Between 1810 and 1830, three denominational families—Methodist, Presbyterian, and Baptist—saw an increase in the proportion of churchgoers to the city population.[72] It is not surprising that these groups also were the most willing to embrace the "new measures" of evangelism.

Revivals also affected the gender composition of city churches. Although the large majority from all denominations were female, and this majority increased over time as greater and greater numbers of males enamored with Baltimore's bustling economy preferred searching for earthly rather than heavenly treasures, revivalistic Methodist and belatedly evangelical Presbyterian congregations slowed the feminization process of Baltimore's religious institutions.[73] Truly, two in three converts during seasons of revival were female. But this substantial majority paled when contrasted with the 80% female majorities found among nonrevivalistic denominations and among the Presbyterian establishments before their acceptance of the controversial "new measures."[74] A consequence, if not intent, of adopting aggressive means of evangelicalism was the stimulating of greater male participation in Baltimore's church life.

Finally, the revivals—at least according to their proponents—improved personal morality within the city. In the midst of the winter 1817–18 revival Stephen Roszel noted:

On Fells Point, where our ears used to be assailed with oaths and imprecations, you will now scarcely hear an improper word. The Sabbath, instead of being spent (as in many instances it formerly was) in rioting, is regarded generally as a day of religious solemnity.[75]

While certainly Roszel's biases influenced his observation, the revival seasons did inspire the eager enthusiasts with visions of a fully Christianized and morally upright society. These millennial expectations contributed toward the establishment and growth of dozens of missionary and benevolent societies, which in turn exerted a powerful moral influence upon the community.[76]

In sum, the revivalism associated with the second great awakening penetrated Baltimore with considerable force, producing an intense and fervent religiosity, mass conversions, and church growth. Before 1815, with rare exceptions, revivalism was a Methodist phenomenon. But this limitation did not make it unimpressive. Baltimore Methodism grew at an astonishing rate—faster than any denomination in the city—and at times even faster than the spectacular growth of Methodism nationwide. Between 1790 and 1830 Baltimore Methodism grew over 1,550%, a remarkable feat for any church in any era. After 1815 the revival became more general and was capped with extensive evangelical activity. Aided considerably by the revival, the proportion of Baltimore churchgoers in 1830 probably doubled the national average.

Why did revival erupt when and where it did? In some ways the Baltimore revival followed unexpected patterns. Unlike the great Philadelphia and New York City revivals, which occurred during the years of the Panic of 1837 and the Panic of 1857, revival in Baltimore during this era did not correlate with times of economic adversity.[77] The Panic of 1819, if anything, dampened the period of evangelical success that began following the War of 1812 and that reappeared in the mid-1820s. Neither did it occur principally in times of the most rapid city growth. The coming of thousands of Santo Domingo refugees during the 1790s and the unsurpassed population growth of nearly 20,000 citizens during the first decade of the century did not trigger city-wide revival. Nor was the revival like Charles Finney's famous Rochester revival of 1830—a revival that according to Paul Johnson was essentially a middle-class bourgeois event.[78] Apparently no social class in Baltimore was exempt from revival participation. The aggressively revivalistic white Methodists throughout the period came overwhelmingly from the artisan class. But one in three Methodists was black and poor. Meanwhile, most Presbyterians—both before and during periods of extensive revival—were white-collar workers, and among the wealthiest Baltimore citizens. While the degree of emotionalism displayed in revivalistic services varied inversely with the social ranking of the denomination, it is remarkable how little the periods of rapid church growth altered the social complexion of congregations.

Methodists embraced revivalism because they perceived a datable, instantaneous conversion as essential for Christians. They learned that a fervent appeal to the emotions was the surest way to induce sinful man to seek assurance of eternal forgiveness. Since evangelism was their top priority, they used all means at their disposal to win new converts. This brought certain results. While a conversion event evoked greater emotional release than a conversion process—and thereby energized Methodist converts with religious zeal—if not properly harnessed, the emotional enthusiasm of Methodists could appear distasteful to the more "respectable," and in the end short circuit their evangelical goal. In time Baltimore Methodists exerted greater effort to tone down the emotional excesses of their services and to improve the image of their meetings among the more respectable classes. This adjustment enabled them to make gains among the wealthiest in the city, though no doubt it also tarnished the Methodist appeal among the lower classes.

Even as the Methodist revival won greater acceptance among the respectable classes, Presbyterians—already similar to the Methodists in the soteriological essentials—became more willing to embrace more aggressive means of church recruitment. The serious decline among contributing male members provided them with added incentive to adopt the evangelistically proven "methods" of the Methodists. High-church Episcopalians, however, who carefully separated themselves from their Methodist rivals by emphasizing the need for greater dignity in religion, denounced the "new measures" as prostituting the true gospel. Hence, instead of advocating revivalism and thereby giving added respectability to their evangelical rivals, they bet their future on their ability to appeal to those who sought "peace and consolation" from the disgust of the Methodist and Presbyterian disorder. Still others, such as the Unitarians, Swedenborgians, and Roman Catholics, rejected outright the "new measures" on doctrinal grounds.

Documenting the causes of religious awakenings has always been tenuous. Perhaps indeed the spirit blows where it wills, and from whence it comes no man knows. But in some ways the Baltimore revival was unmysterious. While not clearly related to economic activity, class, or city growth, it was the result of a carefully designed plan. Revival erupted among those who wanted it, and who labored diligently to promote it. It was one strategy for church survival in a competitive and increasingly materialistic era. Rather than seeking for clues from the demand side of the equation, perhaps Baltimore's awakening more simply can be understood as "supply-side religion."

7
ECUMENISM

ALTHOUGH pastors privately denounced their religious rivals and publicly proclaimed the superiority of their denomination, Baltimore preachers also preferred interdenominational peace to conflict. Of the nearly one thousand religious titles published in Baltimore between 1790 and 1830, surprisingly few were direct attacks against a specific mainline denomination, and as a rule even these publications concerned matters of church polity rather than theology. Mainline churchmen had good reason to join hands rather than cross swords. Common local responsibilities, national loyalties, and millennial visions brought to Baltimore churches a degree of solidarity. Consequently, the age of voluntarism that followed disestablishment was an era of ecumenism as well as competition.

Occasionally, churches even provided financial assistance to their competitors. In 1786 a sudden downpour struck Baltimore. Rising waters rushed over Jones Falls, severely damaging buildings in low areas. Among the structures hit was the partially completed German Reformed Church. Already in debt and disunited over building expenses, the congregation lacked the funds necessary to repair the storm damages. Rather than close its doors, the congregation accepted support from willing sister churches. On three succeeding Sundays, St. Paul's Episcopal, First Presbyterian, and the German Lutheran congregations met for worship in the damaged German house. Each collected an offering to aid the stricken congregation.[1]

This incident was not unique. In 1795 Pastor John Healy and a band of Baptist immigrants from Leicester, England, arrived in Baltimore. After an unsuccessful attempt at securing a house for worship, St. Paul's Episcopal offered the Baptists a room rent free to be used for worship until more permanent quarters could be obtained. In 1796 the Light Street Methodist house burned to the ground. Citizens from several denominations contributed funds toward its replacement. Even more surprising was the willingness of Baltimore Protestants to contribute heavily toward the building of St. Patrick's, a Roman Catholic house in Fells Point.[2]

Church cooperation was not limited to occasional financial assistance. Because Baltimoreans, like most early Americans, preferred to confront such problems as poverty, disease, and crime through voluntary rather than governmental agencies, local churches working both independently and in concert established voluntary associations designed to promote the public welfare.[3] For every nonreligious association stood two church-related ones.[4] More so than the occupational, political, or ethnic club, the local church was the center of associational activity. Here like-minded individuals gathered, discussed common concerns, and devised strategies to combat perceived community problems.

Throughout the colonial era, Maryland churches created benevolent societies of varying descriptions. Baltimore churches carried the tradition into the national era, sponsoring a dozen or more benevolent organizations each decade. Most of the benevolences assisted the indigent poor. The three largest Protestant denominations—the Episcopal, Methodist, and Presbyterian churches—established mutual relief societies for their needy members.[5] Similarly, the Roman Catholic clergy incorporated the Baltimore Benevolent Society, a company providing insurance and retirement benefits to Baltimore and Fells Point Catholics. The society collected monthly fees from its members, and paid pensions to those who through age or infirmity lacked sufficient income. But member or not, only the faithful who met their religious obligations at Christmas and Easter received the benefits. With this restriction, the society not only provided insurance, but also reminded Catholics of their duty to attend public worship.[6] Through such organizations, churches attempted to care for their own. Only in times of extreme financial crises did they send members beyond the local society to the public almshouse.[7]

A few benevolent associations aimed at improving the welfare of American Indians and blacks. In 1795 Baltimore Friends organized the Committee on Indian Affairs. This committee raised funds and sent emissaries to instruct nations of the Miami Confederation in the proper techniques for cultivating crops and raising livestock. When the United States government ordered the removal of the Shawnee tribe beyond the Mississippi River, the Committee advised their Indian friends to demand from the government a solemn guarantee that the new Indian lands would "never, upon any pretext" be taken away. If the United States mistreated the Shawnees, it did not occur without a condemnation from Baltimore Friends.[8]

Friends also joined with city Methodists in establishing the Maryland Society for the Abolition of Slavery. This society lobbied in the state assembly for legislation favorable to slaves and free blacks, and petitioned for the freedom of individuals believed to be unlawfully enslaved. At first the society met with success, for in 1796 the General Assembly repealed a law of 1753 that had prohibited slave owners from manumitting slaves in their wills.[9] But the society's aggressive attempts to secure freedom for certain enslaved blacks aroused strong opposition. In 1798 the General Assembly crippled their efforts when it declared that members of the organization "conducted themselves in a most uncandid, unjustifiable, and oppressive manner." A second and more condemning resolution, which labeled the society as "unnecessary," "subversive to the rights of our citizens," and "repugnant to the laws and constitution of the state" narrowly missed passage by a single vote. Shortly after this incident, the society went bankrupt and suspended its operations.[10]

About two decades later Elisha Tyson and Abner Neal—a Quaker philanthropist and a Methodist local preacher—established another association dedicated to the rights of blacks. Seeking to avoid the stigma of the defunct Abolition Society, they called the new organization the Protection Society of Maryland, and admitted slaveholders into its membership. In 1817 the society successfully pushed two pieces of legislation through the Maryland Assembly. First, an old law requiring black prisoners either to prove their free status or to be sold to pay their jail fees was superseded with an act demanding the release after a given period of time of all blacks jailed as suspected runaways. The second law made it a penitentiary offense to sell a slave who was legally deeded with a contract of manumission to an out-of-state resident. Despite this initial success, the Protection Society, like its predecessor, fell into bankruptcy.[11] As a rule, benevolences designed to care for the needs of churchgoers proved more durable than those intended to protect the rights of minorities.

While hundreds of Baltimore churchmen offered their time, talents, and tithes in support of benevolent projects, thousands endorsed a second type of church-related association—the missionary society. Unlike the benevolent endeavors, the missionary associations were not colonial in origin. No missionary society existed in the city before 1810. During the 1810s Baltimoreans organized seventeen evangelical associations. In the 1820s the number swelled to thirty. Some, such as the Baltimore Baptist Missionary Society, the Baltimore Methodist Episcopal Conference Auxiliary Missionary Society, and the Protestant Episcopal Society for the Advancement of Christianity, were denominationally oriented.[12] But the organizations that struck the nerve of so many Baltimoreans, and excited them with a mission of winning the world for Christ, were the interdenominational missionary associations.

The parent of all the interdenominational missionary associations was the Baltimore Bible Society. Founded in 1810, it was the first such society in Maryland, and among the first in the nation.[13] Throughout its existence, the overwhelming majority of its yearly elected officers were either Protestant clergy or lay officials of Baltimore's various houses of worship.[14] In 1813 the Female Bible Society joined as an auxiliary to the male association. Membership was open to all who subscribed to the constitution and contributed an initial fee of five dollars plus two dollars annually.[15]

The purpose of the Baltimore Bible Society was to spread "the Holy Scriptures more effectually and extensively among the multitudes." To achieve these ends members collected funds and procured and distributed Bibles. Initially, the Baltimore societies purchased their Bibles from the British and Foreign Bible Society or the Philadelphia Bible Society. In 1815 the societies purchased a $4,000 set of octavo plates and began printing their own copies.[16] Members deposited Bibles at the jail, penitentiary, the marine and city hos-

pitals, and the almshouse, and provided Sunday School teachers and clergymen with sufficient copies to distribute to the poor of their congregations.
Also, the bylaws of the Female Auxiliary required that the managers inquire
into the families in need of Bibles, visit the poor, converse with them in regard to the benefits of Bible reading and the necessity of obtaining salvation
through Christ, invite them to attend worship at some city congregation, and
offer to read the Bible aloud to those families unable to read.[17] Besides these
local responsibilities, the Baltimore societies contributed funds toward the
translating of Christian scriptures into Chinese and the languages of the
American Indians, and toward supplying the frontier settlers with English,
German, French, and Spanish translations. Between 1810 and 1820 these
societies jointly collected nearly $20,000 from subscriptions, church collec-
tions, and individual donations.[18]

The establishment of the American Bible Society temporarily disrupted the
Baltimore Bible movement. In 1816 the Baltimore Bible Society, with its
female auxiliary, included about one thousand members, had a yearly income
of nearly $5,000, and was distributing the first edition of its own stereotype
octavo volume. Then enthusiasts organized the American Bible Society and
sent invitations to the Baltimoreans to join the national body. Although a
large and outspoken minority insisted that it was God's will to join, the
majority of the members voted to remain independent.[19] This decision
spurred great controversy, which rapidly resulted in a significant decrease
in the size, income, and public esteem of the organization. Whereas earlier
annual reports reeked with optimism, the 1818 report lamented that the membership of 312 Baltimoreans represented only one two-hundredths of the
population of the city. Likewise, the report of 1819, after noting that New
York City supported five or six Bible organizations, bemoaned: "We should
blush for our city if we were to hear the inquiry, cannot Baltimore support
two?"[20]

To accommodate the dissatisfied faction, and perhaps to restore a measure
of civic pride, a group of Baltimoreans in December 1819 established another
association—the Young Men's Bible Society of Baltimore. This society differed from its predecessors on several counts. First, its entrance fee of only
one dollar per year made membership more easily attainable by the common
masses. Second, it restricted officers to men under thirty-five years of age.
Third, it was affiliated with the American Bible Society.[21]

Joining the national body was clearly a popular decision. The Young Men's
Bible Society rapidly grew and added auxiliary associations. In 1821 Baltimore women established the Ladies Branch Bible Society. This sister
organization held joint quarterly and annual meetings with the Young Men's
Society, and after local expenses, turned over its treasury to them. Also in
1821, the Maryland Auxiliary Bible Society was founded as another Baltimore
affiliate with the national organ. Within three years two additional societies,
the African Branch and the Marine Branch, became partner associations with
the Young Men's Society. Thus by 1824 Baltimore supported seven Bible

societies—five of which were auxiliaries of the American Bible Society.[22]

Although in one sense competitors, the Baltimore societies learned to cooperate. As early as 1821 the Young Men's Bible Society drew an elaborate plan of dividing the city into districts to ascertain and visit those destitute of Christian scripture. The male body then assigned to the Ladies Branch the actual task of visiting, arguing that while "men might be regarded as intruders ... what door would be rudely closed against female loveliness; what heart so hard as to be insensitive to the soft and imploring tones of her voice?" In November 1827 the Young Men's Society established an even broader goal— that of providing a Bible to every family in the state of Maryland within one year. Immediately, they made efforts to establish auxiliary societies in every county of the state. Next they attempted the herculean job of locating and supplying the deficient families with Bibles.[23] In Baltimore alone hundreds of volunteers canvassed the neighbors, soliciting funds for financing the statewide project and identifying those families in direct need. This crusade received the official endorsement of the Protestant Episcopal Convention of the Diocese of Maryland, and the Baltimore Annual Conference of the Methodist Episcopal Church. By the end of 1828 all the active Bible organizations in Baltimore had contributed to this cause, raising over $5,000 and distributing scripture to the 1,600 needy families. Although they failed to reach their statewide goal, they did distribute within the year about $20,000 worth of Bibles.[24]

In 1831, after twelve years of work, the Young Men's Bible Society boasted of distributing 28,267 volumes. Proud of their accomplishments, the managers never fell into complacency. The report of 1831, after noting the transient pattern of the urban poor, recommended beginning another major campaign to resupply every citizen of Baltimore with Christian scripture. Bible business in Baltimore was an endless task of which its promoters never grew tired.[25]

Closely akin to the Bible societies were the religious tract societies. The only interdenominational effort of this kind was the Religious Tract Society of Baltimore, established in 1817. According to its organizers, the objectives of the twelve-page tracts circulated by the society were "to instruct the ignorant in the way that leads to happiness, to comfort the afflicted, alarm the guilty, awaken those who sleep on the enchanted grounds of sin, and ... to spread the glad tidings of salvation."[26] Despite these "noble designs," the fear that others might use the society for circulating sectarian arguments prevented many from endorsing the organization. To remove this stigma, the society closely screened all controverted points of religion from its tracts, and included only those simple evangelical doctrines accepted by the mainline Protestant bodies. In one defense of the publications, the Episcopalian rector J. P. K. Henshaw asserted:

Indeed, we may safely say, that almost every religious Tract which we distribute, points out the fallen state of man and the way of recovery by Jesus

Christ. And any one of them, falling into the hands of a person who had never heard of the gospel before, and might never hear of it again, would teach truths by which his soul might be saved.[27]

Within three years after establishment, the society boasted of 226 subscribers who had distributed some 53,248 religious tracts.[28] Nevertheless, owing to the general bias against tract societies, the organization never attained the widespread support common to the Bible societies.

Winning the world through an intensive media blitz was the common dream of both Bible and tract society promoters. This dream demanded a literate public—a precondition not always met in this age before universal public education. Hence it is not surprising to find city churches actively involved in the task of instructing the masses with basic reading skills. Although church-supported charity schools reached hundreds of indigent children unable to afford private education, this number palled when contrasted with the city's ever-enlarging illiterate populace. Then in 1816, during a time of unprecedented enthusiasm for the Bible movement, city churchmen heard about the "Sunday School" experiments in New York and Philadelphia. This concept of Sunday-morning religious and academic instruction for the poor rapidly won a warm reception among Baltimore churchmen.[29]

The history of the Sunday School movement in Baltimore began on 21 October 1816 at a meeting in Light Street Methodist Episcopal Church. The attenders discussed the reports of the Philadelphia and New York Sunday School associations, and enthusiastically gave them their support. Within two weeks they established the Asbury Sunday School Society, the first such organization in Baltimore. Constitutionally committed to the task of educating "as many white and colored persons as we can until they know their duty to God and man and can read the Holy Scriptures," this society opened its first male school on November 17 in a rented room over the Union Engine House on Hanover Street. On that same day the Methodists also organized the McKendree Sunday School Society in Eutaw Street Church as Baltimore's first female society.[30]

Although other denominations disapproved of many Methodistic "new measures" of evangelism, they soon gave the Sunday School their endorsement. Its success was too impressive to ignore. To illustrate, since the number of students quickly exceeded the space of the Union Engine House, the Asbury School in June 1817 asked the vestry of St. Peter's Protestant Episcopal Church for the use on Sunday of their parochial free schoolroom. In considering their request, the vestry decided that rather than open its facilities to the Methodists, it instead would initiate its own Sunday School. Later that summer the leadership at St. Paul's Christ, First Baptist, First Presbyterian, and the Associate Reformed churches of Baltimore made similar decisions.[31]

The next step was to bring unity to the Sunday School movement. On 18 October 1817 a number of females from several denominations met at Baltimore College for the "purpose of forming a Union Society for the more effectual promotion of Sunday School." After singing, praying, and hearing an address on the value of the proposed association, the women discussed several constitutions of similar societies before ratifying a modified version of the Female Union Society of New York. The final document explicitly stated their objectives:

> to stimulate and encourage the education and religious instruction of the ignorant; ... to improve the methods of instruction; ... to promote the opening of new schools, and to unite in Christian love, persons of various denominations engaged in the same honourable employment.

To achieve the latter goal, the constitution forbade the discussion of any of the "controverted points of religion." At the ensuing meeting they drafted rules and policies for all Sunday Schools to follow, and defined the duties and responsibilities of school managers, superintendents, teachers, and students.[32]

Baltimore males soon followed their example. In December 1817 the men established the "Union Board of Delegates for the Male Sunday School Society of Baltimore." This society—initially consisting of representatives from the Sunday Schools of St. Paul's, Asbury Association, Associate Reformed, St. Peter's Protestant Episcopal, First Baptist, Christ, and the Baltimore Sunday School Association—procured funds for the printing and purchasing of books and stationery supplies necessary for the schools. Like the female interdenominational effort, the society experienced immediate growth. Within its first year the Union expanded to include the Sunday Schools of Second Baptist, Trinity Protestant Episcopal, and the nondenominationally sponsored Federal Hill school, and boasted of a total enrollment of over 1,500 students.[33]

Because the object of all Sunday Schools was to prepare the children to read the Bible, there was little variation among the different denominations in either content or method of instruction. The typical Baltimore Sunday School grouped eight to twelve children in a class according to ability, not age. Children under five years were not admitted. Once enrolled, children were not allowed to transfer from one school to another without proper reason. Classes opened with prayer and singing. Then the voluntary teacher in charge asked questions from the spelling and reading lessons. Teacher responsibilities also included preserving order in the classroom, sitting with the children who attended public worship, and visiting those missing two consecutive Sundays. They were fined for neglecting their duties, or being late to class. Beginning students first memorized the alphabet. When they could spell words of one syllable, they advanced to a higher-level class, and began reading selected portions of the Bible. The more advanced students read and answered questions from the gospels and Old Testament, and in some cases studied special biblically oriented topics such as the geography of the holy land.[34]

In addition to their learning to read, teachers expected students at all levels of achievement to memorize Bible verses and hymns, and to answer questions in the catechism selected by the Sunday School. A typical assignment for students able to read was the memorization each week of five verses of hymns, two questions out of the catechisms, and ten verses of scripture. Teachers motivated students to complete their assignments by awarding points for every perfectly recited lesson. Students received additional points for being punctual, for good behavior in class, and double points for good behavior at worship. Similarly, teachers removed points for disorderly conduct either in class or worship, and for neglecting to bring the lesson book to class. When students accumulated a certain number of points, they won a blue ticket or ribbon; as the number grew, they received a red ticket, and eventually a book.

Judging from the amount of material reported as memorized, the motivational scheme of the Baltimore Sunday Schools proved quite successful. A male school of the Asbury Association reported that during 1823, the 161 boys enrolled memorized a total of 75,962 Bible verses—an average of nearly five hundred verses per student enrolled.[35] Individual accomplishments were even more impressive. One young female in a three-month period reportedly recited 477 Bible verses and sixty-nine pages of catechism.[36]

Most schools provided students with extracurricular activities. Male Sunday scholars often received free instruction in writing and arithmetic on two or three evenings a week. Girls frequently attended a sewing class one afternoon a week. At least one congregation established a weekly night social for the Sunday students to meet casually for conversation and group prayer.

Regardless of the efforts to attract and motivate, teachers constantly complained about the irregular attendance of students. During the initial years of the movement, only approximately one-third to one-half admitted during the year were among the regular attenders by the year's end. In 1819 the improved image of the schools contributed to an upswing in attendance patterns, as better than two in three students admitted during the year remained active at the time of the annual report. However, the persistence rate of this year was unusually high. By the third decade of the century, with the novelty diminishing, both the growth and persistence rates slowed to a significant but far less impressive level.[37]

One reason for the temporary decline in Sunday School scholars was the inability of school superintendents to find a sufficient quantity of volunteer teachers. The schools hardest hit by this difficulty were inevitably the schools for African adults. In 1821 the managers of the Female Union Society suspended the two largest African schools owing to a lack of teachers and meeting places. Until this time some one hundred blacks ranging in age from six to sixty had regularly attended each school.[38] Compounding the difficulty of finding white volunteer teachers for black schools was the vocal opposition from a segment of the community, which paradoxically warned against the futility of educating blacks and against the social dangers of offering Africans educational opportunity. The Sunday School evangelicals, however, never abandoned their ideals to the point of acquiescing in the latter argument. Nor did they accept the assertion that Africans were inherently incapable of learning. Instead, Sunday School Union reports debunked such accusations, occasionally even contrasting the enthusiasm and appreciation of black students with their white counterparts. In one narration on the origins of a African female school, the report wrote that

> [although] originally intended for white adults ... as few as would avail themselves of this opportunity of obtaining instruction, it was thought best to receive those who earnestly plead for admission in such crowds, that they were obliged to limit this number to one hundred and sixty.[39]

Another reporter of an African male school noted: "We have never beheld so much apparent anxiety to learn as the scholars at this school generally evince."[40]

The superlatives used in describing black initiative paralleled the imperatives depicting the urgent need of providing blacks with religious instruction. One Sunday School teacher, astonished in learning that one of her middle-aged African students never knew she had a soul and had never heard the name of God except in profanity, included in her quarterly report the following challenge:

> O friends of Jesus! let these accounts rouse you to diligence ... we beg that your exertions may be continued; and your influence used, to obtain more laborers ... that we may be enabled to admit all in situations similar to those we have mentioned: many who are exposed to temptations of which ye, who are educated in the school of virtue, have no idea. And when you consider that you may be blessed instruments of saving such ... surely you will not need no [sic] other motive to stimulate you to exertion.[41]

While scores of volunteer teachers responded to her plea, the number of blacks eager to take advantage of the rare opportunities of both mass assembly and educational instruction always exceeded the facilities of the Sunday School Unions. Most churches made the education of white children their priority, and in doing so, neglected the needs of the city's most impoverished. Despite this limitation, on any given Sunday after 1818, between one and three thousand males and females—drawn primarily from the laboring classes—received religious instruction while being taught the rudiments of reading.[42]

Besides uniting behind the Bible and Sunday School movements, city churchgoers cooperated in a variety of other outreach programs. In 1817 Baltimore women established the Female Mite Society for the Education of Heathen Children in India. Created to raise funds to support Christian schools in India, the organization carried both feminist and Christian goals. As women, its organizers were alarmed at the publications coming from missionaries to India which described the low status of women in Indian culture.

As Christians they believed that the solution to the social evils there lay in the Christianization of this "heathen" land. And as mothers they longed first and foremost for the conversion of children. Apparently this form of public appeal hit the conscience of many Baltimore women. Within a year after its inception the society embraced some seven hundred female subscribers who contributed a penny a week to the treasury. And before the society officially dissolved in 1856, it had boarded, clothed, and educated over seventy Indian children from the pennies collected each week.[43]

Similarly, in 1823, 325 Baltimore men subscribed to the newly established Seamen's Union Bethel Society. With a board of directors composed of a member from each Protestant denomination, the interdenominational Seamen's Society held Sunday and Tuesday evening worship services in rented rooms at both Fells Point and near the Basin, and hired a clergyman to minister especially to the seamen in the boarding houses and hospitals of the city.[44] In charity sermons the directors asked city residents to give generously to the mission. In these addresses they reminded their hearers how the comforts of society depended upon the seamen's industry, and how merchants and patriots particularly were indebted to their laboring.[45] But improving the public image of seamen was only of secondary importance. The object of the mission clearly was to bring this "profligate and vicious" class to repentance. At least in the opinion of members, the society produced visible results. A reporter in 1830 wrote: "A few years since and sailors had no altars—had no offerings to bring; but now, thanks to our *God*, the night of moral darkness and desolation is passing fast away—'The morning breaks, truth is pouring in apace.' "[46]

The successes of the interdenominational ventures encouraged individual denominations to duplicate their efforts. In 1815 Episcopal women organized the Female Society for the Dissemination of Religious Knowledge. At first it procured funds for the purchase and circulation of Episcopal prayerbooks and catechisms. In 1818 the female society changed its focus and thereafter concentrated on propagating the faith via twelve-page religious tracts. By 1821 the association, now operating under the title of the Protestant Episcopal Female Tract Society of Baltimore, published and circulated 5,000 copies of different evangelical tracts every month.[47] The following year the body founded three juvenile auxiliary societies. The youth belonging to these organizations not only assisted in the distribution of tracts, but also financially supported the cause by giving a penny a week to the treasury. The 1823 report listed 347 subscribing youth. Episcopalians were exuberant over the juvenile societies because of their two side benefits: training children to save so that they might give to worthwhile projects, and leading them "to consider the importance of religious instruction by perusing the Tracts which pass through their hands for distribution." The society hence prepared a future generation of Episcopalians to meet their spiritual and temporal responsibilities, even as it dispersed evangelical literature to the community at large. With the aid of the children, by 1830 the Female Tract Society had distributed to Baltimore residents and visitors well over one million pages of religious instruction.[48]

Although not so predominant as the Episcopalians, Baltimore Friends and Unitarians also established organs for propagating their faith. In 1818 the Quakers instituted the Baltimore Association of Friends for Publishing and Distributing Tracts on Moral and Religious Subjects.[49] In 1820 the Unitarians founded the Baltimore Unitarian Society for the Distribution of Books. The impetus for establishing this society was a vote of the Young Men's Bible Society which excluded the First Independent Unitarian Church from those churches included in its membership. In response to this snub, the Unitarians organized their own independent association, and in January 1821 commenced publishing a religious periodical. During its initial year *The Unitarian Miscellany* experienced unexpected success, requiring the society to double its original order of one thousand copies.[50] A negative compliment was paid to its impact by an opponent, Presbyterian Samuel Miller, when he commented: "Probably in no part of our country out of Massachusetts do these poisoned agents so completely fill the air, or like one of the plagues of *Egypt*, so noisomely come into your house, your chambers, and your kneeling troughs as in Baltimore." Circulating religious literature was a successful, yet involatile means of evangelizing the masses. Hence such churches as the Episcopal, Unitarian, or Friends, who rejected the more emotional Methodistic measures of evangelism, relied heavily upon the printed page as a means of propagating the gospel.

Reform crusades, such as the African colonization movement, also accompanied the missionary excitement of the age. The city's demographic complexion made it particularly receptive to arguments for colonization. In 1800 the 2,771 free blacks in Baltimore represented about 10% of the population. Both the number and percentage increased each decade so that in 1830, 14,783 or 18% of the city were free blacks. Many viewed this large, impoverished, and underemployed class as a threat either to the institution of slavery or to the city's public health and safety. Hence when Washingtonians established the American Colonization Society in 1817, Baltimoreans promptly organized the Maryland Auxilary Colonization Society as an affiliate to the parent body.[51]

Some churchmen questioned the altruistic dimension of this organization. These individuals feared that the underlying object of exporting free blacks to Africa was to tighten the chains of American slavery. But defenders of the venture, such as Unitarian Jared Sparks, unequivocally embraced colonization as the only hope of lessening the "mischiefs of slavery, and . . . the living pestilence of a free black population." Sparks argued that by draining off the free blacks and by replacing them with the influx of white laborers, a "vicious, worthless, dangerous population" would be succeeded by an "intelligent, and thriving class." In the end this change would improve the character and condition of those slaves who remained. Sparks thus foresaw colonization as the means by which "the slaves are made better, and the poisonous influences of the free colored people on society grows weaker as their numbers diminish."[52]

To other Baltimore churchmen the goal of colonization was more than populating a continent of freedmen by depopulating a continent of slaves. It was also to convert Africa to Christianity by sending to it Christianized blacks. Nathaniel Peck, one of the first Baltimore blacks to leave for Africa, clearly understood his missionary responsibility. In a letter to his mother he proudly wrote: "I am now President of a Sunday School Society. The native children receive instruction every day."[53] After more than a decade of struggle—with still only six hundred American blacks colonized in Africa—Baltimoreans attempted to rejuvenate the colonization movement by strengthening its Christian image. In January 1831 they formed the Maryland State Colonization Society to supersede the nearly defunct elder institution. The new organization carried strong missionary overtones. Its constitution explicitly stated that "the extirpation of slavery in Maryland was the chief object of the Society's existence." Moreover, it restricted the colonizers only to those free blacks willing to abstain from alcoholic drink. The organization added these statements in order to detach itself from those auxiliaries which desired to perpetuate American slavery, and to provide a stronger "Christian witness" so that the gospel light would shine in its purest splendor to the black heathen in Africa.[54]

A second reform impulse generated by the missionary enthusiasm was the temperance movement. Christians have always condemned drunkenness, but in Baltimore there was no organized effort to confront the problem of intemperance until the late 1820s. Methodists again took the lead. On 6 October 1829 they joined with a few Presbyterian clergy and city physicians to establish the Baltimore Temperance Society. This organization, unlike many early temperance associations, never advocated moderation in drinking. From its beginning it stood for complete abstinence. The constitution stated that the use of ardent spirits was "not only unnecessary but hurtful," that it produced "intemperate appetites," and that as long as moderate drinking continued, the "evils of intemperance" could "never be prevented." Members thus pledged to "abstain from the use of distilled spirits" and to use "all suitable ways" to discourage its use in the community. This involved publishing and circulating books and tracts intended to awaken the public to the dangers, causes, and remedies of intemperance, and securing to the cause the cooperation of the medical faculty, public press, magistrates, and clergy. It also collected relevant statistical information, organized auxiliary societies in city congregations, and raised funds to carry out the society's mission. At least among Methodists the society met with immediate success. By 1831 more than 1,500 Baltimore Methodists had subscribed to the requirements of its constitution.[55]

The propaganda and social benefits of the missionary ventures reached countless Baltimore residents. But the impact of the voluntary associations

cannot be measured solely in the number of Bibles distributed, children educated, or Africans colonized. The associational activity itself—aside from its
missionary or reform intentions—altered the social landscape of the city.
First it enlarged the sphere of respectable female involvement in the public
arena. Traditionally, males in the pulpit were the soul-winners and, in the
home, the breadwinners. With the proliferation of missionary associations,
women became active fund raisers, Bible distributors, house visitors, and
Sunday School teachers. Although not disrupting the traditional norms of
church or family, they did assume the principal soul- and breadwinning roles
of the city's largest religious organizations. Women increasingly became the
workers, although generally not the creators nor the decision-makers of the
missionary enterprises that characterized the era. Second, the associations
helped integrate families into the larger community. By awakening neighbors
to common concerns, convincing them that their participation mattered,
and sending them out with clearly defined responsibilities, the associations
broadened the base of community involvement and offered stability to residents confronted with rapid demographic change. Third, through the various
denominational and interdenominational Bible, tract, Sunday School, and
missionary societies, religious leaders saturated the community with their gospel message, and as a result extended both the size and moral influence of the
local congregations. Baltimore's experience was not unique. Aided by the
coordinated missionary activities, Protestant churches across the nation made
rapid gains. By the middle decades of the nineteenth century America was
securely Protestant—in terms of both church membership and social values.[56]

Labeling the national network of interdenominational associations the
"Benevolent Empire," historians of early America have noted how the rising
popularity of missionary societies imbued church leaders with greater powers
of social control. Not all, however, view the stewards of the empire as acting
with benevolent or altruistic motives. Clifford Griffen and Charles Foster portray the Benevolent Empire as simply "a soothing oil on social sores," placed
there by pastors and wealthy businessmen who desired to manipulate the
lower clases in order to preserve their wealth and status.[57] What were the
motives of Baltimore's associational leaders? And why did Baltimore's Benevolent Empire grow so rapidly after 1815?

An analysis of 272 managers and elected officers of seven selected civic,
benevolent, and missionary associations indicates that these leaders were
overwhelmingly white-collar workers of high economic standing, the majority
of whom also served as clergymen or lay officials of local congregations.[58]
Probing their motives is a more difficult assignment. Because these leaders
were the same individuals who ran local churches, one might assume that
their motives for associational activity were no different from their reasons
for involvement as leaders of the local congregation. As economic leaders,
perhaps some felt threatened by the enlarging masses of urban poor, and
thereby joined churches and created missionary associations to help pacify the
undisciplined multitudes with tranquil Christian doctrines of submissiveness.

To the degree that this was true, Foster's assertion that the humanitarian's task was "to make the world safe for the conservative" contains an element of truth.[59]

As intriguing as conspiratorial theories may be, it is unnecessary to assume that only ulterior motives lurked behind the statements of Baltimore's benevolent leaders. True, Baltimore pastors voiced distress over the unruly— particularly those from the lower classes—who disturbed the solemnity of Sunday worship. Others griped about the laziness of blacks and the profligate character of sailors. The periods of greatest concern about the poisonous influences of urban transients occurred in times of social crises—such as during the mass migration to Baltimore of Santo Domingo refugees in the 1790s, the yellow fever epidemics of 1798 and 1819, or the tumultuous months of 1812 when political divisiveness among city residents erupted in street rioting and violence. Churchmen responded to these difficulties with additional types of benevolent associations. But the height of the institutionalized missionary activity occurred during the postwar years and the latter years of the 1820s. Rather than correlating with times of social or economic hard times, periods of intensive missionary work paralleled the years that Baltimore experienced city-wide revival. It was the middle-class revivalistic Methodists—not the upper-class Presbyterians or Episcopalians—who took the initiative in establishing the city's first Sunday School, missionary, colonization, and temperance societies.

Moreover, the goals of the missionary associations on occasions challenged rather than embraced the status quo. While many discouraged the education of blacks, Sunday School advocates struggled to find voluntary teachers. Managers of the Young Men's Bible Society disturbed slave owners when they wrote:

When we consider the wrongs and outrages which the sable sons of Africa have suffered from our hands; torn from their parental abodes, from the presence of friends, families, children, and all that the heart holds dear, it is evident that we are bound, not only as Christians, but as men to do all in our power to amend and to repair such glaring injustice.[60]

Seamen's Union supporters blistered residents for leaving seamen "to the mercy of their tormentors." They insisted that merchants offer both temporal and moral support to this forsaken class, and that the sailors' claims to these benevolences rested "not merely upon the general grounds of charity" but were "founded in justice and equity."[61] The Baltimore Bible Society countered popular attitudes toward American Indians when it retorted:

And what right had we to wage a war for a purpose so diabolical as the expiration of the whole race of a peculiar people. Produce the white man's patent to annihilate the race of red men. The all just and merciful sovereign of the Universe had not given us such a right.... If we would turn our generals into missionaries and our swords into Bibles, and convince the

Indians that we had no desire to drive them into the Pacific Ocean, we should make them safe, perhaps serviceable neighbors, and support our claim to the title of a Christian nation.[62]

Given the general insensitivity throughout the period for the plight of the disadvantaged, these appeals for mercy and justice to the downtrodden do not indicate a Benevolent Empire engineered by a self-serving elite desirous only of keeping the underprivileged in their place.

A simpler explanation for the appearance of the "Benevolent Empire" was the one expressed by the stewards themselves—to win Baltimore, if not the world, to Christianity. Methodists and a few others were willing to use all means—including camp and town meetings and emotionally pungent Sunday preaching—to reach this end. Although many rejected these new measures as discrediting true religion, most churchmen embraced the less volatile but effective means of evangelism through organized missionary associations. Circulating evangelical tracts, teaching children to read the Bible, and establishing churches for seamen did not demand an instantaneous conversion experience, nor did it promote ranting emotionalism. But it did present the lost with a gospel message encouraging them to seek regeneration. Since most Protestants during this era agreed in regard to the soteriological fundamentals of "fallen man" and "free grace," and in the acceptance of the Bible as the precise and unadulterated word of God, there were few theological obstacles to an ecumenical missionary thrust. Through missionary societies the ancient Christian goal of making disciples of all nations could be pursued without resorting to "Methodistic fanaticism."

Why Baltimoreans took seriously this goal at this time, and worked with confident diligence to achieve it, was less a function of greed or fear than of American nationalism and rising millennial expectations. Christians since the time of St. Paul have awaited the second advent of Jesus, but they have not always emphasized this doctrine with equal enthusiasm. The decades following the War of 1812 were times in which Baltimoreans preached the doctrine of an imminent second coming with force. Presses printed a variety of pieces that detailed the signs of the times. Booksellers had difficulty keeping these titles in stock. In winter 1817–18, local stores went through two editions of a Methodist songbook filled with millennial imagery, such as that reflected in the chorus:

Don't you see Jesus coming? Don't you see him in yonder cloud?
With ten-thousand angels round him, See how they do my Jesus crowd.[63]

The preface of *The Christian Orator*, a collection of speeches delivered before religious societies, interpreted contemporary events as predecessors to the soon-appearing "millennial kingdom." It began:

We live in a remarkable period of the world; in a period when revolutions ... are occurring with a rapidity altogether without a parallel. The darkness

... is vanishing away, and scenes of unexampled brightness are everywhere opening to our view. The customs, which were generated and nourished by the heathenism and infidelity of former days, are melting away before schools, and Missionaries, and Bibles. Even war ... is beginning to yield its dominion; and in its room a spirit of peace, and a heavenly benevolence has gone forth, to unite in one happy family, all the children of Adam.[64]

Such millennial rhetoric was widespread. A Sunday School reporter wrote: "We cherish the fond hope that the day of millennial glory is fast hastening for the advancement of which we continue to blend our prayers and labours of love, fully confident that they shall not be in vain."[65] In an address before the Seamen's Union, J. P. K. Henshaw asked rhetorically:

Why are the soldiers of the cross buckling on their armour—uniting heart and hand, and coming up to the help of the Lord.... Are not the preparations making for that great battle which is to decide the contest between holiness and sin—Heaven and Hell—which is to establish the supremacy of the church and effect the redemption of the world?[66]

For Henshaw, Armageddon was near. Between 1817 and 1821 Baltimore presses published *The Prophetic History of the Christian Religion Explained*, a two-volume work by John George Schmucker. In the study Schmucker purportedly unlocked the mysteries of the book of Revelation, and demonstrated that indeed the end was at hand. James Kemp of St. Paul's applauded the work. Daniel Kurtz of Zion Lutheran was even more enthusiastic, recommending to the public that "every attempt, by a discerning mind, to explain this prophetic Book, which certainly is drawing near its fulfillment, deserves commendation."[67] Even a member of the New Jerusalem Swedenborgian Church—a church that believed the spiritual second coming had already occurred—felt obliged to thwart the rising millennial zeal. In a pamphlet published in 1816 this Swedenborgian asserted that "surely mankind cannot be so irrational now as to look for a personal appearance of Jesus Christ." Although he admitted that the signs were "striking" and "calculated to arrest the attention of the careless observer," he argued that these signs were a "consequence of, not a cause of, his coming."[68]

Methodists, Baptists, Presbyterians, Episcopalians, Lutherans and even Swedenborgians believed that the ancient prophecies were being fulfilled before their eyes. Biblical scholars viewed the American revolution as the fulfillment of Nebuchadnezzar's dream foretold in Daniel 2. America—the champion of liberty and of republican government—was the "stone made without hands" which smote the "image made of iron and clay" and "became a great mountain which filled the whole earth." Napoleon was the Beast of Revelation 17, who hated and devoured the Whore of Babylon, understood by Protestants to be the Roman Catholic Church. Even more remarkable to contemporary churchmen, the spread of Bible societies in Russia and Britain, the improvements in vital piety in America, the unusual outpouring of the spirit on the American frontier, and the establishment of America's early missionary societies appeared to fulfill the great prophecy that in the latter-day glory, the word of the Lord would cover the land as the waters cover the sea.[69] Since Americans had long believed that they were God's chosen people, that the cause of liberty was the cause of God, and that the triumph of liberty as realized in America would accompany the coming kingdom, it is not surprising that the fervor of millennial enthusiasm erupted with greatest intensity at the conclusion of the War of 1812, during a period characterized by an unprecedented outburst of national unity and patriotism. During this era of political "good feelings," American Protestants united—not organically but through interdenominational missionary associations—to do their part in preparing for the long-promised millennial kingdom. The urgency of the times demanded no less.

In sum, ecumenical unity in the early nineteenth century was reflected in the moderate church cooperation and extensive associational activity. With more than fifty civic and religious benevolences operating around the turn of the century, Baltimoreans were adept in organizing voluntary societies designed to confront perceived community needs. When the ambitious goal of reaching the world with the gospel became a recognized priority, the natural response was to create a network of missionary societies, diverse in object but similar in organization to the renowned benevolent associations. Although the popularity of the associational activity and the theological consensus in the evangelical essentials provided the setting for ecumenical cooperation, the impetus for the burst of activity—which produced at least seventeen missionary societies during the 1810s and no less than thirty during the 1820s—was the growing conviction that the ancient prophecies were being fulfilled, and that the millennial kingdom was near. Understanding their mission in definite cosmic terms, the millennial vision fostered increased missionary activity, which in spreading from community to community convinced more and more that the second advent was imminent and thereby fostered still greater evangelical diligence. The millennial rhetoric that wedded even more tightly the ideals of liberty and republicanism with the coming kingdom of God, accentuated the conviction that churchmen must stand together for the sake of both God and country.

8
SCHISM

BELIEVING that only a virtuous citizenry could maintain the delicate balance of freedom without falling into the pits of tyranny or anarchy, early American churchmen viewed religious institutions as the arbiters of virtue and thereby the fortresses of the republic. Millennial excitement added further incentives for maintaining strong and vigorous churches. Because slanderous accusations slung during nasty church squabbles discredited all religious denominations, unnecessary church conflict appeared both unchristian and unpatriotic. Hence, in the pluralistic society—a fact begrudgingly accepted by Episcopalians, but readily embraced by others—most Baltimoreans agreed that no church had the right to claim an exclusive monopoly upon religious truth, or to charge all its competitors as counterfeits in league with the Antichrist. Mainline churches moderated their hostilities, offered financial assistance to others in times of crises, and cooperated in interdenominational associations because despite their differences they were partners in national and divine missions.

Still, all was not peace. National and millennial enthusiasm fostered interdenominational cooperation, but it also bred church conflict. The competitive aspects of the voluntary church and the seriousness with which churchmen took religious issues discouraged perfect harmony. At some point between 1790 and 1830 virtually every Baltimore congregation experienced acrimonious controversy or even schism. Far from ramdom disturbances, these continuous church squabbles followed several defined and not entirely unexpected patterns.

The most vicious church battles pitted the semi-unified mainline denominations against the few "unorthodox" denominations excluded from interdenominational participation. Baltimore churchmen showed no tolerance for any religious group that rejected the Bible as divine revelation, or that rejected the doctrines of the Trinity and the divinity of Christ. Clearly the gentlemen's agreement to moderate criticism and assist congregations in distress did not apply to deists, Swedenborgians, and Unitarians.

The struggles against the despised deists demonstrated the willingness of

Baltimore churchmen to turn plowshares into swords. Few cowered from battle. In 1791, shortly after coming to St. Paul's, Joseph Bend delivered an eight-part sermon series in which he defended the reasonableness and necessity of revealed religion by attacking what he considered the fallacious arguments of the deists.[1] Meanwhile, Methodists and Baptists attacked the purported spread of "deistic infidelity" with an ardent appeal to the heart. Even the Swedenborgians published polemics designed to convert the rational deist into their understanding of Christian deism. In 1794, for instance, the Swedenborgian James Jones Wilmer published *Consolation: Being a Replication to Thomas Paine and Others on Theologics*, in which he attempted to refute point by point the "irrational principles" expressed in Paine's *Age of Reason*.[2]

The literary attack of the Swedenborgians continued into the next century. In August 1801 Pastor John Hargrove of the Baltimore New Jerusalem Church established a periodical, *The Temple of Truth*, to counter a deistic periodical, *The Temple of Reason*. Although short-lived, Hargrove's journal appeared during the very months that Elihu Palmer, the nationally known exponent of rational religion, visited Baltimore in the hope of establishing permanent deistic societies. The journal offered an interesting portrait of the ideological battles being raged between the Christians and the rationalists. Palmer asserted such typical deistic arguments against Christianity as the inadmissibility of biblical miracles as evidence supporting revealed religion, and the unjustness of the Divine command to believe or be damned. Hargrove retorted that deism rested "upon the sandy foundation of fallacies and mere appearance," and was "subversive" of all "the sweets of experimental religion, and civil government"—"gloomy as the night, wavering as the wind, unsettled as the ocean, destructive as the pestilence, and perishing as the grass."[3] While other clergy applauded Hargrove's attack against the common enemy, they refused to support his periodical. Within four months the weekly journal folded. Much to Hargrove's embitterment, the mainline proved unwilling to accept the unorthodox Swedenborgians as allies in their crusade against "deistic infidelity."[4]

Even without *The Temple of Truth*, Baltimore presses were not silent. Denominational publications continued to remind their audiences of the evils of "liberal religion."[5] Individual laymen published both anonymous and signed pamphlets defending their faith against the opponents of revealed religion. Local clergy also reprinted and circulated popular anti-deistic books, such as David Simpson's *A Plea for Religion and the Sacred Writings*.[6] Then in 1810 the Baltimore Bible Society, the first of many missionary societies designed to rebuff infidelity by reaching the masses with the gospel message, began its propaganda campaign.[7] Although the battle was never really in doubt, by the end of the second decade of the nineteenth century the Christian crusaders felt secure in their triumph. James Kemp of St. Paul's reflected this confidence when in 1817 he pronounced: "The age of infidelity has passed away. The jargon of sophistry and vanity, which assumed the dignified name of philosophy, has in a great measure, with its authors descended into the grave."[8]

The decline of "infidelity" did not arrest the war cry of the orthodox, for alongside the deists were the anti-Trinitarians, who threatened the central dogma of Christendom. The first major controversy in Baltimore over the doctrine of the Trinity occurred during the 1790s, with the establishment of the New Jerusalen Swedenborgian Church. One distinguishing characteristic of the church was its attack on the dogma of the Trinity as formulated at the Council of Nicaea. According to the orthodox, the Swedenborgians were heretical in their teaching of the oneness of God in person as well as in essence. The Swedenborgians rejected the trinity of persons in the Godhead, accepting instead only a trinity of principles—love, wisdom, and power.[9]

The opening of a New Jerusalem Church in Baltimore provoked a nearly universal negative reaction among the orthodox bodies because it attracted members from virtually all religious persuasions. The situation became acute in 1798, when two Methodist clergymen ordained by Bishop Asbury published *A Valedictory Address to the People Called Methodist*. In this publication they announced their intentions of withdrawing from the Methodist Church and joining the New Jerusalem fellowship. Although one soon returned to the Methodist fold, the second, John Hargrove, remained the generating force behind the Baltimore Swedenborgians for three decades.[10]

For several years following Hargrove's conversion to the New Jerusalem Church, the Swedenborgians and their principal foes, the Methodists, debated the reasonableness and merits of their particular theological points of view. The contest soon deteriorated into name-calling, with the participants branding their opponents "false pretenders," "hypocrites," "ignorant understrappers," and "common prostitutes."[11] Perhaps because of the inability of the New Jerusalem Church to emerge as a major denomination, and Hargrove's well-known animosity toward deism, the bitter controversy passed. By the 1820s Protestants accepted even Hargrove as an officer in several of the interdenominational evangelical societies.

Unlike the Swedenborgians, Baltimore Unitarians never won the acceptance of mainline denominations. Their beginnings in Baltimore date from October 1816, when a group of prominent citizens, principally recent arrivals from New England, invited Dr. J. W. Freeman of King's Chapel in Boston to the southern city. Responding to the call, Freeman journeyed to Baltimore and remained three weeks. On October 13, in a rented Gibney Hall, he conducted a worship service for a congregation sympathetic to unitarian doctrines.[12] According to Edward Hinkley, a charter member of Baltimore's First Independent Church, the audience at the initial meetings was "large and respectable," despite the fact that "one minister threatened to excommunicate from his church any member who should presume to hear Freeman." Even more militant was the anonymous female who was overheard stating "that the boys ought to have broken Freeman's windows while he was preaching, and to have stoned him through the streets."[13] Such threats did not stop Freeman. During his three weeks in Baltimore he gave impetus to a movement that four months later led to the creation of the First Independent Church. One year after his initial visit, Freeman returned to Baltimore, this time to dedicate the recently built house of worship. Meanwhile the trustees were in the process of selecting a thirty-year-old graduate of Harvard, Jared Sparks, as pastor of the church.[14]

Persuading Sparks to accept the call to Baltimore was no easy matter. Being simultaneously offered a church in Boston, Sparks had to decide between taking a church where doctrinally unitarian congregations were thriving, or taking the Baltimore charge where no such church previously had existed. Before making his decision, Sparks asked his Baltimore friend Edward Hinkley if unitarian beliefs could prosper amidst the southern bias against liberal religion. Hinkley responded affirmatively, asserting that "no single sect or party has the power to make strong opposition, and ... no one will have the inclination to persecute or oppose." He concluded: "Finally, all know the church will be established and supported by men powerful and respectable, to oppose whom would be useless and disgraceful."[15] Hinkley promised that the power of economic prestige would exceed the power of religious prejudice.

Although Hinkley's optimism was sufficient to induce Sparks to come to Baltimore, the ensuing problems that Sparks confronted suggest that Hinkley may have underestimated the strength of Baltimore's anti-unitarian forces. On 15 January 1819, Sparks wrote:

> There is a vast deal of prejudice and ignorance here, but there is less than there has been. People whose curiosity is so ardent as to drive them to the new church, and who go trembling for fear they shall commit the unpardonable sin, go away astonished that they have not heard anything blasphemous or profane, or even wicked, and they make good report.[16]

Even this cautious optimism soon melted. The event that stirred the anti-unitarian forces was the announcement that the prestigious William E. Channing of Federal Street Church, Boston, would speak at Spark's ordination. On 5 May 1819 Channing delivered the ordination message—an address destined to become nationally known as the "manifesto of a new liberal faith." As a definitive proclamation of principles, this Baltimore sermon spelled out five major confrontations between the orthodox and unitarians. Specifically, Channing rejected: (1) the dogma of the Trinity as "unnatural," "unscriptural," and leading to "idolatry"; (2) the orthodox Christological understanding of the unity of both divine and human natures of Christ as illogical and confusing; (3) the doctrine of total depravity as inconsistent with the moral perfection of God; (4) the orthodox understanding of the atonement, which asserted that Christ's death was necessary to placate God and quench his wrath; and (5) the doctrine of regeneration by irresistible grace.[17]

The "unitarian manifesto" spurred a controversy, both nationally and locally. At first Sparks felt that the attention aroused by his church advanced the cause of unitarianism in Baltimore. In June he wrote:

> A strong spirit of inquiry is rapidly making its way among the people here, and prejudice is certainly sinking by degrees. There are many, however, who still would think it an impardonable sin to enter the vestibule of our church, even on a week day ... and who cannot possibly conceive that a Unitarian can be a Christian.[18]

Then in late summer, a yellow fever epidemic hit Baltimore. Orthodox clergymen, believing the epidemic to be God's punishment on the city, clamored for an official day of fasting, prayer, and humiliation. On this special occasion one clergyman attributed the plague to God's wrath, because the city had allowed a "synagogue of Satan" to be erected. Shortly thereafter, the Young Men's Bible Society excluded the First Independent Church from participation in the organization. The holy war had begun.[19]

The most far-reaching polemical battle began the following year. In October 1820 Dr. Samuel Miller, a noted professor at Princeton Theological Seminary, came to First Presbyterian to preach the ordination sermon of Pastor William Nevins. Miller's discourse, immediately published and circulated nationally, attacked the heresies of unitarianism, asserted that the preachers of such doctrines were universally the "most accepted to the gay, the fashionable, the worldly minded, and even the licentious," and finally denied that Unitarians were in fact Christians.[20]

The attack demanded a stern reply by Sparks, which then triggered another blast by Miller. This literary interchange continued for three years, and climaxed only when both authors published book-length summations of their respective arguments.[21] Although both men held distinguished credentials, the debate was not without its unseemly side. Denouncing Unitarians as the "most delusive and dangerous of all that have ever assumed the Christian name," Miller accused them of being either timid "infidels" or those who respect religion "yet desire to have it so modified as to give them as little trouble ... as possible."[22] Similarly, Sparks's words were so strong that they were condemned even by his Unitarian colleagues in New England as uncharitable and illiberal.[23]

If Miller was the commander-in-chief of the literary crusade against Baltimore Unitarians, he was supported by an army of lieutenants and captains ranging from the prestigious William Wyatt of St. Paul's Episcopal Church to anonymous citizens of the city.[24] In contrast, Sparks, standing alone as the defender of Unitarian thought, grew weary of the constant onslaught from his foes. In August 1821 Sparks confessed to a friend: "I have hard times in Baltimore. They assail me on all hands, and my task is too great. It would be a blessing to me to be in a quiet parish in some country town in New England."[25] Two months later he again complained: "I am goaded all round, and as if my measure were not yet full, the Catholics are beginning to empty their quivers."[26] For four years, Sparks courageously remained as the voice of southern unitarianism. During this period Baltimore rivaled the combined forces of all New England in the printing of unitarian tracts.[27]

In early 1823, however, Sparks, wearied and in poor health, surrendered. Upon stepping down from the pastorate at First Independent, Sparks never again returned to the Unitarian ministry. Leaving theology for a new discipline, Sparks rapidly emerged as an eminent nineteenth-century historian, and eventually capped his distinguished career by serving as president of Harvard College. Meanwhile, Baltimore's First Independent Church lingered as a wealthy but nonagressive congregation. For the three years between 1824 and 1827 the church was without a pastor. In 1827 G. W. Burnap accepted the call, and began his thirty-two-year pastorate.[28] During this era Burnap generally made it a point not to introduce controversial subjects into worship.[29] While theological differences remained, never again was there to be the intensive contest that distinguished the pastorate of the church's first minister.

Roman Catholics also suffered minor harassment. Until the 1830s—when several clergymen of the city began publishing works asserting that the Church of Rome had done "more to corrupt the truth and order of the true Church of Christ than all the rest of its enemies—infidel and pagan combined"[30]—the Protestant attack upon Catholics was relatively mild. The only major Protestant-Catholic conflict before 1830 occurred early in the century when several local Protestants castigated the administrators of St. Mary's College for admitting Protestant pupils and then requiring them to attend the Catholic mass. The storm passed only after Father W. V. Dubourg published a series of five pamphlets in which he rebutted the charges and clarified the institution's policy.[31] Such an incident was minor when contrasted either with the militant accusations against the unorthodox, or against the Catholics in a later era. Indeed, that a substantial number of Protestant families allowed their children to attend the Catholic college attests to the peaceful coexistence of the Catholics and Protestants of the city.

The willingness of Protestants to live under truce with Catholics grew in part from their respect for John Carroll , the archbishop of the Baltimore diocese, who was well-known for his community spirit and ardent nationalism. Perhaps the patriotic mood of churchmen contributed to the holy alliance. Especially after the migration of the Santo Domingo refugees, too many Catholic immigrants populated the city for Protestants—already anxious about their ability to instill the masses with religious virtue—to crusade against the Roman Church. Discrediting the faith of the immigrants might in the long run bring numbers into Protestant churches, but the short-term dangers of irreligion made the cost too high to pay. Anti-Catholicism would have to wait until the young republic had proven its resiliency.[32] In the meantime the Catholic fathers were free to reach their own impoverished masses with the tranquilizing benefits of the gospel without interference from Protestant antagonists.

More frequent than the vicious assaults against the unorthodox and the mild castigations against the Catholics were the intradenominational struggles between congregations of a given denomination, and the internal fights within the membership of a particular congregation. The urban environment was at least partly responsible for these types of church friction. For instance, the proximity of several congregations of the same denomination bred pastoral jealousies and provided discontented members with the opportunity of joining sister fellowships. The history of Baltimore Baptists best illustrates how these conditions produced disunity and schism. In 1795 John Healy and his Baptist followers arrived in Baltimore. Pastor Lewis Richards promptly invited them to join the Baptist Church. They declined, preferring to remain a separate congregation. When Healy's Second Baptist applied for admission into the Baltimore Baptist Association, Richards accused the church of doctrinal irregularities and persuaded the Association to postpone their admittance. Despite Healy's complaint that the Association's refusal stemmed solely from Richard's assertion that "there was no need of more than one Baptist Church in Baltimore," the regional association did not receive Second Baptist until 1807.[33]

Passions cooled, but only temporarily. In 1820 the two churches broke fellowship when Second Church charged members of First Church with circulating slanderous rumors against Healy. The following year differences between the pastor and the associate pastor of First Church split the congregation. E. J. Reiss, the associate pastor, and several families bolted, to establish Ebenezar Baptist Church. In 1825 another name-calling incident between Reiss, now of Ebenezar, and Healy resulted in a broken fellowship between the two congregations. Still another internal dispute within Ebenezar led to the establishment in 1830 of Mt. Zion Baptist. At least among Baptists, pastoral jealousies were clearly seeds of church conflict.[34]

Baltimore's changing ethnic complexion also increased local church tensions. Particularly hard hit were the German-speaking congregations. In 1790 perhaps one in ten citizens and one in six churchgoers spoke German.[35] But as German immigration slowed, and second- and third-generation Germans assimilated into the English-speaking culture, fewer and fewer German Lutherans, Catholics, Reformed, and United Brethren understood the German language. Introducing English into their services of worship, however, inevitably caused considerable conflict.

At Zion Lutheran the language issue appeared as early as 1769 when the newly founded congregation debated whether it should be incorporated solely as a "German" church.[36] Although they solved the problem without schism, the question remained a point of contention for over half a century. In 1800 several members urged the church Council to introduce English in worship. The Council voted down the proposal, thereby forcing several families to leave the congregation.[37] Then in 1808, at the dedication of its newly built sanctuary, the Council reaffirmed its position with the admonition:

You love your forefathers, you love the evangelical teachings; the truth of salvation as you learned it in your mother tongue is especially important to you. Do you want to do less for your children than your parents have done for you when they brought you up in their mother tongue? No! Without doubt you will not let that happen. Do not rest until your school affairs are on a foundation which will assume that this House also remains a House of God for your posterity, where the preaching will be in German and where the name of the Lord will forever be praised in this language.[38]

Again in 1815 Pastor J. Daniel Kurtz asked his nephew Benjamin Kurtz to become his assistant and preach in English. However, within a few months, Benjamin accepted a call to a Lutheran congregation in Hagerstown, Maryland, thus leaving Zion Church without an English service. The next year several members requested the Council for permission to hold English services. They published pamphlets hoping to persuade the Council that the church would slowly die out if the young did not receive religious instruction in English. Once again the conservative Council rejected the innovation.[39] Finally, in 1823 after another unsuccessful attempt of the English faction to secure an English-speaking co-pastor, several families of Zion Church separated to establish the First English Lutheran Church. Even this did not quench the division at Zion. In 1830 the election of the church's vestry split the congregation along German and English lines. After the German faction won by a 135–68 vote, they adopted a new church constitution, which asserted that "the preaching in English is prohibited" and that this "shall never be subject to change."

The controversy between German- and English-speaking Catholics produced not only verbal abuse and disunity but rioting and bloodshed as well. The problem began in February 1797, when Father Frederick Cesarius Reuter, a young German Franciscan, arrived in Baltimore. Upon receiving an appointment by Bishop Carroll to minister to the needs of Baltimore German Catholics, Reuter established a German school, preached in his native language, and won immediate popularity among his constituents. After laboring for a year, he left the city for Europe, only to return in early 1799 with a letter addressed from Archbishop Brancadoro to Bishop Carroll. This letter reprimanded Bishop Carroll for neglecting Baltimore Germans, and authorized Reuter to collect alms to restore the German Catholic house in Baltimore. Embarrassed by the reprimand, Carroll was affronted, since at this time no German house existed in the city. While authorizing Reuter to administer the sacraments to Baltimore Germans for a specified three-and-one-half month period, Carroll refused to accept Reuter's letter as sufficient permission allowing him to collect funds for the building of a German church.[40]

Despite Carroll's order, in the summer of 1799 Reuter and his German followers initiated a subscription campaign that sought both local and national support to establish a German house in Baltimore. Infuriated at this blatant rejection of authority, Carroll censured Reuter, who then left to seek absolution from Rome. Meanwhile, Baltimore Germans associated themselves as St. John's German congregation and sent a formal protest to Rome. This letter, signed by fifty-three German males, accused Carroll and the English priests of plotting "to stamp out the German language" and desiring "to change us all into Englishmen, rapidly and violently."[41] Moreover, the Germans purchased a lot and began building a parsonage and a house of worship. In October 1802, with the house near completion, six appointed members of St. John's appealed to Carroll to consecrate the church, and to appoint Reuter—who by then had been absolved of the censure—as pastor. After receiving a pledge from both the congregation and Reuter to submit to episcopal authority, Carroll consecrated the house and appointed Reuter as rector.

Unfortunately, the Bishop's controversy with Baltimore Germans was not over. Within sixteen months Carroll had suspended Reuter for "scandalous conduct" and appointed Father F. X. Brosius his successor. But Reuter, receiving support from the majority of the congregation, refused to leave the parsonage or cease celebrating the sacraments. Thus, in May 1804, Brosius sought a mandamus from the civil authority to restore him the possession and use of St. John's Church.[42]

While the case was before the court, passions rose to a perilous height. On May 30 an armed force of Catholics who favored Brosius marched to the parsonage, seized Reuter, ransacked and destroyed his property, and then proceeded to the chapel. Meanwhile, upon learning of the incident, Reuter's followers boarded themselves up in the church house. For several hours a verbal battle followed, as Reuter's men attacked the tyrannous conduct of Bishop Carroll, while Brosius's supporters denounced the immoral Reuter. In spite of an effort by the magistrates of the city to arrest the confrontation without violence, when those on the inside came out, the besiegers rushed into the church and a riot ensued. Although calmer heads regained control, throughout the following year, while the case was still pending, the congregation of St. John's remained severely divided. Finally the controversy subsided in May 1805, when the court ruled in favor of Brosius. Reuter left town, never again to return.[43]

Following the departure of Reuter, the Baltimore German Catholics gradually became less sensitive to their ethnicity. In May 1814 several trustees of St. John's protested against their pastor, Father Mertz, for not preaching in German. In defense, Mertz asserted that one-third of the youth were ignorant of the German language, and thus needed occasionally to hear messages in English. Several days later a number of pewholders wrote Bishop Carroll supporting Mertz. The incident passed without further conflict, and English sermons increasingly became a part of worship at St. John's.[44]

Like the Lutherans and Catholics, the German Reformed congregation underwent difficulties in introducing English into their service of worship. The controversy initially erupted in February 1818, when thirty-six members presented the Consistory a signed petition soliciting permission to have English preaching on Sunday afternoon. Five months later they brought the matter before the entire congregation for discussion. Before a settlement was reached, the pastor, C. L. Becker, died. Suddenly the Consistory faced the dilemma of selecting either a pastor sympathetic to an English service, or a traditionalist opposed to the innovation. After seeking advice from the Synod, and being advised to accept both German and English preaching, the Consistory invited Lewis Mayer to visit and preach in both languages. Thus in September 1818, in spite of several threats of violence, Mayer preached in German in the morning and in English in the afternoon to overflowing crowds.[45]

However, bitterness still remained. Although the congregation overwhelmingly elected Mayer as pastor—the German-speaking faction refusing to participate—he declined the invitation for an appointment at a more unified congregation. Early the following year, the pro-English faction unanimously invited Albert Helfenstein to serve as pastor. In July 1819 Helfenstein delivered his inaugural sermons in both languages. Gradually, he preached less and less in German, until in 1817 German sermons stopped altogether. Although some German families left the congregation, the church was weaned from a German- to an English-speaking congregation without a major schism.[46]

Doctrinal disputes also produced intradenominational conflict. The most prolonged doctrinal contest took place among the low-church and high-church Protestant Episcopalians. Although this denominational battle raged throughout the Maryland Diocese, it was particularly intense in Baltimore, since the principal statewide leaders of both factions served neighboring Baltimore congregations. As high churchmen, Joseph Bend, James Kemp, and William Wyatt of St. Paul's argued that the episcopal structure of the church was a divine institution, established by Christ, and passed down through the generations by a succession of bishops. Salvation depended upon incorporating the individual into this divine institution by the reception of church sacraments. In contrast, the low-church advocates such as George Dashiell and J. P. K. Henshaw of St. Peter's, and John Johns of Christ Church, believed that while the episcopacy was scriptural and necessary for the perfection of the church, it was not essential to the validity of the church. Furthermore, salvation—typically evidenced by instantaneous conversion—could be received apart from the church.[47]

Although these doctrinal differences were the underlying causes of denominational warfare, numerous local battles were fought over less-profound but more obvious concerns. Throughout the first decade of the century, Bend and his high-church friends complained that Dashiell was bringing unqualified men into the ministry. While they officially objected that Dashiell's pupils lacked knowledge of the classical languages, their principal concern as expressed in their personal correspondence was that Dashiell was subverting the church by pushing ignorant men of low-church persuasion into the Diocesan Convention.[48] They also castigated Dashiell for omitting some parts of the prescribed service of worship, singing hymns not included in the official hymnal, allowing non-Episcopalians, and on one occasion even a female, to preach from his pulpit, and disrupting the harmony of the church by encouraging party spirit.[49] In return, Dashiell slandered his opponents as mere "formalists" who lacked the essence of vital religion. The bitterness between both factions clearly became evident in 1808 when the St. Peter's vestry passed a resolution that prohibited Bend from speaking from its pulpit.[50]

The St. Paul's-St. Peter's controversy carried into the Diocesan Conventions. In 1811 the elderly Bishop Claggett requested episcopal assistance. Optimistic that within a few years the low church party would dominate the Convention, and yet certain that the favored candidate at this time was the high churchmen James Kemp, Dashiell and his low churchmen opposed any election that would propel a high churchman into the episcopacy.[51] When a two-thirds majority of the clergy at the 1812 Convention nominated Kemp for Suffragan Bishop, Dashiell's lay followers united to prevent the necessary two-thirds majority of the lay delegation from confirming Kemp's election.[52] Dashiell's party received an added boost in 1813 when Bishop Claggett reversed his earlier position and announced his opposition to a Suffragan Bishop. With the moderates now allied with the low-church party, the 1813 Convention voted that an assistant bishop was unnecessary. This victory was short lived. By a narrow margin the 1814 Convention reversed the decision and called for an election. Catching the low-church party off guard, the high churchmen succeeded in nominating and electing James Kemp of St. Paul's as the Suffragan Bishop.[53]

Following this election, Dashiell's men regrouped and made a belated and futile attempt to prevent Kemp's consecration. A *Protest* written by Dashiell and signed by six Maryland clergymen and seventeen laymen was sent to the House of Bishops of the Protestant Episcopal Church. This document argued that the office of Suffragan Bishop was unknown to the Maryland church constitution, that the election in 1814 did not meet the approval of the required two-thirds majority of the clerical and lay delegates at the Convention, that the 1813 Convention expressed the true majority opinion of the church because in that year the question of a Suffragan Bishop was preannounced as a topic for discussion, and that the 1814 election was achieved by surprise and therefore would lead to discord and division. Unconvinced and unwilling to be intimidated, the House of Bishops approved the election, and on 1 September 1814, consecrated Kemp as Suffragan Bishop of the Maryland Diocese.[54]

Dashiell's tirades continued. From both pulpit and press he asserted that the security of the evangelical part of the church was threatened. He declared that the evangelicals could "never for a moment" consider giving Kemp their approbation, and thus would not attend any convention held under his authority.[55] In the summer of 1815 Dashiell's problems multiplied when he was accused of having an illicit affair with a member of his parish. After refusing to stand trial, Dashiell was convicted by Bishop Claggett of "contumacy" and deposed from pastoral duties.[56] Dashiell responded with the most vehement attack yet unleashed. He accused Claggett of treating him "with flagrant injustice and unexampled cruelty," and even warned the Bishop of the eternal consequences of his action:

> The darkness of death must quickly gather around your head, and without you repent and make amends for your criminal *partiality* and *inhumanity*, your *injustice* and *cruelty*, the awful light of eternity beaming through the darkness will shew you the mysterious hand tracing upon the wall in legible characters your eternal destiny.[57]

Despite his excommunication and a subsequent legal mandamus that sought to require St. Peter's vestry to remove him from the rectorate, Dashiell remained at St. Peter's until Easter 1817. At this time Dashiell and his remaining followers left the congregation to establish the independent St. John's Evangelical Episcopal Church of Baltimore. Although rid of their turbulent leader, St. Peter's demonstrated their low-church sympathies by selecting the evangelical J. P. K. Henshaw as Dashiell's successor.[58] Temporarily the open hostilities between the factions of the Episcopal Church subsided. For several years thereafter—with the single exception of a relatively minor confrontation between Henshaw and Kemp over the use of extemporaneous prayer in worship—harmony appeared to exist between the Episcopal houses in Baltimore.[59]

The latent party spirit reemerged in 1821 over whether to endorse a diocesan seminary for Maryland or to contribute solely to a General Theological Seminary of the denomination. Henshaw and other members of the low-church party favored a separate seminary for Maryland that would be under the auspices of a local Board of Trustees. Under Henshaw's leadership the 1821 Diocesan Convention drafted and endorsed a constitution for a Maryland seminary. Despite this resolution, Bishop Kemp opposed Henshaw's plan, believing that it would open the door to schism by perpetuating certain "Calvinistic doctrines" intended to "multilate and change the liturgy of the church."[60] A specially called General Convention meeting in Philadelphia in October 1821 accepted a constitution for a General Theological Seminary in New York City. Kemp warned that those who resisted this endorsement of the highest council of the church would be subject to punishment. Eventually Kemp's pressure pulled the Maryland Diocese back into line as the 1823 Convention resolved that it was inexpedient to carry into operation any plans for establishing a Maryland diocesan seminary.[61]

Although virtually every major issue brought before the Diocesan Convention after 1823 divided along party lines, the two factions worked harmoniously under the leadership of Kemp. The era of good feelings ended abruptly in November 1827, following the tragic carriage accident that took the life of Bishop Kemp.[62] Now faced with the task of selecting a new bishop, the cold war among the two factions warmed. In 1828 the Convention convened and disbanded without settling the matter, because neither the low-church candidate, John Johns of Christ Church, nor the high-church candidate, William Wyatt of St. Paul's, received the necessary two-thirds majority of votes. After one more year of political maneuvering, which at times broke down into name-calling brawls, the Convention reconvened. Once again neither Johns nor Wyatt emerged victorious. Finally, after another year without a bishop, the 1830 Convention unanimously elected William Stone, a compromise candidate selected by a committee of leaders of the two factions, as the Bishop of Maryland.[63]

The doctrinal disagreements among Episcopalians reveal the limitations of the ecumenical activity of the era. Low-church Episcopalians, like most mainline Protestants, placed greater emphasis on soteriological than ecclesiastical doctrines. They stressed the need for the individual first to seek salvation, and then find the most appropriate church. High-church Episcopalians were less willing to separate the choices. Believing that scripture confirmed their position, high churchmen did not oppose the interdenominational Bible societies. But generally they were less enthusiastic about other interdenominational missionary activities. Sermons by high-church Episcopalians inevitably were the more sectarian discourses of Baltimore Protestants. If ultimately the high-church position prevailed, it was not without three decades of bitter struggle against low-church Episcopalians, who more closely approximated the evangelical consensus of many mainline Protestants.

Even the interdenominational unity among evangelicals occasionally provoked contention at the congregational level. Some evangelicals imbued with millennial enthusiasm forsook the customs of their church for innovations more in line with their vision of the coming kingdom. The controversies among Baltimore Presbyterians, Friends, and Methodists provide cases in point.

On 27 May 1824 John M. Duncan, of the Associate Reformed Church and a recently appointed director of Princeton Theological Seminary, delivered a controversial lecture to the seminarians. After asserting that the interdenominational Bible societies had "created a new era in the moral world," he pronounced: "The anticipation of the millennium ought now to seize the bosom, and ... ought now to occupy the attention of every minister.... Sectarianism is now falling, like the worn-out economy of Moses in the days of Paul."[64] So far most Protestants could agree. But Duncan carried his enthusiasm to a dangerous degree when he next asserted that the traditional creeds and confessions of the church were inappropriate for the millennial age.[65]

Duncan's arguments against the use of creeds did not go unchallenged. Six weeks later Samuel Miller addressed the Princeton seminarians with a lecture in which he denied Duncan's assertion that creeds superseded the scriptures and generated discord. Miller insisted that creeds were "lawful," "expedient," "necessary," and "indispensable" to the purity of the church of Christ.[66] Duncan then retorted with a 278-page defense of his position.[67] Before the theological quarrel subsided, Duncan and Miller, plus several outside critics, published additional pamphlets that restated and summarized their respective arguments.[68]

The Duncan-Miller contest had an unfortunate impact upon Duncan and his congregation. While the literary debate was in progress, the Second Presbytery of Philadelphia to which Duncan belonged dissolved, and instructed its members to become connected with other Presbyteries under the General Assembly of the denomination. When Duncan applied to the Presbytery of Baltimore, the Presbytery questioned his credentials, refused him admittance, and referred the matter to the General Assembly. Affronted by this unexpected development, Duncan promptly withdrew his application for admittance.[69]

Although Duncan protested that the General Assembly had no jurisdiction in the matter, the Assembly created a committee headed by Miller to study the question. Before this committee took official action, Duncan formally withdrew from the Presbyterian Church. The Assembly, in turn, announced that the pastoral connection between Duncan and the Associate Reformed Church of Baltimore was officially dissolved.[70] But supported by the majority of the congregation, Duncan continued his ministerial duties as their pastor. In January 1827 the anit-Duncan minority petitioned the Baltimore County Court for a mandamus requiring that the church property be turned over to those members acquiescing to the decision of the General Assembly. The ensuing court case attracted attention as spectators jammed the courthouse. Distinguished counselors for each side contributed to the excitement. William Wirt, the prominent Baltimore lawyer and politician who was to be the standard-bearer of the Anti-Masonic Party in the presidential election of 1832, represented Duncan's faction. Roger Taney, who soon would win renown as President Jackson's Attorney General, then Secretary of Treasury, and eventually as the Chief Justice of the Supreme Court, defended the minority. The long-standing controversy subsided only when the judge decided in favor of the majority party.[71] Duncan remained as a popular pastor of the independent congregation until shortly before his death in 1851. His millennial vision of a creedless church was too radical for most of his denomination, but he could take consolation in knowing that his congregation was the fastest-growing Presbyterian church in Baltimore. Duncan's belief that liberty and Christian unity should replace bigotry and sectarian divisiveness was shared by many American churchmen.

Related issues of religious liberty also provoked schisms among Baltimore Friends. In the 1820s the more evangelical Quakers, who like mainline Protestants emphasized the infallibility of the Bible and an orthodox Christology, drew apart from the supporters of Elias Hicks, who emphasized the "inner light" of divinity within every individual. Although Friends had always embraced the principle of the inner light, supporters of Hicks were labeled Hicksites, while their opponents were known as "orthodox." At the Philadelphia Yearly Meeting in 1827 the Hicksite faction, which included a large majority of the membership, split from the "orthodox" and established a separate Yearly Meeting. After this separation, the "orthodox" in Baltimore "disowned" all members who failed to attend their meeting. The issue came to a head in the Baltimore Yearly Meeting of 1828 when George Jones, an orthodox traveling minister from England, left the meeting after asserting he could not remain in fellowship with those who had departed from the purity of Quaker doctrine. Approximately one-fifth of the Baltimore Friends followed Jones, and established an "orthodox" branch of the Baltimore Yearly Meeting. Many who remained among the Hicksites did so not because of their commitment to Hicks's doctrines, but because of the principle of religious liberty.[72]

Like the Presbyterians and Friends, during the 1820s a number of Baltimore Methodists broke with their fellowship in a fight over religious liberty. According to the Methodist Episcopal polity, the supreme governing agency of the church was the Quadrennial General Conference. With delegates to this conference limited to traveling itinerants, and with much power vested solely in the hands of the bishops, a minority of Methodists from across the nation began to desire a lessening of the autocratic structure of the denomination.[73]

Baltimore was the center of the reform movement. In 1824 city station churches sent petitions to the General Conference advocating the admission of lay delegates to the governing body. When the conference failed to take positive action on the memorials, the disappointed reformers resolved to start a pro-reform periodical entitled *Mutual Rights*, and to establish Union Societies to disseminate the principles of reform.

Despite both local and nationwide opposition, in 1826 the Baltimore Union Society proposed to host a national convention of friends of reform in order to coordinate their efforts to achieve reform at the next quadrennial convention. Although this ambitious plan did not materialize, in November 1826 a convention was held for the state of Maryland. When the trustees of Baltimore's Methodist churches refused the reformers the use of Methodist houses, the convention met in the English Lutheran house. In addition to providing a forum for the discussion of structural change, the convention intensified the division between the advocates and opponents of reform.[74]

In April 1827 the issue came to a head when the Baltimore Annual Conference censured the reformist Reverend Dennis B. Dorsey for circulating "an improper periodical work," *Mutual Rights*. Although opponents had long accused the periodical of breeding dissension, the editors of *Mutual Rights* repeatedly denied any disloyalty to the church, and insisted that their object was "to prevent secessions and divisions" by promoting reform within the structural framework of the denomination. Thus when the Conference censured Dorsey for circulating the journal, the Baltimore Union Society members erupted in outrage. Nicholas Snethen reflected the reformers' wrath when he urged all Methodists "to resist this inquisitorial power, this attempt to renew in America the old, the exploited principle of torture, this monstrous outrage upon the principle of civil and religious liberty."[75]

Alexander McCaine complicated the controversy in May 1827, when he delivered a lecture before the Baltimore Union Society entitled "History and Mystery of the Methodist Episcopal Church." This revisionist history of the origins of American Methodism argued that John Wesley, the beloved founder, did not approve of the form of church government of American Methodists. After the address was published, Thomas Bond, the leading anti-reform local preacher of Baltimore, denounced it as inaccurate and disgraceful. Moreover, Bond asserted that Methodists had no spiritual or natural right in lay representation, and that those dissatisfied with the structure of the church should withdraw.[76]

A literary battle continued throughout the summer of 1827. Finally, on August 7 the itinerants of the city announced from the pulpits that a meeting would be held to consider the expulsion of the rebellious reformers. In September, church officials charged ten local preachers and twenty-two laymen with "endeavoring to sow dissension." Subsequently the officials tried and convicted these men for three specific offenses: belonging to the Union Society, supporting the *Mutual Rights*, and approving Alexander McCaine's "History and Mystery."[77]

While the expelled members awaited their appeal, a "General Convention of Reformers" convened in Baltimore for the purpose of preparing grievances at the 1828 General Conference. In addition to petitioning for lay- and local-preacher representation in the General Conference, the reformers also demanded that the rule of 1796 regarding "sowing dissension" be modified so as to prevent its alleged abuse. Their pronouncements made it clear that the battle line between the reformers and anti-reformers had been clearly drawn. Unity through reform or schism would depend upon the outcome of the 1828 General Conference.[78]

Meanwhile, the local crisis in Baltimore continued to a crescendo. In December the District Conference controlled by traditionalists convened and promptly dismissed without hearing the appeal of the expelled members. Insisting that the rightful place for appeal was unlawfully dissolved, the suspended preachers sent a protest to the presiding elder of the conference delineating their reasons for not appealing their case to the Quarterly Conference, the next level of appeal.[79] While awaiting the 1828 General Conference to determine their ultimate relation with the Methodist Episcopal Church, the suspended men associated themselves under the General Rules of the Union Societies. Furthermore, in January 1828 forty-three reform-minded Baltimore women formally withdrew from the Methodist Episcopal Church to join the expelled male leaders.[80]

The decisive General Conference of 1828 agreed to restore the suspended reformers on the condition that they discontinue the periodical *Mutual Rights* and the Union Societies. Upon rejecting these terms, the reform faction of the Methodists called a meeting in Baltimore in November 1828. The convention drafted and ratified the constitution of the schismatic Associated Methodist Church. Two years later the name was changed to the Methodist Protestant Church. Over two hundred Baltimore Methodist Episcopalians withdrew to associate with the newly created denomination.[81]

Although always a minority even within the city, the Baltimore reformers were largely responsible for the birth of a Methodist church that abolished the episcopacy and introduced the equal representation of lay and clerical leadership at all levels of ecclesiastical authority. This branch remained independent for 111 years, until its 197,996 members reunited with the main body in 1939.[82]

In conclusion, church life in early national Baltimore was characterized by both consensus and conflict. Motivated by the commitment to preserve a virtuous citizenry, and usher in the millennial kingdom, mainline Protestants and, to a lesser degree, Catholics worked in harmony to build a Christian nation. Their rules of fair play, which tempered interdenominational confrontations, did not apply to all religious bodies. With one voice the mainline denounced the deists, Swedenborgians, and Unitarians because they rejected one or more of the fundamental doctrines of Biblical revelation, the Trinity, and the divinity of Christ. Petty jealousies, ethnic tensions, and theological disagreements intensifed by the diversity and spatial density of urban congregations, also disrupted church unity at the intradenominational and congregational levels. Moreover, nationalism and millennialism, the very forces that generated ecumenical cooperation, inspired some evangelicals with visions beyond the dreams of most mainline churchmen. Inevitably, the result was schism. In an age saturated with holy causes, both holy alliances and holy wars were common. In doing battle for the Lord, Baltimore's awakened crusaders did not hesitate to convert the churches militant into militant churches.

CONCLUSION
THE BALTIMORE AWAKENING IN PERSPECTIVE

STANDARD treatments of the second great awakening generally include the following scenario. Organized religion in postrevolutionary America was in a state of decay. For several decades the national mind had focused on political rather than religious matters. Partisan strife, the years of warfare, Indian terrorism of the frontier, incessant geographical mobility, and rapid socioeconomic changes all contributed to the disruption of normal religious activity and church organization. Orthodox Christian leaders, appalled that the newly ratified constitution made no reference to God, expressed deep concern over the growing popularity of deism. And with only five percent of the population official church members, Protestant clergymen warned that without renewal, the nation would follow the churches into ruin.[1]

Following this night of despair, so the script reads, the dawn of a new century brought light and glory to the nation floundering in spiritual darkness. The heavenly glow, appearing first among New England Congregationalists, moved westward across the Alleghenies into the barbaric frontier. This religious quickening, the forerunner to the coming age of mass revivalism, found expression in two distinct styles of piety. On the western frontier camp meetings flourished, and with them the wild and emotional piety of uneducated Methodists and Baptists. Meanwhile, on the eastern seaboard, more dignified and orderly Presbyterians and Congregationalists expressed their new-found faith by joining scores of benevolent, moral reform, and missionary societies.[2]

In the 1820s, Charles Finney, a New England lawyer turned evangelist, bridged the gulf between the rowdy western and urbane eastern religiosities.[3] By mitigating the aggressive tactics of frontier religion and making them palatable to the more respectable urban classes, Finney brought added respectability to the emerging evangelical profession. From town to city Finney took his revival caravan, and wherever he landed, droves of new converts entered the churches. His revival fires eventually cooled, but not before they had left an indelible mark upon American religion. By the 1830s the percentage of churchgoers had increased fivefold from the spiritually barren 1790s.

134

Protestant values, once on the endangered list, now permeated American culture. And frontier revivalism, previously discarded as the enthusiasm of the ignorant, now was embraced by many American denominations as the normal mode of church recruitment.

Why the sons and daughters of our founding fathers became so religious has puzzled historians for generations. In the 1950s scholars emphasized the ideological origins of the awakening because they viewed the revivals as a Protestant counteroffensive against the threat of infidelity in the east and barbarism in the west.[4] By the 1960s scholars began to look more to sociology than to theology for explanations of the revivals. In a seminal 1969 essay Donald Mathews asserted that evangelical religion prospered because it gave meaning and direction to a people suffering from the social strains of a nation moving in new political, economic, and geographical directions.[5] Building upon Mathews's insights, a number of cultural (as opposed to church) historians in the last decade armed themselves with statistical methodologies and social science models in an attempt to isolate the specific pressures that produced a generation so susceptible to mass revival. While no consensus has emerged, the studies have produced insightful hypotheses. For example, Paul Johnson, who interpreted the awakening as a middle-class bourgeois phenomenon, associated church growth with the rapid advancement of the capitalistic market. In essence Johnson concluded that urban revivalists won converts primarily because wage earners worked for men who insisted on seeing them at church.[6] Mary Ryan, in contrast, linked the rise of evangelical religion with the movement from farm to city and the corresponding breakup in the intergenerational patriarchal family unit.[7] Similarly, Nancy Cott, who identified women as the principal participants in the revivals, argued that revivalism flourished because it satisfied the emotional needs of the growing numbers of single women stranded in the cities without either familial support or economic opportunity.[8]

Historians also disagree in their assessment of the consequences of the awakening. According to the social-control theorists, the revivals and reform associations were perpetrated by an unholy alliance of ministers and wealthy businessmen who exploited the power of religion to keep the masses in order and to preserve their personal status and wealth.[9] Some feminist scholars also accentuate the conservative tone of the awakening as they condemn evangelical religion as the architect of the restrictive and dehumanizing nineteenth-century "cult of true womanhood."[10] Other scholars, however, see within the reforms and revivals of the awakening the strains of both the American progressive tradition and the modern women's liberation movement.[11] Still others, noting the predominance of women in the revivals, the growing female majorities in the churches, and the transition in theology from a masculine Calvinism to a sentimental Arminianism, have labeled this spiritual movement a "woman's awakening" and asserted that it resulted in the "feminization of American religion."[12]

While conforming to the broad contours of contemporary scholarship, this study of Baltimore calls into question several commonly held assumptions about religion in early national America. In the following pages I shall highlight five areas in which the Baltimore experience deviates from patterns of religious life described in other histories of the period. In some ways these differences simply reflect the unique character of Baltimore's religious heritage and social environment during this era of rapid city growth. To some extent, however, the differences underscore the need to reconstruct our paradigms of the awakening so as to take into account the anomalies of the Baltimore past. Intended to be more provocative than definitive, these conclusions offer a new approach for the study of early national religion and suggest how the shifted focus can broaden our definition of the awakening.

First, with four in nine Baltimoreans at least nominally attending church in the 1790s, it is apparent that Baltimore did not experience the extreme religious despair that allegedly characterized late eighteenth-century America. This is not to say that Baltimore clergymen were pleased with the vitality of their congregations. Indeed, if the statistical records were ignored and the history of the era was drawn solely from literary sources, the myth of the great declension could very well be supported. How, then, does one explain the distance between fact and rhetoric? Perhaps, as some have suggested, the cries of gloom were simply strategic ploys intended to pressure churchgoers to avoid petty disagreements and unite under clerical leadership in a holy war against the phantom forces of evil. But if only a ploy, why was their despair as explicit in personal correspondence as in public pronouncement? An understanding of the gender profile of late eighteenth-century Baltimore congregations points us to a second and more likely hypothesis. In an age of voluntarism, the ability to attract contributing male members was paramount; yet, at this very time, Baltimore churches were failing miserably in this critical task. Hence, in looking into church pews filled increasingly with women, Baltimore's male clergymen genuinely feared for the future of their churches. And unless Baltimore was remarkably unique, it is likely that the jeremiad tradition of postrevolutionary America was largely a consequence of clerical worries that the church was becoming a feminine institution.

Second, the Baltimore experience suggests that recent scholarship has overmagnified Charles Finney's role in inaugurating a new era of mass revivalism, even as it has neglected the Methodist influence in fomenting urban revivals.[13] Two decades before Finney left his law office for the ministry, virtually every revival technique and emotional manifestation associated with western revivals had penetrated the Baltimore community. Sectarian Methodists, not nondenominational professional evangelists, invariably were both the instigators and the most avid defenders of the controversial "new measures." Camp meetings, although generally considered a frontier phenomenon, stood with protracted meetings and weekly revivalistic services as the principal means of Methodist recruitment. Methodists also brought to Baltimore such revival institutions as the Sunday School, and foreign missionary associations, and assisted the willing ministers of sister denominations in establishing men's Bible studies, young people's prayer meetings, and lay testimonial services. By the 1820s Methodist piety even affected the structure of worship in neighboring denominations, as Episcopal and Presbyterian houses, in an attempt to keep pace with the successful Methodists, enlivened their Sunday services by embracing extemporaneous praying and by hiring trained musicians to stimulate more fervent congregational singing. In sum, without the aid or the need of Charles Finney, frontier religion made its way into America's third largest city by way of impoverished but pious Methodist itinerants.

Third, this study cautions future students of the period against defining the awakening primarily as a season of revival that resulted in the "churching" of the American people. Church growth, of course, was an integral component of the awakening, and thus should be analyzed by historians as an index of the strength of the awakening. But as Baltimore's history demonstrates, often the more radical transformations both in the institutional structure and in the expression of early national religion had little to do with the overall increase in the size of the churchgoing population.

To illustrate, between 1790 and 1830, Baltimoreans built over thirty-five houses of worship, and added some 34,000 nominal members to their church roles. These figures indicate growth rates, respectively, of approximately 400% and 650% in the number of congregations and nominal churchgoers in the city. While impressive when interpreted in isolation, when viewed in the light of Baltimore's extraordinary growth, these statistics actually belittle the magnitude of the Baltimore awakening. Specifically, the 34,000 additional churchgoers translate into only a modest proportionate gain in the church-going community, from about four in nine to about one in two. But to deduce from this data that the evangelical excitement of the period had only marginal impact upon city congregations is to miss the greater story and institutional significance of the Baltimore awakening. For at least in America's most rapidly growing city, mass revivalism had far more to do with filtering churchgoers into given denominations than in enlarging the proportion of the churchgoing community.

The awakening, in sum, spurred church growth, but not uniformly. Instead, growth rates during this era of intense evangelical activity were largely a function of denomination. Methodists, far and away, were the winners in the competition for new members, although Roman Catholics, Presbyterians, and Baptists also enlarged their shares of the market. With the exception of the Roman Catholics (whose growth largely was a consequence of immigration), the churches with the most rapid growth rates were those which most enthusiastically embraced the new measures of evangelicalism, and accepted revivalism as the normal mode of church recruitment. In contrast, the denominational losers of the period were: (1) the ethnic churches, which relied most heavily on parental socialization as the primary means of church retention, and (2) the nonorthodox bodies, which held doctrinal positions deemed incompatible with the soteriological essentials embraced by the mainline.

Meanwhile, the Episcopalians, who remained highly selective in their acceptance of the new measures, continued to grow, but at a slower pace than their more evangelical neighbors or than the city at large.

Another consequence of the awakening that cannot be measured simply in terms of church growth is illustrated in the paradox expressed in the public statements of Baltimore Episcopal clergymen. During the 1790s, when the Episcopal church was the largest Baltimore denomination, Episcopal rectors complained about the deadness of their congregations. Forty years later, although the percentage of Episcopalians in the city had declined, and this once-dominant denomination ranked only third in the total number of churchgoers, Episcopal ministers no longer were prophets of doom. Instead, they boasted about the rising health of their church, and optimistically foretold the imminent return of Jesus Christ.

It is this flight to hope from despair—not the cold facts of church membership—that touches upon the true meaning of the Baltimore awakening. For at least to this generation of churchgoers the term *awakening* referred less to the noise of mass revivals than to the silent, personal conviction that God was at work awakening the attention of his people. Used more as a verb or adjective than a noun, the word *awakening* implied a movement of the spirit that was convincing this generation of believers of the social and personal dangers of religious neglect.[14] The ironic sentiments expressed by Baltimore Episcopalians offer ample testimony to the power of the awakening to alter the world view of early national churchgoers, and to the extent that this heightened religious consciousness permeated evangelical and non-evangelical churches alike.

Fourth, the study suggests that scholars seeking to understand the dramatic religious changes of the early nineteenth century should not underestimate the importance that denominational competition played in altering institutional religion. In stating this conclusion, I am not dismissing or undervaluing the insights of cultural historians of the past decade. For instance, Paul Johnson's argument that participation in church life brought shopkeepers financial rewards provides us with greater understanding into why so many in Baltimore's rising middle class were found among revival participants. Likewise Nancy Cott's assertion that the anxieties of displaced, single women made them receptive to evangelical preaching helps us understand more fully the presence of Baltimore women within city revivals. The problem with such explanations, however, is that in Baltimore the revivals were truly general, embracing among others youth, free blacks, single women, aspiring artisans, wealthy merchants, and public officials. While clearly a function of creed, the revivals were not overly influenced by age, gender, race, or class. In fact, as well as altering the comparative sizes of Baltimore denominations, revivals broadened the churchgoing population to reflect more nearly the gender, racial, and class ratios of the city at large. Thus, rather than being the purview of a clearly definable group, Baltimore revivals reached a wide spectrum of the city, and in so doing actually retarded the religious trends that were moving toward a female and white-collar male congregational profile. This popularity of revivalism across gender and class lines poses methodological dilemmas for scholars attempting to explain the rise of early-nineteenth-century evangelism in terms of a common psychological profile of the converts.

In a mechanical sense, however, the appearance, location, and institutional consequences of Baltimore revivals can be explained apart from the psychological orientation of early national churchgoers. In a pluralistic society the decision to associate with a given church is an act of free choice. But in any economy of exchange, individual choice is influenced by the supply of goods or services being offered and the marketing skills of the competing venders. In the decades following disestablishment, when the virgin denominational market was unusually fluid, voluntary churches fiercely competed with each other for contributing members. The nature of this struggle encouraged churches to implement new strategies to enlarge their share of the population. As previously stated, evangelical churches embracing the more aggressive measures of recruitment prospered, while those reluctant to compete on such terms declined. Hence, to use this market analogy, large numbers of Baltimoreans bought into evangelical religion largely because the price was right and the streets were filled with venders.

To summarize, revivals erupted primarily because churchgoers of particular denominations expected them and labored diligently to promote them. Methodists, and eventually evangelicals of other denominations as well, established the conversion of the city if not the world as their top priority. Committed to this task and cognizant that the first step to converting the masses was winning their attention, evangelicals introduced camp and town meetings, fast days, street preaching, Bible societies, and a host of other innovative measures designed to awaken the apathetic from their spiritual slumber. And while noise alone did not guarantee church growth, the fact that both the location of revivals and growth rates proved to be more sensitive to denomination than to class or gender indicates that religious change in Baltimore was as related to the dynamics of the transmitters of evangelical religion as to the psyches of the receivers.

This supply-side interpretation of the awakening, however, does not address the question of motive. What historic circumstances inspired churchgoers of this particular generation to take so seriously the great commission to take the gospel to all peoples? Without attempting a definitive response, I find that the motives undergirding the leadership of this intensive missionary thrust are to be found in a complex web of theological and social pressures peculiar to the era. First, throughout this period Baltimore pulpits across denominational lines resounded with warnings of a terrible judgment day at which every individual would give an account of his or her earthly actions. Unlike the later, emasculated sermons of mid-century, which euphemized death and softened the demands of God to make him fit more comfortably into the modern world, the messages of early nineteenth-century Baltimore ministers warned parishioners of the ever-present reality of death, which catapulted its victim before the bar of a transcendent, incomprehensible deity who hated sin as much as he cherished obedience.[15] The centrality of this theology of stewardship and accountability at the very least served to remind Baltimore churchgoers of their religious obligations not only to family and friends but to the world at large. Second, augmenting this religious concern was the acute awareness of growing social tensions within the city and nation. Perceiving that these local and national perplexities threatened both morality and social stability, and believing that the ultimate solution to the problem lay in individual spiritual regeneration, the religiously minded recognized that it was their Christian and patriotic duty to take the gospel to the masses. To fail in this task was to threaten the very survival of the nation and the grand republican experiment it had so nobly begun. Third, millennial enthusiasm that erupted with intensity at the conclusion of the War of 1812 energized evangelicals to help fulfill the prophecy that in the final days all mankind would hear the gospel message. No longer motivated by fear, they professed victory as they, like John the Baptist of old, prepared the way for the coming of their Lord.

Fifth, without negating what previously has been asserted, a time leap into mid-nineteenth-century Baltimore suggests that the impact of the second great awakening upon American culture has been overstated. Admittedly, the awakening left its imprint upon both church and society. Revival preaching escaped the confines of Methodism to become accepted by the most distinguished Presbyterian congregations. Missionary associations provided women and blacks with rare opportunities for community leadership and involvement. The heightened religious fervor spurred reform crusades to educate the masses, colonize blacks, and combat intemperance. It encouraged greater ecumenical cooperation among the mainline, and aroused more militant resistance to the unorthodox. The missionary excitement enlarged the size of the churchgoing community, and added to city maps dozens of new houses of worship, all of which would survive well beyond the brief seasons of revival that gave them birth. Moreover, by fortifying the size and influence of local congregations, the awakening minimized the social disorientation that accompanied the city's rapid growth and thereby lessened the harsh realities of urbanization.

But after all this is acknowledged, the Baltimore awakening still fell short of the glorious goals erected by its perpetrators. For underlying their patriotic and millennial rhetoric was a twofold ambition: (1) to "masculinize" Protestantism in verve and person so that the church again could compete against the glittering world of economic opportunity for the allegiance of the best and the brightest of men; and (2) to Christianize the culture so that the collective powers of individual piety could curtail the corrupting and dehumanizing pressures of the modern world. Yet, notwithstanding their dreams, the missionary enterprisers slowed but could not break the tide toward a female domination of the church. And in their pursuit to capture the world, they themselves became captive. By mid-century the uncompromising zeal against slaveholding and the too-eager pursuit of gain were softened with the acknowledgments that slaveholders also were among God's chosen, and that the acquisition of great wealth could ultimately accomplish the greatest good. Meanwhile, evangelical ecumenism and the Protestant-Catholic truce gave way to American nativism and the splintering of Protestantism into its warring, effeminate-liberal, and compassionless-conservative factions. And despite the liberating potentials within a theology that placed human spirit over divine decree, nineteenth-century evangelicalism lengthened the leash but never severed the chain that confined women to their domestic sphere.

In the end the awakened Baltimore crusaders failed because they promised a millennium that never dawned. Future generations would perpetuate their denominational names and, at least for a time, their methods. But their original evangelical message of stewardship and accountability ultimately was replaced with the promise that God would help those who helped themselves. American religion along with mid-century culture was consumerized, but not as a product of the second great awakening. Instead, this "feminization of American culture" was a monument to the failure of the evangelicals to transform America into the promised land.

APPENDIX A
NOTES ON METHODOLOGY

SEVERAL obstacles preclude a precise estimation of the status and number of churchgoers in the early national period. First, there is the problem of interpreting the meaning of church membership. Some denominations such as the Roman Catholics, Lutherans, and Episcopalians included as members all nominal affiliates, youth and adult, who escaped the rare stigma of excommunication. Other groups, like the Baptists, limited membership to adult believers. Still others, like the Methodists, required weekly attendance at class meetings and dismissed from membership lists those who were consistently negligent. To alleviate this problem of definition, I include as members—or perhaps more appropriately, churchgoers—all individuals willing to allow one particular denomination to baptize, marry, or bury their immediate family members. Using this least-stringent requirement for church membership not only allows for meaningful comparisons of denominational strength, but it also maximizes the utility of the most prevalent sources of data—the church registers.

Estimating the number of nominal members then becomes similar to the task of piecing together a puzzle with two-thirds of the pieces marred and the remainder missing. Even where congregation records are extant, the precision of the estimates varies, depending upon the types of data reported. For example, I accept with confidence the self-estimates of Methodist and Baptist membership, since both denominations tended to leave excellent records. Thus, to estimate the total population of a community associated with these denominations, I simply multiply the number of members recorded by a corrective constant, which adjusts the figure to include children of members under the normal eligible age of membership.[1]

In contrast, for the Episcopalians, Presbyterians, Lutherans, and Catholics, whose church registers generally recorded only the yearly baptisms, marriages, and deaths, and occasionally the communicants, the techniques for estimating size of membership are more complex and less precise. A comparison of the number of communicants, while helpful in contrasting the styles of piety, is less helpful as an indicator of quantity of membership since the proportion of adults nominally associated with a church who were active com-

142

municants varied from nearly 100% to only 10%.[2] Although still not direct indicators of size, the yearly counts of baptisms, marriages, and deaths are suggestive as to the relative size of the congregations. When taken independently, the best of the three indicators is the number of persons yearly interred, especially if the age of the interred member is recorded. In an analysis of the published records of the Baltimore Baptist Association, and the manuscript class registers of Baltimore and Fells Point Methodists, I found that approximately two percent of the adult population for each urban congregation perished every year.[3] Assuming that this mortality rate held for other denominations, I estimated the size of the various congregations by multiplying the average number of adults interred by a corrective constant based upon the above mortality rates and the proportion of children under the normal age of membership. Next, I compared this estimate with a second one based soley on the percentage of deaths in the city from a particular congregation.[4] Although the above methods of estimating membership size are filled with uncertainties, when taken together and compared with occasional contemporary estimates made by local pastors, and the comparative number of yearly baptisms and marriages, a rough figure for the membership of the several congregations can be ascertained. Counting the yearly baptisms, marriages, and deaths is time-consuming and tedious, but it allows for closer approximations of denominational strength than do those estimates taken solely from the rare "official" membership counts, or from the seating capacity of the church houses.

Like the problem of estimating denominational size, comparing the status structure of different churches is complicated by the varying types of church records. For example, comparing the occupations and wealth of Catholic pewholders, Episcopal communicants, and Lutheran contributors would be meaningful as an index of denominational class structure only if one erroneously assumed that pewholders, communicants, and contributors were equally synonymous with nominal religious affiliation.[5] The way to minimize this type of error is to standardize the source from which the subjects of all denominations are drawn. When possible, I selected the heads of households of those families who had their children baptized. This source is useful because (1) baptismal records are among the most numerous extant early records, and (2) because the families who had their children baptized best approximate my definition of nominal membership. With few exceptions, notably the Friends and Baptists, churchmen viewed the baptism of infants as a minimal requirement for a family's affiliation with a denomination. For most Protestants and Catholics, rich and poor, white slave master and black slave, baptism was a basic requirement. Hence, despite the bias against the unmarried and the married beyond childbearing age, the status profile of families of baptized children approximates the general status structure of a denomination as a whole.

To establish the status profile of churchgoers, I first collected a sample of some 3,000 Caucasian heads of families, most of whom were fathers who had their infants baptized during the years 1800–03, 1813–16, or 1827–30.[6] Inadequate sources of data necessitated the exclusion of black churchgoers and of white churchgoers before 1800. I examined church registers over three-year rather than one-year intervals in order to enlarge the sample size from smaller congregations. I drew only every n[th] father listed in the registers of the larger churches, but in all cases the sample size was such that the sampling error was minimal. Next I traced the individuals through the city directories and tax assessment records for the years surrounding the period of inquiry, and ascertained the occupation, residence, and taxable wealth for each churchgoer. Unidentified individuals with such common names as William Brown or James Smith were eliminated from the sample.

For analytical purposes I classified the occupations of the churchgoers in fourteen trade categories, and the trade groups into one of three status rankings: (1) white collar, (2) skilled artisan, and (3) unskilled laborer. This vertical code of occupations was an adaptation from the model used by Theodore Hershberg, Michael Katz, Stuart Blumin, Lawrence Glasco, and Clyde Griffen in their joint project that studied occupation and ethnicity in five nineteenth-century American cities.[7] A listing of the occupations comprising each of the categories as used in this study is provided in Appendix B.

Assuming that the compilers of the city directories were biased against the lower classes, I arbitrarily classified those individuals not found in city directories as unskilled laborers. If not error free, several types of statistical evidence validate this assumption. First, only 10% of those listed in city directories were semi-skilled or unskilled laborers. It is unlikely that Baltimore's mercantile economy—which centered around the dock, the wharf, the counting-house, and the warehouse—could have functioned with such a low percentage of the work force employed as manual laborers.[8] Second, the significantly high Spearman rho rank correlation between the congregations with the highest percentage of not-listed samples and the congregations with the highest percentage of samples listed as rank-three workers, suggests a close relationship between the samples not listed and unskilled laborers.[9] Third, only about 7% of those individuals across all denominations not listed in the city directories were listed as property holders in the 1804 tax records. This low percentage compares closely with the percentage of property owners among rank-three workers.

The occupational and wealth data for each churchgoer was coded and entered on a computer terminal. Using the SPSS programs, I analyzed the relationship between religious preference and status. Tables 2–4 report the percentages of churchgoers classified in each status rank. Tables 5–7 provide a more detailed breakdown of churchgoers into the trade categories. In the latter tables I compare the percentages of churchgoers classified in a trade with the percentage of Baltimoreans listed in the city directories within the trade. I assumed that the percentage of churchgoers not listed equaled the percentage of the total population not listed in the directory. Positive figures denote an overrepresentation of churchgoers within the trade; negative figures designate an underrepresentation. Each integer signifies a 25% variation from the expected norm. To illustrate, the value 0 indicates that the observed percentage of churchgoers in a trade differs from the overall percentage of the work force in the trade by less than 25%. Similarly, a +2 value indicates that the observed percentage exceeded the expected percentage by 50 to 75%. Table 8 summarizes the actual percentage differences in status rankings between the subgroup, churchgoers, and the overall working force. My data file is stored on tape at the Sam Houston State University Computer Center.

APPENDIX B
VERTICAL CATEGORIES: BY RANK AND TRADE

Rank I: White-Collar Occupations

Innkeeper
Hotel Keeper
Tavern Keeper

Proprietor
Bank/Factory President
Botanist
Builder
Chemist/Druggist
China Store
Clothier
Commission Merchant
Dry Goods/Fancy Store
Farmer
Furniture Store
Gentleman
Grocer
Ironmonger
Jeweler
Liquor Dealer
Lumber Merchant
Manufacturer
Math Instrument Maker
Proprietor
Rope Store
Salesman
Shipbuilder
Sea Captain/Master
Stationery/Bookseller
Storekeeper
Sugar Refiner

Proprietor, cont'd
Tallow Chandler
Tobacconist

Professional
Clergy
Lawyer
Physician
Teacher

Public Servant
Bath Keeper
Beef/Fish/Flour Inspector
Constable
Custom Officer
Deputy Collector of Port
Deputy Sheriff
Judge
Justice of Peace
Military Office
Notary
Pump Superintendent

Low White Collar
Accountant
Agent
Bookkeeper
Clerk
Dentist
Land Surveyor
Teller

Rank II: Skilled Artisans

Miscellaneous
Barber
Boiler
Bookbinder
Clockmaker
Conductor
Engineer
Engraver
Glassblower
Peddler
Potter
Sexton
Stonecutter/Mason
Soap/Candle Chandler

Food
Baker
Brewer
Butcher
Cigar Maker
Confectioner
Victualer
Sugar Maker

Leather
Comb/Brush Maker
Currier
Dyer
Furrier
Morocco Dresser
Saddle/Harness Maker
Saddler
Tanner
Upholsterer

Clothing
Boot/Shoe Maker
Cordwainer
Hatter
Mantua Maker
Merchant Tailor
Tailor
Weaver
Woolendraper

Shipping
Net Maker

Shipping, cont'd
Rigger
Ropemaker
Sailmaker
Ship Carpenter
Shipwright
Stevedore
Wharf Builder
Whipmaker

Metal
Bellhanger
Blacksmith
Brass Sounder
Coppersmith/Printer
Founder
Goldsmith
Gunsmith
Locksmith
Machinist
Silversmith
Whitesmith

Wood
Cabinetmaker
Carpenter
Carriage Maker
Chair Maker
Cooper
Joiner
Piano Maker
Pump/Block Maker
Turner
Wheelwright

Construction
Bricklayer/Mason
Brick Maker
Building Measurer
Japaner
Millwright
Molder
Nail Maker
Painter
Paperhanger
Plasterer
Plumber

Appendix B

Rank III: Unskilled Laborers

Bartender	Mariner
Boatman	Pilot
Bottler	Porter
Carman	Quarryman
Carter	Sailor
Coachman	Seaman
Drayman	Servant
Driver	Stable Keeper
Ferryman	Teamster
Fisherman	Trader
Furnaceman	Waiter
Gardener	Watchman
Hostler	Waterman
Laborer	Yardman

APPENDIX C
ESTIMATED DATES OF ESTABLISHMENT OF HOUSES OF WORSHIP

1739   St. Paul's Protestant Episcopal
1750   German Reformed
1764   First Presbyterian
1770   St. Peter's Roman Catholic
1771   Old Otterbein Evangelical United Brethren
1773   Zion Lutheran
1774   Lovely Lane Methodist Episcopal
1774   Strawberry Alley Methodist Episcopal
1781   Old Town Society of Friends
1785   First Baptist
1785   Light Street Methodist Episcopal
1789   Exeter Street Methodist Episcopal
1791   St. Mary's Roman Catholic
1792   St. Patrick's Roman Catholic
1792   New Jerusalem
1797   Second Baptist
1797   Christ Protestant Episcopal
1797   Associate Reformed
1800   St. John's Roman Catholic
1801   Wilks Street Methodist Episcopal
1802   St. Peter's Protestant Episcopal
1802   Sharp Street Methodist Episcopal (African)
1803   Second Presbyterian
1805   Lombard Street Society of Friends
1806   Trinity Protestant Episcopal
1807   Eutaw Street Methodist Episcopal
1808   Bethel Methodist Episcopal (African)
1817   First Independent Unitarian
1817   St. John's Evangelical Episcopal

1818   Caroline Street Methodist Episcopal
1818   Third Baptist
1818   Reformed Presbyterian
1819   Third Presbyterian
1821   Cathedral of the Assumption of the Virgin Mary Roman Catholic
1821   Ebenezar Baptist
1821   Grace Protestant Episcopal
1822   Wesley Chapel Methodist Episcopal
1822   Franklin Street Methodist Episcopal
1822   Potter Street African Methodist Episcopal
1823   Seamen's Bethel
1823   First English Lutheran
1824   Asbury African Methodist Episcopal
1824   St. James Protestant Episcopal (African)
1826   First United Presbyterian
1828   St. John's Methodist Protestant
1829   East Baltimore Methodist Protestant
1830   Mt. Zion Baptist
1830   Jewish Synagogue
1830   Orthodox Society of Friends

APPENDIX D
CLERGY OF BALTIMORE, 1790–1830

BAPTIST
Lewis Richards (First Baptist, 1784–1818)
Edmond J. Reiss (First Baptist, 1814–21; Ebenezar Baptist, 1821–?)
John Finlay (First Baptist, 1821–34)
John Healy (Second Baptist, 1795–1848)
James Osbourne (Third Baptist, 1818–21)
William Wilson (Third Baptist, 1821–23?)
J. P. Peckworth (Third Baptist, 1823–26)
Sater T. Walker (Ebenezar Baptist, 1824–27?)
Edmund I. Ironmoner (Mt. Zion Baptist, 1830)

CATHOLIC
John Carroll (Perfect Apostolic, Bishop, Archbishop, 1786–1815)
Leonard Neale (Archbishop, 1815–17)
Ambrose Marechal (St. Mary's Seminary, 1799–1803, 1812–17; Archbishop, 1817–28)
Charles Sewall (St. Peter's, 1784–93)
Francis Beeston (St. Peter's, 1793–1809)
Matthew O'Brien (St. Peter's, 1809–11)
Enoch Fenwick (St. Peter's, 1810–20)
Mr. Ryan (St. Peter's, 1812)
James Whitfield (St. Peter's and Cathedral, 1818–28)
Mr. Burgess (St. Peter's, 1819–21)
Charles C. Pise (Cathedral, 1827–32)
Roger Smith (Cathedral, 1828–33)
Michel Levadoux (St. Mary's Seminary, 1791–92, 1802–03)
Antonie Garnier (St. Mary's Seminary, 1791–1803; St. Patrick's, 1792–95, 1797–1803)
Francis Charles Nagot (St. Mary's Seminary, 1791–1810)
Marie Jean Tessier (St. Mary's Seminary, 1791–1829)
Jean Baptiste Chicoisneau (St. Mary's Seminary, 1792–96)
Benoit Flaget (St. Mary's Seminary, 1799–1809)

Jean Baptiste David (St. Mary's Seminary, 1804–11)
Mr. Coupe (St. Mary's Seminary, 1813)
Mr. Tiphaigne (St. Mary's Seminary, 1813)
Louis Regis Reluol (St. Mary's Seminary, 1817–49)
Edward Damphoux (St. Mary's Seminary, 1820–29; Cathedral, 1829–33)
Nicholas Kearney (St. Mary's Seminary, 1821–25; St. Patrick's, 1825–41)
Francois Lhomme (St. Mary's Seminary, 1827–50)
Augustin Verot (St. Mary's Seminary, 1830–53)
John Moranville (St. Patrick's, 1794–1824)
John Floyd (St. Patrick's, 1795–97)
Michael Cuddy (St. Patrick's, 1803–04)
Francis J. Van Horsigh (St. Patrick's, 1824–26)
Ceasarius Reuter (St. John's, 1800–06)
Francis X. Brosius (St. John's, 1806–20)
J. W. Beschter (St. John's, 1820–28)
L. Barth (St. John's, 1828–38)

Episcopal
William West (St. Paul's, 1779–91)
Joseph Bend (St. Paul's, 1791–1812)
John Ireland (St. Paul's, 1796–1801)
Elijah Rattoone (St. Paul's, 1802–06; Trinity, 1809–12)
James Whitehead (St. Paul's, 1806–08)
Frederick Beasley (St. Paul's, 1807–12)
James Kemp (St. Paul's, 1812–27)
William E. Wyatt (St. Paul's, 1814–64)
Thomas Billopp (St. Paul's, 1827)
John Johns (Christ, 1828–38)
George Dashiell (St. Peter's, 1804–16)
John P. K. Henshaw (St. Peter's, 1816–44)
George Ralph (Trinity, 1810–12)
Galen Hicks (Trinity, 1812–14)
John V. Bartow (Trinity, 1815–36)
H. H. Pfieffer (Grace, 1820–?)
William Levington (St. James African, 1824–36)

German Reformed
George Troldenier (First German Reformed, 1791–1800)
John H. Dreyer (First German Reformed, 1802–06)
Christian L. Becker (First German Reformed, 1806–?)
Albert Helfenstein (First German Reformed, 1819–35)

Lutheran
J. Daniel Kurtz (First German Lutheran, 1785–1833)
John Uhlhorn (First German Lutheran, 1823–34)

Jacob Medtart (First English Lutheran, 1824–25)
J. Kranch (First English Lutheran, 1824–25)
John A. Morris (First English Lutheran, 1827–60)

METHODIST EPISCOPAL
Jeremiah Cosden (Methodist City Station [MCS], 1790)
John Hagerty (MCS, 1791, 1793; Fells Point, 1790)
Emory Prior (MCS, 1791)
Richard Whatcoat (MCS, 1792)
John McClaskey (MCS, 1793, 1794, 1795)
George Cannon (MCS, 1794)
Robert Sparks (MCS, 1794)
Chris Spry (MCS, 1794)
Daniel Hitt (MCS, 1796)
Henry Willis (MCS, 1796, 1797, 1798, 1799)
John Harper (MCS, 1797, 1798)
Nelson Reed (MCS, 1797, 1819; Fells Point, 1796, 1798)
Thomas Lyell (MCS, 1798)
L. Mansfield (MCS, 1799)
Thomas Morrell (MCS, 1799, 1800)
Philip Bruce (MCS, 1800)
George Roberts (MCS, 1800, 1801, 1804, 1805)
Lawrance M'Combs (MCS, 1801, 1802; Fells Point, 1803)
Samuel Coate (MCS, 1802, 1803)
Joshua Wells (MCS, 1802, 1803; Fells Point, 1815, 1816)
Nicholas Snethen (MCS, 1803, 1810; Fells Point, 1800)
John Bloodgood (MCS, 1804, 1808)
Thomas F. Sargent (MCS, 1804, 1805)
Alexander McCaine (MCS, 1805; Fells Point, 1800)
Seely Bunn (MCS, 1806)
John Pitts (MCS, 1806, 1807, 1811)
Michael Coate (MCS, 1807, 1808)
Stephen G. Roszel (MCS, 1808, 1816, 1817)
Robert Burch (MCS, 1810)
Asa Shinn (MCS, 1810, 1811, 1812, 1821)
Thomas Everard (MCS, 1811)
Joseph Frye (MCS, 1811, 1812, 1828, 1829; Fells Point, 1830)
John Swartzwelder (MCS, 1811)
Ezekiel Cooper (MCS, 1812)
J. Smith (MCS, 1812)
James M. Hanson (MCS, 1813, 1827, 1828; Fells Point, 1829, 1830)
William Ryland (MCS, 1813, 1814; Fells Point, 1812)
Daniel Stansbury (MCS, 1813)
Beverly Waugh (MCS, 1813, 1818, 1825, 1826; Fells Point, 1819, 1820, 1827)
Jacob Gruber (MCS, 1814)

Job Guest (MCS, 1814; Fells Point, 1813, 1823, 1824)
James Stevens (MCS, 1814)
Thomas Burch (MCS, 1815, 1819, 1820)
Lewis R. Fechtige (MCS, 1815, 1816)
Alfred Griffith (MCS, 1815; Fells Point, 1814)
Frederick Starr (MCS, 1815)
Andrew Hemphill (MCS, 1816)
Richard Hunt (MCS, 1816)
Samuel Montgomery (MCS, 1817)
Tot Prea (MCS, 1817)
Joshua Wells (MCS, 1817, 1818)
Christopher Frye (MCS, 1818, 1828)
John Bear (MCS, 1819, 1830; Fells Point, 1822)
M. Force (MCS, 1819)
Frederick Stier (MCS, 1820)
Richard Tydings (MCS, 1820, 1821)
Samuel Davis (MCS, 1821)
James M'Cann (MCS, 1821, 1822)
William Hamilton (MCS, 1822, 1827, 1829; Fells Point, 1828)
William Prettyman (MCS, 1822)
Joshua Soule (MCS, 1822, 1823)
Charles A. Davis (MCS, 1823)
John Emory (MCS, 1823)
Sam Kennerly (MCS, 1823)
Sam Merwin (MCS, 1824, 1825)
Yelverton T. Peyton (MCS, 1824, 1825, 1827; Fells Point, 1828)
Norval Wilson (MCS, 1824, 1825)
John Summerfield (MCS, 1825)
French C. Evans (MCS, 1826, 1827)
James Paynter (MCS, 1826)
Henry Slicer (MCS, 1826)
David Steele (MCS, 1826)
Sam Bryson (MCS, 1827, 1828; Fells Point, 1826)
Thomas J. Dorsey (MCS, 1827, 1828)
John A. Gere (MCS, 1828)
John L. Amiss (MCS, 1829)
Thomas B. Sargent (MCS, 1829)
John Smith (MCS, 1829)
Joseph White (MCS, 1829)
Henry Furlong (MCS, 1830)
George Hildt (MCS, 1830)
Marmaduke Pierce (MCS, 1830)
Sylvester Hutchinson (Fells Point, 1791)
Joseph Cromwell (Fells Point, 1792)
Joseph Wyatt (Fells Point, 1793)

Benton Riggin (Fells Point, 1799)
Leonard Cassell (Fells Point, 1806)
Thomas Budd (Fells Point, 1807)
Henry Smith (Fells Point, 1807, 1820)
Abraham Daniels (Fells Point, 1808)
Robert Roberts (Fells Point, 1810)
John Davis (Fells Point, 1817, 1818, 1825, 1826)
Richard M'Allister (Fells Point, 1819)
Eli Henkle (Fells Point, 1821, 1822)
Jacob Larkin (Fells Point, 1821)
Charles Cooke (Fells Point, 1823)
Daniel Parish (Fells Point, 1824)
Charles B. Tippit (Fells Point, 1825)
Philip D. Limpscomb (Fells Point, 1829)
John Poisal (Fells Point, 1830)

METHODIST PROTESTANT
Thomas Dunn (East Baltimore, 1830)
Thomas H. Stockton (St. John's, 1830)

NEW JERUSALEM
J. J. Wilmer (New Jerusalem Church, 1792–?)
Mr. Mather (New Jerusalem Church, 1798?)
John Hargrove (New Jerusalem Church, 1799–1830)
Robert Carter (New Jerusalem Church, ?)

PRESBYTERIAN
Dr. Patrick Allison (First Presbyterian, 1763–1802)
Dr. James Inglis (First Presbyterian, 1802–19)
William Nevins (First Presbyterian, 1820–35)
John Glendy (Second Presbyterian, 1803–29)
John Breckenridge (Second Presbyterian, 1826–31)
W. C. Walton (Third Presbyterian, 1822–24)
Dr. George Washington Musgrave (Third Presbyterian, 1830–?)
Nicholas Patterson (Third Presbyterian, ?)
Robert Annan (Associate Reformed, 1803–11)
John Mason Duncan (Associate Reformed, 1812–49)
William Gibson (Reformed Presbyterian, ?)
A. D. Crowe (Reformed Presbyterian, ?)
Archibald White (First United Presbyterian, 1827–33)

UNITARIAN
Jared Sparks (First Unitarian, 1819–23)
Francis William Pitt Greenwood (First Unitarian, 1823–26)
George Washington Burnap (First Unitarian, 1828–60)

UNITED BRETHREN
Philip William Otterbein ("Old Otterbein" Evangelical, 1774–1813)
Frederick Schaffer ("Old Otterbein" Evangelical, 1813–14?)
Joseph Hoffman ("Old Otterbein" Evangelical, 1814–17)
Johann Schneider ("Old Otterbein" Evangelical, 1817–25)
Wilhelm Braun ("Old Otterbein" Evangelical, 1825–28)
Johann Neidig ("Old Otterbein" Evangelical, 1828–31)

TABLES

Table 1
Churchgoers by Denomination

	1790		1810		1830	
City Population	13,503		46,555		80,990	
Roman Catholic	900	7%	5,550	12%	10,000	12%
Non-Roman Catholic		37%		35%		37%
English Protestant		24%		24%		31%
Presbyterian	700	5%	2,000	4%	4,000	5%
Episcopal	1,000	8%	3,500	8%	6,000	7%
Methodist	900	7%	4,500	10%	14,000	17%
Friends	400	3%	1,000	2%	1,000	1%
Baptists	100	1%	300	1%	1,000	1%
German Protestant		14%		11%		4%
German Reformed	700	5%	1,200	3%	1,000	1%
Lutheran	900	7%	3,300	7%	1,500	2%
United Brethren	300	2%	400	1%	500	1%
Non-Trinitarian				1%		1%
New Jerusalem	–	–	300	1%	300	1%
Unitarian	–	–	–	–	400	1%
Total Percentage		44%	47%		49%	

157

Tables

Table 2
Church by Rank, 1800

| | Size | Rank I | | Rank II | | Rank III | | Overall |
		% White Collar	Mean Tax 1804	% Skilled Artisan	Mean Tax 1804	% Unskilled Laborers	Mean Tax 1804	Mean Tax 1804
Estimated City-wide Totals		33		31		35		
Roman Catholic (St. Peter's)	187	17	£575	33	£ 47	51	£ 4	£113
Non-Roman Catholic	810	34	436	38	130	28	7	200
English Protestant	692	36	450	37	122	27	8	209
Presbyterian (First)	116	54	798	31	110	15	2	468
Episcopal (St. Paul's)	205	35	515	32	117	33	12	220
Methodist	309	32	237	43	124	24	6	132
City Station	263	35	248	43	124	22	7	141
Fells Point	46	20	127	46	126	35	0	82
Baptist (First)	24	21	50	21	98	58	1	31
Friends (Old Town)	38	29	160	34	165	37	2	103
German Protestants	92	21	414	46	181	34	11	172
German Reformed	20	10	865	15	133	75	0	107
Lutheran (Zion)	45	24	310	47	101	29	26	131
United Brethren	27	22	453	67	281	11	0	288
Non-Trinitarian (New Jerusalem)	26	31	47	42	122	27	0	66
Total Churched Sample	997	31	450	37	116	32	6	184

Table 3
Church by Rank, 1815

	Size	Rank I		Rank II		Rank III		Overall
		% White Collar	Mean Tax 1815	% Skilled Artisan	Mean Tax 1815	% Unskilled Laborers	Mean Tax 1815	Mean Tax 1815
Estimated City-wide Totals		38		30		33		
Roman Catholic (St. Peter's)	196	26	$172	28	$ 80	46	$ 1	$ 66
Non-Roman Catholic	665	38	654	33	218	29	17	330
English Protestant	548	42	648	33	239	26	34	356
Presbyterian	92	53	517	30	116	16	0	311
First	49	65	665	20	68	14	0	448
Associate Reformed	43	40	239	42	142	19	0	154
Episcopal	196	47	562	20	476	32	38	376
St. Paul's	120	51	681	19	589	30	67	479
Trinity	76	42	337	22	324	36	0	214
Methodist	232	34	870	44	186	22	43	388
City Station	208	35	886	43	203	22	47	408
Fells Point	24	25	674	58	75	17	0	213
Baptist (First)	28	25	191	29	165	46	19	104
German Protestant	108	22	774	34	132	44	0	217
German Reformed	78	24	544	28	36	47	0	143
United Brethren	30	17	1649	50	274	33	0	412
Non-Trinitarian (New Jerusalem)	9	33	133	44	94	22	0	86
Total Churched Sample	861	35	575	32	191	33	25	270

Tables

Table 4
Church by Rank, 1830

	Rank I %	Rank II %	Rank III %	Size
Estimated City-wide Totals	36	36	28	
Roman Catholic	28	32	39	148
Non-Roman Catholic	45	34	21	647
English Protestant	36	37	27	692
Presbyterian	67	22	11	90
First	69	14	16	49
Associated Reformed	63	32	5	41
Episcopal	51	22	27	232
St. Paul's	51	22	28	107
Trinity	44	20	35	54
St. Peter's	58	24	18	71
Methodist	33	50	18	212
City Station	33	50	17	192
Fells Point	25	50	25	20
Baptist (Ebenezar)	59	29	12	17
German Protestant	33	41	26	85
German Reformed	39	34	27	56
United Brethren	21	55	24	29
Non-Trinitarian (Unitarian)	73	18	9	11
Total Churched Sample	42	34	24	795

Table 5
Church Representation by Trade, 1800

	Rank I					Rank II								Rank III		
	INNKEEPERS	PROPRIETORS	PROFESSIONALS	PUBLIC SERVANT	LOW WHITE	MISC ARTISAN	FOOD	LEATHER	CLOTHING	SHIPPING	METAL	WOOD	CONSTRUCTION	SEMI-SKILLED	NOT LISTED	SIZE
City-Wide Percentage Estimates	3.3	22.8	2.6	1.4	3.2	2.9	2.0	1.9	6.3	3.2	2.8	8.9	3.4	8.5	26.6	
Variation from City-wide Estimates																
Roman Catholic (St. Peter's)	−3	0	−3	0	−2	−1	+2	−4	+1	−4	0	0	−1	+1	+2	185
Non-Roman Catholic	−3	0	0	+2	0	−2	+1	0	+2	0	−1	+1	+1	−1	0	790
English-speaking Protestant	−3	+1	0	+2	−2	−2	0	−1	+2	+1	−1	+1	0	−1	0	673
Presbyterian (First)	−4	+4	+4	+2	−2	−2	0	−2	+1	−3	−1	+1	0	−2	−2	114
Episcopal (St. Paul's)	−4	+1	−1	+2	0	−1	0	0	0	+3	−1	0	−1	0	0	203
Methodist	−3	0	0	+5	+1	−3	0	−1	+5	+1	0	+1	+2	−1	−1	299
City Station	−3	0	0	+6	+2	−2	0	−1	+5	−2	0	+1	+2	−1	−1	253
Fells Point	−4	−1	−4	−4	−1	−4	0	−4	+2	+20	0	−1	−1	0	0	46
Baptist (First)	−4	0	−4	−4	−4	+1	−4	−4	−1	−4	+2	0	−4	−1	+4	23
Friends (Old Town)	−2	0	0	+4	0	−4	−4	+8	0	0	−4	0	−4	−4	+2	34
German-speaking Protestant	−3	0	−4	+2	−4	0	+11	+5	+1	−4	0	0	+8	−2	0	91
German Reformed	−4	−2	−4	−4	−4	−4	+6	−4	−4	−4	−4	−1	−4	−1	+6	19
Lutheran (Zion)	−1	0	−4	+2	−4	+2	+22	−4	0	−4	0	+4	+10	−2	0	45
United Brethren (Otterbein)	−4	0	−4	+6	−4	−4	+10	+26	0	−4	+1	+6	+10	−4	−2	27
Non-Trinitarian (New Jerusalem)	−4	−2	+18	+6	0	−4	−4	−4	+3	+5	−4	−4	−4	−4	0	26
Total Churched Sample	−3	0	0	+2	0	−2	+1	0	+1	0	−1	0	0	0	0	995

Table 6
Church Representation by Trade, 1815

	INNKEEPERS	PROPRIETORS	PROFESSIONALS	PUBLIC SERVANT	LOW WHITE	MISC ARTISAN	FOOD	LEATHER	CLOTHING	SHIPPING	METAL	WOOD	CONSTRUCTION	SEMI-SKILLED	NOT LISTED	SIZE
City-Wide Percentage Estimates	1.7	29.6	3.4	1.5	1.3	2.3	1.9	1.7	6.5	3.1	3.3	8.0	2.7	6.1	27.1	
Variation from City-wide Estimates																
Roman Catholic (St. Peter's)	−3	−1	−1	0	0	0	−1	0	0	−1	0	0	0	0	+1	191
Non-Roman Catholic	−4	0	0	+4	+2	−3	0	0	+1	0	0	0	0	0	0	650
English-speaking Protestant	−4	0	0	+5	+2	−3	−1	0	+2	0	0	0	0	0	−2	537
Presbyterian	−4	+1	+1	+7	+6	−4	0	−1	+3	−1	−2	0	−2	−4	−1	91
First	−4	+2	0	+6	+8	−4	0	0	+2	−4	−4	+3	−3	+4	−3	49
Associate Reformed	−4	0	+1	+8	+2	−4	0	−4	+4	+2	−1	−1	0	0	0	42
Episcopal	−4	+1	0	0	0	−3	−1	0	0	0	−3	−1	−3	0	0	192
St. Paul's	−4	+3	+2	0	0	−4	0	+2	0	0	+2	−2	−2	+1	0	116
Trinity	−4	0	0	+2	−4	−1	−4	−4	+5	+2	0	+2	−4	−1	−1	76
Methodist	−4	0	−1	+11	+2	−4	−1	0	+4	0	+6	+2	+5	−1	−1	226
City Station	−4	−1	−1	+7	+3	−4	0	−4	+11	−2	0	−1	+6	−1	−2	202
Fells Point	−4	−1	−4	+7	−4	−4	−4	+4	+2	+22	−1	+1	−4	0	+1	24
Baptist (First)	−4	−1	−1	−4	+7	−4	−4	−1	0	−4	0	0	−4	0	+1	28
German-speaking Protestant	−4	−1	−1	−1	+1	−4	+14	0	0	−2	−1	−2	−1	0	+2	104
German Reformed	−4	−2	−2	−4	+2	−4	+21	−4	+2	−2	0	+8	−4	0	0	77
United Brethren	−4	0	0	+5	−4	−4	−4	−4	+2	−4	−4	+7	+6	0	−2	27
Non-Trinitarian (New Jerusalem)	−4	0	−4	−4	−4	−4	−4	−4	+2	−4	+9	+7	−4	+3	−2	9
Total Churched Sample	−3	0	0	+3	0	−2	0	0	+1	0	0	0	0	0	0	841

Table 7
Church Representation by Trade, 1830

	Rank I					Rank II								Rank III		
	INNKEEPERS	PROPRIETORS	PROFESSIONALS	PUBLIC SERVANT	LOW WHITE	MISC ARTISAN	FOOD	LEATHER	CLOTHING	SHIPPING	METAL	WOOD	CONSTRUCTION	SEMI-SKILLED	NOT LISTED	SIZE
City-Wide Percentage Estimates	1.6	26.9	3.2	2.2	2.3	3.6	3.4	1.9	9.5	2.6	2.9	8.5	3.2	8.3	19.9	
Variation from City-wide Estimates																
Roman Catholic Cathedral	−1	0	−1	−2	0	−3	+1	−4	0	−2	0	0	−1	+1	+2	139
Non-Roman Catholic	−2	0	+4	+2	+1	−1	+1	0	0	0	0	0	+2	−2	0	624
English Protestant	−3	0	+5	+3	−1	−2	−2	0	0	+1	0	0	+2	−2	0	532
Presbyterian	−4	+3	+4	+2	+8	−2	+1	−4	−2	0	0	−1	−1	−1	−2	86
First Church	−4	+4	+6	−4	+3	−4	−4	−4	−2	0	−1	0	−1	−4	−1	47
Associate Reformed	−4	+1	+2	+10	+13	−1	+2	−4	−1	0	+3	−2	0	−1	−3	39
Episcopal	−3	+1	+7	+4	+2	−3	−2	0	0	0	−2	−1	−1	−1	0	226
St. Paul's	−4	+1	+5	+4	0	−3	−3	−2	0	−2	−1	−3	−3	0	0	106
Trinity	−4	+1	+4	+2	0	−4	−1	−4	−2	+7	−1	−2	−1	−2	−1	52
St. Peter's	−4	+12	+4	+6	+2	−4	+5	−2	0	−4	−4	+2	+1	−2	0	68
Methodist	−4	0	0	+3	−1	−1	−1	+3	+1	−2	0	+2	+7	−2	0	203
City Station	−4	0	0	+2	−1	−1	−1	+4	+1	−3	0	+7	+7	0	0	183
Fells Point	−4	−1	−4	+5	−4	−4	−4	−4	0	+3	−4	+1	+8	−4	0	20
Baptist (Ebenezar)	−4	+3	+3	+2	−4	−4	−4	−4	0	−4	+4	+1	−4	−1	−1	17
German Protestant	−4	0	0	−4	0	0	+1	+3	−1	−4	+2	−1	+2	−2	0	81
German Reformed	+2	0	0	−4	+2	+2	+1	+4	−1	−4	+6	+9	+3	0	0	53
United Brethren	+5	0	−4	−4	−4	−4	+8	+3	−1	−4	−4	−4	0	0	0	28
Non-Trinitarian (Unitarian)	−4	+4	+18	−4	−4	+16	−4	−4	−4	−4	−4	−4	−4	−4	−2	11
Total Churched Sample	−2	0	+3	+1	+1	−2	−1	0	0	−2	0	0	+1	−1	0	763

Tables

Table 8
Rank Profile of Baltimore Denominations

	Rank I			Rank II			Rank III		
	1800	1815	1830	1800	1815	1830	1800	1815	1830
City-wide Percentage Estimates	33	38	36	31	30	36	35	33	28
Roman Catholic	−16	−12	−8	+2	−2	−4	+16	+13	+11
Non-Roman Catholic	+1	0	+9	+7	+3	−2	−7	−4	−7
English Protestant	+3	+4	0	+6	+3	+1	−8	−7	−1
Presbyterian	+21	+15	+31	0	0	−14	−20	−17	−17
First	+21	+27	+33	0	−10	−22	−20	−19	−12
Associate Reformed	na	+2	+27	na	+12	−4	na	−14	−23
Episcopal	+2	+9	+15	+1	−10	−14	−2	−1	−1
St. Paul's	+2	+13	+15	+1	−11	−14	−2	−3	0
Trinity	na	+4	+8	na	−8	−16	na	+3	+7
St. Peter's	na	na	+22	na	na	−12	na	na	−10
Methodist	−1	−4	−3	+12	+14	+14	−11	−11	−10
City Station	+2	−3	−3	+12	+13	+14	−13	−11	−11
Fells Point	−13	−13	−11	+15	+28	+14	0	−16	−3
Baptist	−12	−13	+23	−10	−1	−7	+23	+13	−14
First	−12	−13	na	−10	−1	na	+23	+13	na
Ebenezer	na	na	+23	na	na	−7	na	na	−14
Friends	−4	na	na	+3	na	na	+2	na	na
German Protestant	−12	−16	−3	+15	+4	+5	−1	+11	−2
German Reformed	−23	−14	+3	−16	−2	−2	+40	+14	−1
Lutheran	−9	na	na	+16	na	na	−6	na	na
United Brethren	−11	−21	−15	+36	+20	+19	−24	0	−4
Non-Trinitarian	−2	−5	+37	+11	+14	−18	−8	−11	−19
New Jerusalem	−2	−5	na	+11	+14	na	−8	−11	na
Unitarian	na	na	+37	na	na	−18	na	na	−18
Total Churched Sample	−2	−3	+6	+6	+2	−2	−3	0	−4

na = not applicable

Table 9
Occupational Status among Congregational Leadership, 1790–1830

Congregation	% Rank I	% Rank II	% Rank III
1st Presbyterian Committeemen (n–38)	95	0	5
2d Presbyterian Committeemen (n–28)	95	3	3
St. Paul's PE Vestrymen (n–43)	93	2	5
St. Peter's PE Vestrymen (n–18)	72	22	6
Trinity PE Vestrymen (n–25)	72	16	12
Meth. City Sta. Stewards (n–14)	79	21	0
St. Peter's RC Trustees (n–26)	88	12	0
St. Patrick's RC Trustees (n–8)	88	12	0
Old Otterbein UB Vestrymen (n–38)	40	47	13
German Reformed Committeemen (n–16)	63	37	0
New Jerusalem Trustees (n–7)	86	14	0
1st Independent Trustees (n–8)	100	0	0
Totals (n–269)	79	16	5

Table 10

Property Ownership among Congregational Leadership, 1804 & 1815

Congregation	% Property Owners 1804	% Property Owners over £600 1804	Average per capita Assessment 1804	% Property Owners 1815	% Property Owners over $1000 1815	Average per capita Assessment 1815
1st Presbyterian Committeemen	100.0	64.3	£2606	96.0	65.2	$5887
2d Presbyterian Committeemen	100.0	58.3	1437	95.0	78.9	4750
St. Paul's Vestrymen	87.0	60.9	994	83.0	60.9	3556
St. Peter's PE Vestrymen	100.0	42.9	786	83.0	5.0	1600
Trinity PE Vestrymen	...	...	...	89.0	66.7	1942
Meth. City Sta. Stewards	92.9	50.0	999	85.7	64.3	2450
St. Peter's RC Trustees	91.6	58.3	811	100.0	50.0	3829
St. Patrick's RC Trustees	100.0	33.3	426	100.0	66.7	1192
Old Otterbein UB Vestrymen	71.4	14.3	434	83.3	50.0	1594
German Reformed Committeemen	na	na	na	70.0	30.0	1010
New Jerusalem Trustees	85.7	28.6	263	na	na	na

na = not applicable

Table 11
Occupation and Wealth of Methodist Leaders by Office, 1790–1830

Office	% Rank I	% Rank II	% Property Owners 1804	Average Per Capita Assessment 1804	% Property Owners 1815	Average Per Capita Assessment 1815
Stewards & Trustees (n–20)	75.0	20.0	100.0	£999	86.0	$2450
Local Elders (n–21)	71.4	19.0	na	na	na	na
Local Deacons & Exhorters (n–23)	47.8	43.5	na	na	na	na
Class Leaders Only (n–108)	41.7	48.1	56.5	304	62.1	1045
Total	50.0	40.7	66.1	474	66.7	1332

Table 12
Wealth of Baltimore City Station Methodist Episcopal White-Collar Members and Leaders, 1815

	No. in Sample	% Property Owners	Average Per Capita Assessment
Class Leaders	31	71	$1053
Class Members	69	60	772
General Membership (all denominations)	287	54	561

Table 13
Wealth of Baltimore City Station Methodist Episcopal Skilled Artisan Members and Leaders, 1815

Class Leaders	24	71	$1090
Class Members	93	38	279
General Membership (all denominations)	259	29	236

Table 14
Tenure of Baltimore Clergy by Denomination in Years

Denomination	Overall Average Tenure	Average Tenure of Pastors Ordained before 1810	Average Tenure of Pastors Ordained after 1810
Baptist	13	44	5
Catholic	11	12	10
Protestant Episcopal	12	7	16
German Reformed	10	7	18
Lutheran	12	48	4
New Jerusalem	11	11	–
Presbyterian	17	23	13
Unitarian	13	–	13
United Brethren	10	39	4
Total Non-Methodist	11	15	8
Methodist	2	2	2

Table 15
Tenure of Non-Methodist Protestant Clergy by Congregational Size in Years

	Pastors Ordained before 1810	Pastors Ordained after 1810	Total
Largest Congregation of Each Denomination	17 (n–16)	11 (n–17)	14 (n–33)
Smaller Congregations of Each Denomination	19 (n–5)	8 (n–20)	10 (n–25)
Total for all Congregations	18 (n–21)	9 (n–37)	12 (n–58)

Table 16
Percentage Religious Titles from Baltimore Presses 1775–1819

	Total Titles	Religious Titles	% Religious Titles
1775–79	50	3	6
1780–84	35	5	14
1785–89	48	8	17
1790–94	108	31	28
1795–99	184	26	14
1800–04	361	80	22
1805–09	384	110	29
1810–14	509	150	29
1815–19	594	210	35

Table 17
Membership Growth Patterns among Baltimore Congregations

Congregation & Interval of Years Data Available	Number of Years Data Available	Average Number Members Received (Annual Gross)	Average % of Annual Variance	Years Members Received Doubled Annual Average
1st Baptist (1796–1822)	19	11	75	1802, 1816, 1818
2d Baptist (1808–30)	20	10	67	1816, 1818
3d Baptist (1819–26)	6	8	48	. . .
1st Presbyterian (1802–30)	19	22	67	1817, 1827
Associate Reformed (1812–30)	19	46	44	1818, 1819, 1824
St. Peter's PE (1818–30)	13	27	27	1818**
Trinity PE (1820–30)	11	13	52	1830
Meth. City Sta. (whites) (1800–30)	29	71*	161	1801, 1812, 1814, 1816, 1817, 1818, 1824, 1826, 1828
Meth. City Sta. (blacks) (1800–30)	27	60*	101	1814, 1815, 1825, 1828
Meth. Fells Pt. (whites) (1800–30)	25	32*	232	1801, 1818, 1826
Meth. Fells Pt. (blacks) (1800–30)	25	10*	272	1801, 1802, 1811, 1813, 1814, 1818, 1822, 1824, 1828, 1829

*Designates net membership growth
**Slightly less than double average

Table 18
Number and Types of Voluntary Associations Active Each Decade, 1790–1829

	1790–99	1800–09	1810–19	1820–29
Civic Associations	11	26	32	40
Ethnic Associations	2	5	4	7
Occupational Associations	1	5	6	7
Political Associations	1	2	4	4
Subtotal	15	38	46	58
Religious Associations	31	39	66	93
Local Congregations	18	27	33	46
Benevolent Type	13	12	16	17
Missionary Type	0	0	17	30
Grand Total	46	77	112	151

Table 19
Statistical Annual Reports of Sunday Schools of the Female Union Society of Baltimore*

Sunday School	1819	1820	1821
St. John's	52	66	30
1st Presbyterian	57	56	50
Associate Reformed	93	70	85
1st Baptist	48	44	30
2d Presbyterian	50	100	80
Hookstown Road	25	24	23
Powhattan Factory	50	49	52
Colored Adults (1st)	160	180	0
Franklin St.	. . .	80	79
York Turnpike Road	. . .	30	70
Colored Adults (2d)	. . .	55	0
Pennsylvania Ave.	. . .	. . .	70
Total	535	726	569
Estimated Average Weekly Attendance	350	470	375

* Not affiliated with the Female Union Society was the McKendrean Society of the Baltimore City Station Methodist Episcopal Church.

Table 20
Statistical Annual Reports of Male Sunday Schools of Baltimore

Sunday School	1818		1819		1823	
	Enrolled	Regulars	Enrolled	Regulars	Enrolled	Regulars
Asbury Association						
#1–City Spring	200	170	174	150	161	116
#2–Franklin St.	53	24	75	60	77	44
#3–Old Town	45	25	36	25 (est)	164	83
#4–S. Howard St.	…	…	69	42	89	51
#5–Powhattan Factory	…	…	100	83	92	71
#6–Sharp St.	…	…	40	30 (est)	77	63
#7–Pearl St.	130 (est)	100	130	110	57	42
Subtotal	428 (est)	319	624	500 (est)	706	470
Wesleyan Association						
St. Paul's	…	…	50	40	…	…
Christ	78	60 (est)	75	60 (est)	…	…
St. Peter's	91	60	125	50	…	…
Trinity	114	92	200 (est)	155	…	…
Associate Reformed	250	87	200 (est)	60 (est)	…	…
1st Baptist	120	50	150	80	…	…
2d Baptist	229	75 (est)	255	65 (est)	…	…
Federal Hill	179	45	0	0	…	…
	71	60	138	118	…	…
Estimated Total	1,560	850	1,820	1,130	…	…

Table 21
Denominational Leadership & Occupation among Benevolent Empire Officers

Managers & Officers of Benevolent Societies	% Identified as Clergy or Lay Officers	% Rank I	% Rank II	% Rank III
General Dispensary (n–10)	60	90	0	10
House of Industry (n–34)	53	80	9	9
Maryland Colonization Society (n–62)	35	94	6	0
Bible Society of Baltimore (n–42)	79	96	2	2
Young Men's Bible Society (n–78)	12	51	26	24
Maryland Auxiliary Bible Society (n–23)	65	79	22	0
Religious Tract Society of Baltimore (n–23)	48	87	9	4
Total (n–272)	50	82	11	7

NOTES

Introduction

1. Thomas W. Griffith, *Annals of Baltimore* (Baltimore: printed by William Woody, 1833), p. 97; U.S. Bureau of the Census, *A Century of Population Growth* (Washington, D.C.: Government Printing Office, 1909), pp. 11, 84, 272, and *Negro Population in the United States 1790–1915* (Washington, D.C.: Government Printing Office, 1918), p. 55.

2. Charles Varle, *A Complete View of Baltimore With a Statistical Sketch* (Baltimore: n.p., 1833), p. 11; Griffith, *Annals*, pp. 294, 304.

3. *Century of Population Growth*, p. 57; Griffith, *Annals*, pp. 294, 304.

4. For a summary of the causes of growth in early national Baltimore, see David Gilchrist, ed., *The Growth of Seaport Cities: 1790–1825* (Charlottesville: University of Virginia Press, 1967), pp. 34–36. Also see Sherry H. Olson, *Baltimore: The Building of an American City* (Baltimore: The Johns Hopkins University Press, 1979); Gray L. Browne, *Baltimore in the Nation* (Chapel Hill: University of North Carolina Press, 1980); and Charles G. Steffen, *The Mechanics of Baltimore: Workers and Politics in the Age of Revolution, 1763–1812* (Urbana: University of Illinois Press, 1984).

5. *Century of Population Growth*, p. 198; Griffith, *Annals*, p. 294.

6. See Tables 2 and 3.

7. *The Catholic Encyclopedia* (New York: Encyclopedia Press, Inc., 1913), 2: 228–35; [Michael J. Riordan, comp.], *Cathedral Records: From the Beginning of Catholicity in Baltimore to the Present Time* (Baltimore: The Cathedral Mirror Publishing Co., 1906), p. 107.

8. Charles C. Goss, *Statistical History of the First Century of American Methodism* (New York: Carlton & Porter, 1866), pp. 56–102; "Proceedings of the General Convention of November 12–22, 1828," *Mutual Rights and Christian Intelligencer* 1 (5 December 1828): 25–27; *At A Meeting or Convention of Clergy and Lay Delegates of the Protestant Episcopal Church of Maryland at Baltimore, May 29, 1788* (Baltimore; n.p., 1788); see also the convention journals of the Protestant Episcopal Church, Maryland Diocese, for the years 1788–1830; John J. Gardner, Jr. *The First Presbyterian Church of Baltimore; A Two Century Chronicle* (Baltimore: First Presbyterian Chruch, 1962), pp. 39–40; Klans G. Wust, *Zion in Baltimore 1755–1955* (Baltimore: published by Zion Church of the City of Baltimore, 1955), pp. 48–50; and Paul E. Holdcraft, "The Old Otterbein Church Story," typescript located at the Maryland Historical Society, Baltimore, Md. (hereafter cited as MdHi), pp. 29–34.

9. Marguerita B. Block, *The New Church in the New World: A Study of Swedenborgians in America* (New York: Henry Holt & Co., 1932), p. 87; and Herbert B. Adams, *The Life and Writings of Jared Sparks* (Boston: Houghton, Mifflin, and Co., 1893), 1: 125–32.

Chapter 1. Membership

1. John H. B. Latrobe, *Picture of Baltimore Containing A Description of All Objects of Interest in the City; and Embellished With Views of the Principal Public Buildings* (Baltimore: F. Lucas, Jr., 1832), pp. 126–47; J. Thomas Scharf, *History of Baltimore City and County With a New Introduction by Edward G. Howard* (Baltimore: Regional Publishing Co., 1971), pp. 517–92; and Varle, *Complete View*, pp. 45–54. For the dates of establishment for all houses of worship built before 1830, see Appendix C.

2. Joseph Bend to William Duke, 21 April 1795; 8 July 1799; 14 May 1802; 9 June 1802; 5 May 1804, Maryland Diocesan Archives on Deposit at Maryland Historical Society, Baltimore (hereafter cited as MdBD). Also see William Duke, *Observations on the Present State of Religion in Maryland* (Baltimore: n.p., 1795).

3. All estimates of size of church membership are summarized in Table 1. For the method used in determining the estimates, see Appendix A.

4. For national estimates, see Donald G. Mathews, *Religion in the Old South* (Chicago: University of Chicago Press, 1977), p. 47; and Edwin S. Gaustad, ed., *The Rise of Adventism: Religion and Society in Mid-Nineteenth-Century America* (New York: Harper & Row, 1974), p. xiii.

5. Clayton Colman Hall, ed., *Baltimore, Its History and Its People* (New York: Lewis Historical Publishing Co., 1912), p. 657; *Sesquicentennial St. Patrick's Parish, Baltimore, Maryland, 1792–1942* (Baltimore: St. Mary's Industrial School, 1942)), pp. 11–18.

6. Gaustad, *Rise of Adventism*, p. xiii.

7. See Dieter Cunz, *The Maryland Germans, A History* (Port Washington, N.Y.: Kennikat Press, 1972). The story of how Baltimore Germans struggled to maintain their native language in services of worship is discussed in chapter 8.

8. For the struggle of blacks to obtain a separate house for worship, see Alfred Z. Hartman, "History of Methodism in Maryland, 1770–1912," typescript located at MdHi; Bettye J. Gardner, "Free Blacks in Baltimore, 1800–60" (Ph.D. diss. George Washington University, 1974), pp. 66–67; and Scharf, *History of Baltimore*, pp. 569, 581.

9. See Appendix A. The analysis below of the relationship between religious preference and status is based upon the findings summarized in Tables 2–8.

10. U.S. Bureau of the Census, *Return of the Whole Number of Persons Within the Several Districts of the United States, According to "An Act Providing for the Second Census or Enumeration on the Inhabitants of the United States." Passed February the twenty eighth, one thousand eight hundred. Printed by order of the House of Representatives* (Washington, D.C.: William Duane & Son, 1802), p. 68; *U.S. Bureau of the Census, Fifth Census; or Enumeration of the Inhabitants of the United States, as Corrected at the Department of State, 1830* (Washington, D.C.: Duff Green, 1832); Griffith, *Annals*, p. 294; "Baltimore City Station Methodist Episcopal Records," Microfilm reel M 408; "Annual Register for the Methodist Episcopal Church on Fells Point," Microfilm reel M 411, located at the Maryland Hall of Records, Annapolis (hereafter cited MdHR); Annie Burns, "Register of the First Presbyterian Church, Baltimore," typescript located at the Library of Congress, Washington, D.C. (hereafter cited DLC), 2: 298–320; "Register of the Associate Reformed Congregation in Baltimore, 1812–1865," 1: 1–30, 236–66, and "Register of the First German Reformed Church, Baltimore," 2: 184–209 (MdHR); "Ebenezar Baptist Church Minutes," Microfilm reel M 159 (MdHR); "Trinity Protestant Episcopal Church, Register," 1: 48–55, and vol. 2, MS 850; "St. Peter's Protestant Episcopal Church, Register," pp. 47–62 (MdHi).

11. "Trinity Protestant Episcopal Church, Register," 1: 48–55, and vol. 2, MS 850; St. Peter's Protestant Episcopal, Register," pp. 47–62 (MdHi); Baltimore City Station and Fells Point Methodist Episcopal Church Records, Microfilm reels M 408–M 411 (MdHR).

12. Ibid.; Annie Burns, "Register of the First Presbyterian Church, Baltimore," 2: 298–320 (typescript at DLC); "Register of the Associate Reformed Congregation in Baltimore, 1812–1865," 1: 1–30, 236–66, and Register of the First German Reformed Church, Baltimore," 2: 184–209 (MdHi); and "Ebenezar Baptist Church Minutes," Microfilm reel M 159 (MdHR).

13. For example, the notations "moved," "expelled," "dead," or "withdrawn" were inscribed

beside the names of some 270 white-class members of Baltimore City Station between 1803 and 1805. This suggests a loss of over 9% of the membership annually. See Class Lists of 1803, Baltimore City Station Methodist Episcopal Records, Microfilm reel M 408 (MdHR).

14. These two separate congregations, St. Paul's Church and Christ Church, shared the same vestry and pastors until their official separation in 1828. See Francis F. Beirne, *St. Paul's Parish: A Chronicle of the Mother Church* (Baltimore: Horn-Shafer Co., 1967), pp. 49–50, 95. For an account of the establishment of Trinity and St. Peter's, see chapter 3.

Chapter 2. Leadership

1. First Baptist Church, Baltimore, *A Church Covenant; Including a Summary of the Fundamental Doctrines of the Gospel; Compiled by Elkanah Holmes, and Unanimously Adopted by the First Baptist Church, Baltimore* (Baltimore, 1818); New Jerusalem Church, Baltimore, *A Copy of the Incorporated Constitution of the New Jerusalem Church* (Baltimore, 1804), pp. 2–8; Rebecca Funk, *A Heritage to Hold in Fee 1817–1917, First Unitarian Church of Baltimore* (Baltimore: Garamond Press, 1962), pp. 113–15. Also see Arthur C. Pierkorn, *Profiles in Belief: The Religious Bodies of the United States and Canada* (New York: Harper & Row, Pub., Inc., 1978), 2: 651–59; and Gustave Weigel, *Churches in North America* (New York: Schocken Books, 1965), pp. 63–66, 118–21.

2. Baltimore Yearly Meeting Society of Friends, *Discipline of the Yearly Meeting of Friends Held in Baltimore, 1806* (Baltimore, [1806]), pp. 33–39. For Quaker polity during the era, see Richard Bauman, *For the Reputation of Truth: Politics, Religion, and Conflict Among the Pennsylvania Quakers, 1750–1800* (Baltimore: The Johns Hopkins University Press, 1971).

3. *Journal of Presbyterian History* 3, no. 4 (Winter 1974): 474–77; Pierkorn, *Profiles in Belief*, 2: 275–96; and Weigel, *Churches*, pp. 35–36.

4. Julius Hofmann, *A History of Zion Church of the City of Baltimore 1755–1897* (Baltimore: C. W. Schneidereith & Sons, 1905), pp. 20–24, 40–43; Wust, *Zion in Baltimore*, pp. 118–23; Lars P. Qualben, *The Lutheran Church in Colonial America* (New York: Thomas Nelson and Sons, 1940), pp. 272–314.

5. William E. Wyatt, *Sermon Exhibiting Some of the Principal Doctrines of the Protestant Episcopal Church of the U.S., by which that Church is Distinguished from Other Denominations of Christians* (Baltimore: Robinson, 1820), pp. 11–21, 39–42; S. D. McConnell, *History of the American Episcopal Church From the Planting of the Colonies to the End of the Civil War* (New York: Thomas Whitaker, 1890), pp. 173–189, 215–276; Spencer Ervin, "The Established Church of Colonial Maryland," *Historical Magazine of the Protestant Episcopal Church* 24 (1955): 232–92; Pierkorn, *Profiles in Belief*, 2: 147–65; Weigel, *Churches*, pp. 50–54.

6. Robert Emory, *History of the Discipline of the Methodist Episcopal Church* (New York: G. Lane & P. P. Sandford, 1844), pp. 46, 59, 137, 235; Pierkorn, *Profiles in Belief*, 2: 593–95; Weigel, *Churches*, pp. 54–58.

7. Holdcraft, "Old Otterbein," pp. 1–17; Edward Drinkhouse, *History of Methodist Reform* (Norwood, Mass.: J. S. Cushing & Co., 1899); Harry V. Richardson, *Dark Salvation: The Story of Methodism as It Developed Among Blacks in America* (Garden City, N.Y.: Anchor Press, 1976), p. 31; Pierkorn, *Profiles in Belief*, 2: 603–4, 618–20, 3: 52; Weigel, *Churches*, pp. 59–63.

8. *Sesquicentennial Saint Patrick's*, pp. 98–99; [Riordan], *Cathedral Records*, p. 19. See also H. Burn-Murdock, *The Development of the Papacy* (London: Faber & Faber Ltd., 1954).

9. James Kemp, *Episcopacy Vindicated: In a Series of Letters to the Rev. Dr. Miller* (New Haven: n.p., 1808), "The Ordination of the Apostles" and "A Sermon on Church Government," MS Kemp Sermons, MdBD; Wyatt, *Sermon Exhibiting Some of the Principal Doctrines* (Baltimore, 1820); J. P. K. Henshaw, *The Apostolic Ministry: Views of Calvin and the Early Presbyterians, Wesley, Clarke, and Others Upon the Apostolic Succession* (New York: Protestant Episcopal Tract Society, n.d.). For examples of the Methodist arguments, see Thomas E. Bond, *Methodism Not a Human Contrivance; But a Providential Arrangement* (Baltimore: Isaac P. Cook, 1839); and David M. Reese, *A Letter to the Rev. G. W. Musgrave, "Bishop!" of the Third*

Presbyterian Church of Baltimore, Being a Reply to His Late Work Entitled "Polity of the Methodist Episcopal Church in the U.S." & c. (Baltimore: Armstrong, Berry & Isaac P. Cook, 1843).

10. George Bourne, *Remarks Upon a Pamphlet Entitled "An Inquiry into the Validity of Methodist Episcopacy"* (Baltimore: Geo. Dobbin & Murphy for John Hagerty, 1807), p. 36.

11. William Nevins, *Thoughts on Property* (New York: American Tract Society, 1836), pp. 64, 69.

12. For example, in 1821 the preface of the initial volume of *The Presbyterian Magazine* established the goal of promoting harmony among the various denominations. While the editors promised to "co-operate with all who love the Lord Jesus in sincerity," and to avoid controverted issues, they reserved the right as the occasion required "to vindicate the Presbyterian system of church government." For further discussion, see chapter 7.

13. On the preoccupation of postrevolutionary America with matters of constitutional theory, see Russel Blaine Nye, *The Cultural Life of the New Nation, 1776–1830* (New York: Harper & Row, Publishers, 1960), pp. 3, 9, 101, 154–56, 201–5.

14. Hofmann, *History of Zion Church*, pp. 40–44; Funk, *A Heritage to Hold in Fee*, pp. 113–14; *Sesquicentennial St. Patrick's*, pp. 99–100; *A Copy of the Constitution of the New Jerusalem Church*, pp. 7–8; "First Rules and Discipline" in Holdcraft, "The Old Otterbein Church Story"; Norman H. Maring, "A Denominational History of the Maryland Baptists: 1742–1882," (Ph.D. diss., University of Maryland, 1948), pp. 30–33; Gardner, *First Presbyterian*, p. 16; *Constitution and Canons of the Protestant Episcopal Church, Maryland* (Easton, Md.: Cowan, 1802), pp. 3–17.

15. Funk, *A Heritage to Hold in Fee*, pp. 113–14.

16. Maring, "Denominational History," p. 33n.

17. *Discipline of the Yearly Meeting of Friends, 1806; Constitution of the First Philosophical and Evangelical Association of Baltimore* (Baltimore, 1825), pp. 117–25; Baltimore First Philosophical Evangelical Association, *Constitution* ([Baltimore], 1825), pp. 209–15.

18. Approximately 35% of the Methodist, 15% of the Roman Catholic, and 6% of the Presbyterian and Episcopal nominal churchgoers were black. "Journal of the Baltimore Annual Conferences 1800–1833," typescript located at Wesley Theological Seminary, Washington, D.C. (hereafter cited DWyT), pp. 57, 68, 77, 83, 90, 102, 114, 121, 130, 144, 154, 165, 172, 182, 190, 204, 213, 231, 238; Annie W. Burns, "Cathedral of the Assumption of the Virgin Mary, Burial Records," 2 vols., and "Register of the First Presbyterian Church, Baltimore," typescripts located at DLC; "Register, St. Paul's Parish, vol. 1," MdHi.

19. For example, a list of official members of Baltimore City Station in 1815 includes 8 black class leaders, 10 black exhorters, and 9 black local preachers. "Baltimore City Station Methodist Episcopal Records," Microfilm reel M 408, MdHR.

20. Emory, *History of Discipline*, p. 279. However, since Maryland law prohibited black suffrage, Methodist Negroes were prohibited from voting in church elections.

21. The proportion "one-seventh" is based upon a count of approximately 215 notations "gone to Coker" on the class membership rolls of 1815. "Baltimore City Station Methodist Episcopal Records," Microfilm reel M 408, MdHR.

22. Gardner, "Free Blacks in Baltimore," pp. 66–67. The conflict between Sharp Street and Bethel congregations is mentioned in Daniel Coker's *Journal of Daniel Coker, A Descendant of Africa, From the Time of Leaving New York, in the Ship Elizabeth, Capt. Sebor, on a Voyage for Sherbro, in Africa in Company with Three Agents and about Ninety Persons of Color. With an Appendix.* (Baltimore: Edward J. Coale, 1820), p. 42.

23. *Origination, Constitution, and By-Laws of St. James First African Protestant Episcopal Church in the City of Baltimore, Adopted April 23, 1829* (Baltimore, William Woody, 1829), pp. 3–20.

24. Ibid., p. 7.

25. James Kemp, *A Pastoral Letter Addressed to the Members of the Protestant Episcopal Church in the Diocese of Maryland* (Baltimore: William Woody, 1824), pp. 7–12; *Constitution and Canons: A Compilation for the Use of the Members of the Protestant Episcopal Church in Maryland, Consisting of the Constitution and Canons of the Church in the United States* (Balti-

more: Robinson, 1822); Beirne, *St. Paul's Parish*, pp. 261–72.

26. "Trinity Protestant Episcopal Church, Register," I: 48–55, and vol. 2, MS 850, "St. Peter's Protestant Episcopal Church, Register," MdHi, pp. 47–62.

27. The conclusions below are based upon a status analysis of Baltimore church leaders. The results are summarized in Tables 9–10. The method is the same as that described in Appendix A.

28. Beirne, *St. Paul's Parish*, pp. 261–72; George Buck, *Christ Protestant Episcopal Church, Baltimore, Maryland* ([Baltimore]: Meyer & Thalheimer, 1937), p. 5.

29. For these elected officials of First Presbyterian, See Gardner, *First Presbyterian*, pp. 185–90.

30. Of the 867 samples from the general membership of all congregations around 1815, only 5 or 0.6% were assessed over $5,000 in property value. Thus, the average elected official was well within the upper 1% of society.

31. "Second Presbyterian Church Records, Baltimore," MdHi, 2: 74–81.

32. For Roman Catholic officials, see [Riordan], *Cathedral Records*, p. 108.

33. "Trustees Book, Fells Point Methodist Episcopal Church"; Methodist Episcopal Church Books, Baltimore City Station, 1818–23, 1823–32, Lovely Lane Museum, Baltimore (hereafter cited MdBL); Fielder Israel Papers, MS 488, MdHi; Emory, *History of the Discipline*, pp. 235–36.

34. For example, in 1801, 43 of the 295 white males at Baltimore City Station were local officers in the church. See "Baltimore City Station Methodist Episcopal Records," Microfilm reel M 408, MdHR; "Methodist Episcopal Church Book, Baltimore City Station, 1818–1823"; "Local Preacher's Plan of Appointment for the County for 1832" (Broadside), MdBL; Fielder Israel Papers, MS 488, MdHi.

35. Fielder Israel Papers, MS 488, MdHi; Methodist Episcopal Church Books, Baltimore City Station, 1818–23, 1823–32, MdBL; Wade Crawford Barclay, *History of Methodist Missions, Part I, Early American Methodism, 1769–1844. Vol. 2, To Reform the Nation* (New York: The Board of Missions and Church Extension of The Methodist Church, 1950), pp. 337–40.

36. "Baltimore City Station Methodist Episcopal Records," Microfilm reel M 408, MdHR.

37. See Tables 11–13.

Chapter 3. Clergy

1. *Minutes of the Annual Conferences of the Methodist Episcopal Church*, vol. 1, 1773–1828, vol. 2, 1829–38 (New York: T. Mason & G. Lane, 1840).

2. [Riordan], *Cathedral Records*, pp. 18, 107; *Sesquicentennial St. Patrick's*, pp. 68–103; *St. Mary's Seminary, Baltimore. List of the Superiors, Professors, and Students Ordained, 1791–1916* (New York: The Encyclopedia Press, 1917), pp. 1–4.

3. See Tables 14–15.

4. Donald Scott, *From Office to Profession: The New England Ministry 1750–1850* (Philadelphia: University of Pennsylvania Press, 1978).

5. Gardner, *First Presbyterian*, pp. 49–54.

6. Ibid., pp. 49–54; Thomas H. Walker, *One Hundred Years of History, 1802–1902: Second Presbyterian Church, Baltimore, Maryland* (Baltimore: Sun Printing Office, 1902), pp. 37–49; "Second Presbyterian Church Records, Baltimore," MdHi, 2: 74–81.

7. Beirne, *St. Paul's Parish*, pp. 50–51.

8. Joseph Bend to William Duke, 9 November 1801, MdBD.

9. Joseph Bend to William Duke, 1 August 1801; 30 November 1801; 14 May 1802; 9 June 1802, MdBD.

10. Joseph Bend to James Kemp, 3 March 1803; Joseph Bend to William Duke, 8 January 1802, MdBD.

11. Joseph Bend to William Duke, 4 March 1802; 8 April 1802; 14 May 1802, MdBD.

12. Testimonials for the Rev. Dr. Rattoone, 1805, MdBD.

13. Dr. James Smyth's certificate regarding Mrs. Rattoone, 10 October 1805; Elijah Rattoone to the Gentlemen of the Vestry of St. Paul's Parish, 21 September 1805, Elijah Rattoone to Bishop Clageett, 21 November 1805, Joseph Bend to Bishop Claggett, 8 September 1805; 21 November 1805; 17 May 1806, MdBD.

14. Joseph Bend to William Duke, 17 May 1806; 26 April 1809; Joseph Bend to James Kemp, 26 June 1809; Elijah Rattoone to Bishop Claggett, 13 September 1808; 26 September 1808, MdBD.

15. William Buell Sprague, *Annals of the American Pulpit*, vol. 5 (New York: Robert Carter & Brothers, 1857–[69]), pp. 353–55; Hugh Davey Evans, *The Future of St. Paul's Parish. Baltimore* (Baltimore: n.p., 1878), pp. 25–36; Beirne, *St. Paul's Parish*, pp. 43–60; "Society for the Promotion of Useful and Ornamental Knowledge, Minutes," MdBD.

16. *Baltimore Telegraph* (5 December 1815), quoted in [Riordan], *Cathedral Records*, p. 46.

17. The five Baltimore pastors elected as bishops for their denominations were Philip Otterbein (United Brethren), John P. K. Henshaw and James Kemp (Protestant Episcopal), and John Carroll and Ambrose Marechal (Roman Catholic). Two Baltimore itinerants, Beverly Waugh and John Emory, were also elected as bishops of the Methodist Episcopal Church.

18. Account of the Rev. William West with St. Paul's Parish, Baltimore, 1790; Inventory of the Rev. William West, 1791, MdBD.

19. Baltimore, Maryland, St. Paul's Church, *To the Pewholders and Other Contributors of St. Paul's Parish in Baltimore Co.* (Baltimore: n.p., 1804), pp. 7–8; Joseph Bend to William Duke, 3 April 1799; Joseph Bend to James Kemp, 2 April 1799, MdBD; Howard E. Wooden, "The Rectory of St. Paul's Parish, Baltimore: An Architectural History," *Maryland Historical Magazine* (September 1962), pp. 210–23.

20. St. Paul's Church, *To the Pewholders of St. Paul's*, p. 4.

21. George Dashiell, *Address of the Vestry to the Members of the Protestant Episcopal Church of St. Peter's, in the City of Baltimore* (Baltimore: Warner & Hanna, 1806), p. 7.

22. Joseph Bend to William Duke, 17 May 1806, MdBD.

23. Nicolas Brice and James Kemp, *To the Members of the Congregation of St. Paul's Church in the City of Baltimore. July 22, 1819* (Baltimore: n.p., 1819). For reports on the financial difficulties of rural pastors, see Ethan Allen, *The Garrison Church, Sketches of the History of St. Thomas Parish* (New York: James Pott & Co., 1898), pp. 50–51, 58, 62, 67–68, 76, 80–81; Report of Joseph Bend to the Standing Committee, 1791–92, James Kemp to Joseph Jackson, 10 February 1815, Joseph Bend to William Duke, 3 November 1798, 8 April 1802, Thomas J. Claggett to James Kemp, 22 January 1812, MdBD.

24. "Second Presbyterian Church Records, Baltimore," 2: 123–25.

25. Adams, *Life and Writings*, 1: 126–31.

26. Funk, *A Heritage to Hold in Fee*, p. 114.

27. William Nevins, *Select Remains of the Rev. William Nevins, with a Memoir* (New York: John S. Taylor, 1836), pp. 20–21.

28. J. F. Weishampel, Jr., *History of Baptist Churches in Maryland Connected with the Maryland Baptist Union Association* (Baltimore: published by Weishampel, 1885), pp. 31–34; Maring, "Denominational History," p. 38.

29. Ibid., pp. 37–39; "Ebenezer Baptist Church Minutes," Microfilm reel M 159, MdHR.

30. Joshua Wills, *Historical Sketch of the Second Baptist Church of Baltimore, Maryland* (Philadelphia: George F. Lasher, 1911), pp. 8–12; Maring, "Denominational History," p. 37.

31. Block, *The New Church in the New World*, p. 93. *First African Protestant Episcopal Church in the City of Baltimore World Most Respectfully Solicit the Attention of the Christian Public* (Broadside), (Baltimore: n.p., 1829).

33. Robert E. Coleman, "Factors in the Expansion of the Methdist Church From 1784 to 1812" (Ph.D. diss. University of Iowa, 1954), pp. 208–9.

34. Ibid., p. 209.

35. Fielder Israel Papers, MS 488, Box 13, MdHi.

36. Coleman, "Factors," pp. 211–12; Abel Stevens, *History of the Methodist Episcopal Church in the United States of America* (New York: Carlton & Porter, 1867), 2: 114; W. W.

Sweet, *Circuit-Rider Days Along the Ohio: Being the Journals of the Ohio Conference from Its Organization in 1812 to 1826*, edited with Introduction and Notes by W. W. Sweet (New York & Cincinnati: Methodist Book Concern, 1923), p. 34; Fielder Israel Papers, MS 488, Box 13, MdHi; "Journal of the Baltimore Annual Conference, Methodist Episcopal Church, 1800–1833," typescript located at DWyT, pp. 10, 15, 19, 24–25, 32, 37, 39–40, 44, 50, 58–59, 66, 75–76, 104–5.

37. The above findings are based upon the clergymen listed in Ethan Allen's *Clergy in Maryland of the Protestant Episcopal Church Since the Independence of 1783* (Baltimore: James S. Waters, 1860), pp. 2–48.

38. Sprague, *Annals*, 3: 257–62; 4: 229–37, 278–84, 629–40, 645–51.

39. Adams, *Life and Writings*, 5: 435–44.

40. Wust, *Zion in Baltimore*, p. 49.

41. Weishampel, *History of Baptist Churches*, pp. 31–35; Sprague, *Annals*, 6: 201–2.

42. Coleman, "Factors," p. 453.

43. Sprague, *Annals*, 7: 486–93.

44. *Minutes of the Several Conversations between the Rev. Thomas Coke, LL.D., the Rev. Francis Asbury, and Others at a Conference begun in Baltimore, in the Year 1784. Composing a Form of Discipline for the Minister, Preacher, and Other Members of the Methodist Episcopal Church in America* (Philadelphia: Charles Cist, 1785), p. 11.

45. James Kemp to Joseph Jackson, 8 March 1814. See also James Kemp to Joseph Jackson, 11 April 1814, MdBD.

46. "Journal of the Baltimore Annual Conference, Methodist Episcopal Church, 1800–1833," typescript located at DWyT, p. 23.

47. Gardner, *First Presbyterian*, pp. 73–75.

48. William E. Wyatt to St. Paul's Parish, Baltimore, ca. 1820; William E. Wyatt to James Kemp, 1 July 1820; 20 July 1820, MdBD.

49. For a discussion on the differences between low churchmen and high churchmen at this period, see Nelson W. Rightmyer, "The Episcopate of Bishop Kemp of Maryland," *Historical Magazine of the Protestant Episcopal Church* 28, no. 1 (1959): 66–84.

50. Joseph Bend to William Duke, 3 September 1810, MdBD.

51. Charles Worthington, *Reply to the Circular of the Vestry of St. Peter's Church* (Baltimore: n.p., 1815), pp. 16–18.

52. Ibid., pp. 1–16.

53. Francis Hollingsworth, *Explanation of the Reasons and Motives for the Advice Given on a Late Occasion* (Baltimore: n.p., 1815), pp. 4–6.

54. *Journal of a Convention of the Protestant Episcopal Church 1816, Held in St. Anne's Church, Annapolis, June 12–14, 1816* (Annapolis: Green, 1816), pp. 5–14; James Kemp to Joseph Jackson, 13 December 1815, MdBD. For a running account of the Dashiell scandal seen through the eyes of an opponent, see James Kemp to Joseph Jackson, 3 October 1815; 28 November 1815; 13 December 1815; 20 February 1816; 6 March 1816; 5 April 1816; James Kemp to James Claggett, 15 September 1815; 25 December 1815; 16 January 1816; 21 March 1816; 23 April 1816; 13 July 1816; James Kemp to William Duke, 22 January 1816; 22 August 1816; 26 June 1817; James Kemp to William Hemsley, 22 February 1816, MdBD. For Dashiell's defense, see George Dashiell, *An Address to the Protestant Episcopal Church in Maryland* (Baltimore: n.p., 1816).

55. *The State of Maryland Against the Vestry of St. Peter's Church, in which a Portion of the Members of the Church Prayed for a Mandamus to be Directed to the Vestry* (Baltimore: J. Robinson, 1817), pp. 1–58.

56. James Kemp to William Duke, 25 March 1817; 24, April 1817, MdBD.

57. *A Correct Narrative of the Rise and Progress of the Religious Fracas which Took Place in the German Roman Catholic Church of St. John in Baltimore on Wednesday the 30th of May, 1804* (Baltimore: n.p., 1804), pp. 10–11.

58. Ibid., pp. 12–15; "General Court, May Term 1804. Rev. Francis X. Brasius vs. Rev. Caesarius Reuter and Others," in *The State of Maryland Against the Vestry of St. Peter's*, pp. 59–72.

59. Richardson, *Dark Salvation*, p. 85.

60. Gardner, *First Presbyterian*, pp. 62–67.

61. An argument emphasizing the centrality of the doctrine of accountability will be presented in chapter 5.

62. Joseph Bend to William Duke, 20 November 1792. See also Joseph Bend to William Duke, 22 September 1800; 2 February 1801; 30 November 1801; and Joseph Bend to James Kemp, 6 February 1796, MdBD.

63. Jared Sparks to Miss Storrow, 7 May 1819, quoted in Adams, *Life and Writings*, I: 142–43.

64. Nevins, *Select Remains*, pp. 20–21.

65. Ibid., pp. 17–18; see also John Smith, *Lectures on the Nature and Ends of the Sacred Office, and on the Dignity, Duty, Qualifications, and Character of the Sacred Office* (Baltimore: Magill & Cline, 1810), pp. v–viii, 109–13.

66. John Holland, *Memoirs of the Life and Ministry of the Rev. John Summerfield. AM* (New York, 1846), p. 438.

Chapter 4. Discipline

1. Thomas O'Brien Hanley, *The American Revolution and Religion: Maryland 1770–1800* (Washington, D.C.: The Catholic University of America Press, Consortium Press, 1971), pp. 25–73.

2. Nathan O. Hatch, *The Sacred Cause of Liberty and Republican Thought and the Millennium in Revolutionary New England* (New Haven: Yale University Press, 1972), pp. 97, 138. See also Sidney Mead, "From Coercion to Persuasion," *Church History* 25 (1956): 317–37.

3. For Washington's farewell address, see Henry Steele Commager, ed., *Documents of American History* (New York: Appleton-Century-Crofts, Inc., 1948), pp. 169–75.

4. Alexis de Tocqueville, *Democracy in America*, vol. 1, The Henry Reeve Text, the Rev. Francis Brown, ed. Philips Bradley (New York: Alfred A. Knopf, 1956), pp. 305–6.

5. John Horace Pratt, *An Authentic Account of All the Proceedings on the Fourth of July, 1815, with Regard to Laying the Cornerstone of the Washington Monument, Now Erecting in the City of Baltimore, Accompanied by an Engraving of the Monument* (Baltimore: John Horace Pratt, 1815), pp. 10–14.

6. James Inglis, *A Sermon Delivered in the First Presbyterian Church, Baltimore, On Thursday, September 8, 1808, Being a Day of Fasting, Humiliation, and Prayer Appointed by the General Assembly of the Presbyterian Church in the U.S.A.* (Baltimore, 1808), p. 12.

7. John Johns, *The Annual Sermon Before the Bishops, Clergy and Laity Constituting the Board of Missions of the Protestant Episcopal Church in the U.S.A., Preached in St. Paul's, Boston, June 20, 1838* (New York: William Osborn, 1838), p. 16. For similar accounts, see John D. Dreyer, *Concord and Religion; the Principal Sources of Civil Prosperity: A Discourse Delivered in the German Reformed Church in the City of New York, on Sunday Succeeding the 36th Anniversary of the Independence of the U.S.* (New York: E. Conrad, 1812); John Hargrove, *Sermon Delivered in the City of Baltimore at the New Jerusalem Temple, October 20, 1814, the Day Appointed and Set Apart for Public Thanksgiving; for the Late Deliverance of that City and Its Inhabitants from the United & Formidable Attack of the British Fleet and Army* (Baltimore: Munroe & French, 1814); Frederick Beasley, *A Sermon Delivered Before the Convention of the Protestant Episcopal Church in the State of New York, October 4, 1808* (New York: Swordses, 1808); John Glendy, *An Oration on the Death of Lieut, Gen. George Washington, Composed on the Special Request of the Commandant and His Brother Officers, of the Cantonment in the Vicinity, and Delivered at Staunton, on the 22d Day of February, 1800* (Baltimore: Sands & Neilson, 1835); Inglis, *Sermon Delivered ... September 8, 1808*; James Inglis, *Sermons of the Late Dr. James Inglis, Pastor of the First Presbyterian Church in Baltimore, With Some of His Forms of Prayer* (Baltimore: N. G. Maxwell, 1820); Joseph Bend, "Sermon for the Thanksgiving of February 19, 1795," MS Bend Sermons, MdBD.

8. *The Key of Paradise, Opening the Gate to Eternal Salvation* (Baltimore: Wane & Murphy, 1804), p. 20.

9. Nevins, *Thoughts on Popery*, pp. 24, 94.

10. *Journal of a Protestant Episcopal Convention 1827, Held in ChesterTown, Kent Co., June 13–15, 1827* (Baltimore, 1827), p. 11. See also William Nevins, *Practical Thoughts* (New York, 1836), p. 110; and Joseph Bend, "On the Observance of the 7th Day," MS Bend Sermons, MdBD.

11. For condemnations directed toward the evils of Sabbath-breaking, see E. L. Finley, *An Address Delivered by Request of the Managers of the Sunday School Union, for the State of Maryland, at Their Annual Meeting, Held on the 30th Day of November 1830 in the First Presbyterian Church* (Baltimore, 1831); Protestant Episcopal Female Tract Society of Baltimore, *The Benefit of Affliction, A Visit to the Sunday School, The Sabbath Evening, and The Friendly Visit* (Baltimore: J. D. Toy, 1823); John Summerfield, *Sermons and Sketches of Sermons by the Rev. John Summerfield with an Introduction by the Rev. Thomas E. Bond* (New York: Harper & Brothers, 1845), p. 228.

12. Gardner, *First Presbyterian*, pp. 43–44; Wills, *Historical Sketch*, pp. 65–69; [Riordan], *Cathedral Records*, pp. 26–27; Historical Records Survey, "Inventory of Church Archives in the District of Columbia" (Washington, D.C.: District of Columbia Historical Records Survey, 1940), pp. 84–85; Scharf, *History of Baltimore*, pp. 540–41; Funk, *A Heritage to Hold in Fee*, p. 53; Beirne, *St. Paul's*, p. 40; "Second Presbyterian Church Records, Baltimore," vol. 2, MdHi; *Discipline of the Baltimore Yearly Meeting, 1806*, p. 39; "Journal of the Baltimore Annual Conference, Methodist Episcopal Church, 1800–1833," p. 206; Maring, "Denominational History," pp. 45–46; *Maryland Gazette & Baltimore Advertiser*, 17 March 1789.

13. *Advice to the People Called Methodists With Regard to Dress* (Baltimore: Butler for Hagerty and Kingston, 1808), pp. 3–16. See also Jesse Lee, *A Short History of the Methodists in the United States* (Baltimore: Magill and Clines, 1810), p. 97; and *Practical Piety, a Sermon Preached at the Watchnight Held in Johnstown, Delaware* (Baltimore: Hagerty, 1814), pp. 5–7.

14. *Epistle of the London Yearly Meeting Society of Friends* (Baltimore: Sower, 1802), p. 2; *Epistle of the London Yearly Meeting Society of Friends* (Baltimore: Gray, 1803), pp. 2–3.

15. *Mutual Rights and Christian Intelligencer*, 20 August 1829, 2: 96.

16. *Minutes of the Baltimore Baptist Association, Held in the City of Washington, District of Columbia, on the 14th, 15th, 16th and 17th Days of October, 1808* (Baltimore: n.p., 1808), p. 9; *Minutes of the Baltimore Baptist Association Held in the Brick Meeting House, Forks of Winter's Run, Harford County, State of Maryland, on the 18th, 19th, 20th, and 21st Days of October, 1810* (Baltimore: n.p., 1810).

17. *The War Dance No War Whoop: Being a Reply to a Letter from the Rev. George Dashiell to an Invisible Clergyman, alias the Rev. on the Subject of the War Dance as Lately Exhibited in Baltimore, by the Chiefs and Warriors of the Osage Tribe of Indians, in a Series of Letters, by a Layman* [Baltimore, 1804], pp. 5–6.

18. Ibid., p. 6.

19. Ibid., pp. 7–9.

20. Ibid., p. 10.

21. *The War Dance*, no. 2, p. 7.

22. Ibid., pp. 22–23. See also *A Short Reply to Burk and Guy with Some Ripe Fruit for a Friend to Truth, by a Layman of the New Jerusalem Church* (Baltimore, 1804).

23. *Catholic Encyclopedia*, 2: 239–41.

24. *Journal of a Protestant Episcopal Convention 1811, Held at St. Paul's, Baltimore, June 19–21, 1811* (Baltimore: J. Robinson, 1811), p. 6.

25. George Dashiell, *A Sermon Occasioned by the Burning of the Theatre in the City of Richmond, Virginia, on the 26th of December, 1811, Delivered in St. Peter's Church, Baltimore, January 12, 1812* (Baltimore: J. Kingston, 1812), p. 2.

26. John Dallas Robertson, "Christian Newcomer, Pioneer of Church Discipline and Union Among the United Brethren in Christ, the Evangelical Association, and the Methodist Episcopal Church" (Ph.D. diss., George Washington University, 1973), p. 77n.

27. For a general account, see Thomas E. Drake, *Quakers and Slavery in America* (New Haven: Yale University Press, 1950). For a contemporary account of the activities of Baltimore Friends, see John S. Tyson, *Life of Elisha Tyson the Philanthropist, By a Citizen of Baltimore* (Baltimore: B. Lundy, 1825).

28. For the story of the Methodist struggle against slavery, see Donald G. Mathews, *Slavery and Methodism: A Chapter in American Morality, 1780–1845* (Princeton: Princeton University Press, 1965).

29. Maring, "Denominational History," p. 47.

30. Wills, *Historical Sketch*, p. 61.

31. *Journal of a Protestant Episcopal Convention 1807 in St. Paul's Church, Baltimore, May 20–24, 1807* (Baltimore: J. Robinson, 1807), p. 6; James Kemp, "On Marriage and Divorce," 23 October 1804, MS Date file, MdBD.

32. *An Address of the General Conference of the Methodist Episcopal Church* [Baltimore, 1800], Broadside.

33. *A Mission to the Indians from the Indian Committee of Baltimore Yearly Meeting to Fort Wayne, in 1804, Written at the Time by Gerard T. Hopkins, with an Appendix Compiled in 1862 by Martha A. Tyson* (Philadelphia: T. E. Zell, 1862), pp. 175–76.

34. William C. Dunlap, *Quaker Education in Baltimore and Virginia Yearly Meetings with an Account of Certain Meetings of Delaware and the Eastern Shore Affiliated with Philadelphia* (Philadelphia: University of Pennsylvania, 1936), pp. 446–47, 484–88.

35. *An Address of the Baltimore Yearly Meeting to Thomas Jefferson* (New York, 1807), Broadside; *Epistle of Baltimore Yearly Meeting to Subordinate Meetings* (n.p., 1809), pp. 1–2.

36. *An Address to Christians of Every Denomination on the Subject of the Ensuing Presidential Election* [n.p., 1808], pp. 2–16.

37. William Jennings, *An Address to the Catholic Voters of Baltimore* (Baltimore, 1828), pp. 3–15.

38. Nevins, *Select Remains*, pp. 331–32.

39. Minutes of Leaders Meeting, 11 April 1820, 'Church Book, Baltimore City Station, 1818–1823," MdBL.

40. *Journal of the Protestant Episcopal Church General Convention 1808, in Baltimore, May 17–26, 1808* (New York: Swordses, 1808), pp. 15–16.

41. MS Trials and Judgments, 1816–22, Baltimore City Station, Methodist Episcopal Church, MdBL.

42. Minutes of the Baltimore City Station Quarterly Conference, 12 April 1820, MS Methodist Episcopal Church Book for Baltimore City Station 1818–23, MdBL.

43. *Discipline Yearly Meeting of Friends 1806.*

44. Proverbs 22: 6.

45. Wust, *Zion in Baltimore*, pp. 35–36.

46. *Discipline Yearly Meeting of Friends 1806*, pp. 94–95; Dunlap, *Quaker Education*, p. 508.

47. For a detailed account of the attempts to establish a permanent day school sponsored by the Baltimore Monthly Meeting, see Dunlap, *Quaker Education*, pp. 487–515 passim.

48. Hall, *Baltimore*, p. 657; *Sesquicentennial St. Patrick's*, pp. 11–18; Joseph Bend, "For the Free School," and "For the Episcopal Charitable Institution," MS Bend Sermons, MdBD; see also William E. Wyatt, *A Discourse on Christian Education Delivered Before the Association of the Alumni of Columbia College at Their Anniversary, October 9, 1833* (Baltimore, 1833); Finley, *An Address Delivered.*

49. *A Brief Account of the Baltimore Female Humane Association Charity School of the City of Baltimore* (Baltimore: Warner & Hanna, 1803), pp. 2–23; *A Plan of the Baltimore Female Charity School* (Baltimore: n.p., 1800), Broadside.

50. Joseph Bend, *The Past History and Present Condition of the Institution of St. Paul's Parish, Originally Incorporated under the Title of the Benevolent Society of the City and County of Baltimore* (Baltimore: J. Robinson, 1860), p. 39; Joseph Bend, "For the Free School," MS Bend Sermons, MdBD.

51. The two schools referred to above were sponsored by the Washington Society and the

Tammany Society of Baltimore.

52. *Memorial Volume of the Centenary of St. Mary's Seminary of St. Sulpice, Baltimore, Maryland, 1791–1891* (Baltimore: John Murphy & Co., 1891), pp. 8–9; *Strictures on the Establishment of Colleges, Particularly that of St. Mary's, in the Precincts of Baltimore, as Formerly Published in the Evening Post and Telegraph* (Baltimore: n.p., 1806), pp. 57–58; William V. Dubourg, *St. Mary's Seminary and Catholics at large Vindicated against the Pastoral Letter of the Ministers, Bishops, &c. of the Presbytery of Baltimore* (Baltimore: Bernard Dornin, 1811).

53. Francis Asbury, *The Journal and Letters of Francis Asbury*, 3: 143.

54. "An Address to the Annual Subscribers for the Support of Cokesbury College," printed in Asbury, *Journal*, 3: 54–60.

55. Ibid., 3: 65.

56. Ibid., 3: 62, 72–73, 88, 93, 102–3, 106, 110, 123–24, 134.

57. Ibid., 2: 75.

58. John Owen Gross, *Methodist Beginnings in Higher Education* (Nashville: Board of Education, 1959), pp. 25–26.

59. Asbury, *Journal*, 2: 110–11.

60. *The Methodist Magazine* 1 (1818): 89–93.

61. Ibid., pp. 109–10; For Jennings's career, see Thomas H. Stockton, *A Discourse on the Life and Character of the Rev. Samuel K. Jennings, M.D., Delivered at St. John's Church, Liberty St., Baltimore, Sabbath Evening, March 11, 1855* (Baltimore: John Toy, 1855).

62. Minutes of Leaders Meeting of 12 November 1817; Minutes of Male Members Meeting of 12 November 1817, Fielder Israel Papers, MS 488, Box 13, MdHi.

63. *The Methodist Magazine* 1 (March 1818): 110; "Journal of the Baltimore Annual Conference, Methodist Episcopal Church, 1800–1833," pp. 113, 115, 118.

64. Minutes of Male Members Meeting of 4 March 1819; 10 May 1819; 3 June, 1819; Minutes of a Leaders Meeting, 15 December 1819, Fielder Israel Papers, MS 488, Box 13, MdHi.

65. "Journal of the Baltimore Annual Conference," p. 135.

66. See chapter 7 for an in-depth account of Baltimore's missionary tract associations.

67. For the percentages of religious titles by five year intervals, see Table 16.

68. Francis de Sales, *Devout Life* (Baltimore: Robinson for Dormin, 1816); John Milton, *Paradise Lost* (Baltimore: Palmer for Lucas, 1813); William Percy, *True Christian Character* (Baltimore: Dobbin & Murphy, 1809); Hannah More, *Practical Piety* (Baltimore: Palmer for Kingston, 1812); Mason Lock Weems, *God's Revenge Against Murder* (Baltimore: Bell & Cook, 1814); idem, *God's Revenge Against Adultery (Baltimore: Pomeroy, 1815); idem, God's Revenge Against Gambling* (Baltimore: Hagerty, 1815).

69. John Wesley, *A Compendium of Logic, Directions to Penitents and Believers for Renewing Their Covenant with God, The Doctrine of Salvation, Faith, and Good Works, The Principles of a Methodist, Salvation By Faith, Wandering Thoughts* (Baltimore: Butler, 1808); John Fletcher, *Fletcher's Appeal to Matter of Fact and Common Sense..., The Posthumous Works of the Rev. John Fletcher ...* (Baltimore: Edes, 1814), *A Rational Vindication of the Catholic Faith ...* (Baltimore: Toy for Neal, 1818); Emanuel Swedenborg, *Queries Concerning the Trinity* (Baltimore: Adams, 1792).

70. *Account of the Life and Death of John Fletcher* (Baltimore: Butler, 1805); Jesse Lee, *A Short Account of the Life and Death of the Rev. John Lee* (Baltimore: Butler, 1805); *Memoirs of the Dead* (Baltimore, 1806); George Bourne, *Life of the Rev. John Wesley* (Baltimore: Dobbin & Murphy, 1807); Mary Fletcher, *An Account of the Death of Sarah Lawrence* (Baltimore: Butler, 1808); *The Methodist Magazine* 2: (August 1819): 284–89; *The Methodist Magazine* 4: (June 1821): 205–8; *The Methodist Magazine* 5 (November 1822); *The Methodist Magazine* 6 (June 1823): 210–14, 249–56.

71. Patrick Allison, *A Discourse Delivered in the Presbyterian Church in the City of Baltimore, February 22, 1800, the Day Dedicated to the Memory of Gen. George Washington* (Baltimore: Pechin, 1800); Glendy, *An Oration on the Death of Lieut. Gen. George Washington*; John Ireland, *Funeral Panegyric of George Washington Pronounced February 22, 1800 in the United Churches of St. Paul's and Christ Church, Baltimore, State of Maryland* (London: S. Rousseau for

Cuthell & Martin, 1802); James Kemp, *A Sermon, Delivered in Christ Church, Cambridge, Maryland, February 22, 1800, being the Day of Mourning Appointed by Congress for the Death of Gen. George Washington, Late President of US* (Easton, Md.: Cowan, 1800); Joseph Bend, "Sacred to the Memory of George Washington," MS Bend Sermons, MdBD; John Carroll, *A Discourse on General Washington Delivered in the Catholic Church of St. Peter's, in Baltimore, February 22, 1800* (Baltimore: Warner & Hanna, 1800); Thomas Morrell, *A Sermon on the Death of General Geo. Washington ... Delivered on February 22, 1800 in the City of Baltimore, and Published at the Request of Many of the Hearers* (Baltimore: Warner & Hanna, 1800).

72. Joseph Bend, "Sacred to the Memory of George Washington," MS Bend Sermons, MdBD, p. 8.

73. Kemp, *Sermon Delivered ... February 22, 1800*, p. 12.

74. Allison, *Discourse Delivered ... February 22, 1800*, p. 24.

75. Morrell, *A Sermon on the Death of ... Washington....*, pp. 3–29.

76. Carroll, *Discourse on General Washington ... February 22, 1800*, p. 24. Also see James H. Smylie, "President as Republican Prophet and King: Clerical Reflections on the Death of Washington," *Journal of Church and State* (Spring 1876), pp. 232–52.

Chapter 5. Worship

1. See R. D. Whitehorn, "The Church at Worship," in Ronald C. D. Jasper, ed., *The Renewal of Worship: Essays by Members of the Joint Liturgical Group* (London: Oxford University Press, 1965), pp. 13–20. For the same concept stated by an early national Baltimore pastor, see Inglis, *Sermons*, pp. 61–74.

2. Julius Melton, *Presbyterian Worship in America: Changing Patterns Since 1787* (Richmond: John Knox Press, 1967), pp. 13–15.

3. Weigel, *Churches*, pp. 76–80.

4. *Hymns for the Use of the Catholic Church in the U.S.A. A New Edition, with Additions and Improvements* (Baltimore: Butler, 1807), p. ii.

5. Popular titles that underwent more than one edition included Jeremiah Minter's *Hymns and Spiritual Songs for the Use of Christians* (1801, 1802, 1806, 1809), John Rippon's *A Selection of Hymns* (1803, 1804, 1814, 1818), the official hymnal of the Protestant Episcopal Church, entitled *The Whole Book of Psalms with Hymns* (1800, 1808, 1812, 1814), and Isaac Watts, *Divine Songs* (1799, 1801).

6. James E. P. Boulden, *The Presbyterians of Baltimore: Their Churches and Historic Grave Yards* (Baltimore: Wm. K. Boyle & Son, 1875), p. 131; Sharf, *History of Baltimore*, p. 551.

7. Holdcraft, "The Old Otterbein Church Story," pp. 13–19; George Hedley, *Christian Worship: Some Meaning and Means* (New York: The Macmillan Co., 1953), pp. 102–26.

8. *Social and Camp Meeting Songs for the Pious*, 2nd ed. (Baltimore: Toy for Lucas and Harrod, 1818), p. 73.

9. Bond, *Methodism, Not a Human Contrivance*, pp. 20–22.

10. Joseph Bend, "Church Musick," p. 19. See also "On Psalmody," MS Bend Sermons, MdBD.

11. Sharf, *History of Baltimore*, p. 519; [Riordan], *Cathedral Records*, p. 101; Wust, *Zion in Baltimore*, p. 36.

12. Brief Sketch of the History of Christ Church, Baltimore (Baltimore, [1898]), pp. 2–5; St. Paul's Church, *To the Pewholders of St. Paul's*.

13. *Sesquicentennial St. Patrick's*, p. 31; Elias Heiner, *Centenary Sermon Delivered in the Second Street Church, on Sabbath Morning, December 8, 1850, on the Occasion of the Centenary Celebration of the 1st German Reformed Congregation of Baltimore* (Baltimore: Sherwood & Co., 1850), p. 28.

14. See Tables 2–8.

15. Wust, *Zion in Baltimore*, pp. 45–49. In contrast to the emphasis on liturgical order at

Zion, the first English Lutheran Church used no liturgy, molding its order of worship after a "plain Presbyterian style." John G. Morris, *Life Reminiscences of an Old Lutheran Minister* (Philadelphia: 1896).

16. The assertion that St. Peter's did not have an organ is based upon the omission of such in the listings of the property holdings of the congregation. See Dashiell, *Address of the Vestry*; and John P. K. Henshaw, *Address of the Trustees of St. Peter's School to the Congregation of St. Peter's Church and To the Public* ([Baltimore], 1822), pp. 1–6.

17. Gardner, *First Presbyterian*, p. 60; Melton, *Presbyterian Worship*, p. 35.

18. *The Baltimore Collection of Sacred Musik, Selected and Compiled Under the Direction of a Committee of the Associate Reformed Presbyterian Church of Baltimore* (Baltimore: Cushing & Jewett, 1819), pp. ii–iii; Latrobe, *Picture of Baltimore*, pp. 126–47; "Trinity Church Register, Baltimore," MdHi, 1: 67.

19. Wust, *Zion in Baltimore*, p. 36.

20. [Riordan], *Cathedral Records*, p. 101.

21. *Brief Sketch of the History of Christ Church*, pp. 6–7; Funk, *Heritage to Hold in Fee*, pp. 15, 63; Beirne, *St. Paul's Parish*, p. 73.

22. "Second Presbyterian Church Records, Baltimore," vol. 2, MdHi.

23. John Cole, *The Rudiments of Music, or an Introduction to the Art of Singing, Compiled for the Use of Schools* (Baltimore: Dobbin & Murphy, 1810), p. iv. Cole's other works included: *Sacred Harmony* (1799); *The Beauties of Psalmody* (1804, 1805, 1806); *Program for Sacred Music* ... (1807); *Divine Harmonist* (1808); *Episcopal Harmony* (1809, 1810, 1811); *The Minstrel* (1811, 1812); *Devotional Harmony* (1814); *Songs of Zion* (1818).

24. Samuel Cole, comp., *Sacred Music: Published for the Use of the Cecilian Society Established Under the Patronage of the Clergy and Vestry of St. Paul's Parish* (Baltimore: Cole, 1803), pp. 1–16.

25. *The Baltimore Collection of Sacred Musik*, pp. i–vii.

26. Frank Baker, *John Wesley and the Church of England* (Nashville: Abingdon Press, 1970), pp. 249–54.

27. Melton, *Presbyterian Worship*, pp. 21–27.

28. Inglis, *Sermons*, p. iii.

29. *Journal of a Convention of the Protestant Episcopal Church in Maryland Held in St. Paul's Church, Baltimore, May 20th, 21st, and 22nd, MDCCCXVIII* (Annapolis: Jonas Green, 1818), p. 10. See also *The Beauty of Holiness in the Common Prayer, as Set Forth in Four Sermons Preached at the Rolls Chapel in 1816, by Thomas Pissee, D.D., Adapted to the Protestant Episcopal Church in the U.S. with an Introduction by James Kemp* (Baltimore: Smith & Coleman, 1817), p. iii; and John P. K. Henshaw to Bishop Kemp, 5 January 1818, MdBD.

30. George Dashiell, *An Address to the Protestant Episcopal Church in Maryland* (Baltimore, 1816), p. 1.

31. Quotation from William West to Bishop White, 1 March 1790, MdBD. See also James Kemp, "For the Repertory," located under the Subject File of Joseph Kemp, MdBD; and *Review of the Rev. Jared Sparks' Letters on the Protestant Episcopal Church in Reply to the Rev. Dr. Wyatt's Sermon* (Baltimore: N. G. Maxwell, 1820).

32. Melton, *Presbyterian Worship*, pp. 21–27. For examples, see Inglis, *Sermons*, pp. 377–89.

33. Benjamin Carr, *Masses for the Use of the Catholic Churches in the United States* (Baltimore, 1805), p. 94.

34. Lee, *Practical Piety*, pp. 22–23.

35. Gardner, *First Presbyterian*, p. 43; Heiner, *Centenary*, p. 20.

36. Methodist Episcopal Church Book, Baltimore City Station, 1823–32, MdBL; Wust, *Zion in Baltimore*, p. 35.

37. Wills, *Historical Sketch*, pp. 40–57; John Johns, *Valedictory Discourse Delivered at Christ Church Baltimore, October 3, 1832* (Baltimore: N. Hickman, James Young printer, 1842).

38. Heiner, *Centenary Sermon*, p. 20.

39. Gottlieb Shober, *A Comprehensive Account of the Rise and Progress of the Blessed Reformation of the Christian Church* (Baltimore: Shaeffer & Maund, 1818), pp. 144–207.

40. *The New Week's Preparation for a Worthy Receiving of the Lord's Supper, Recommended to the Devout in General and Particularly to the Members of the Protestant Episcopal Church of the U.S.A.* (Baltimore: Warner & Hanna, 1803). See also Joseph Bend, "For Christmas," p. 30, "For the Ascension," p. 29; "For Easter," p. 31, "Nature, Ends, and Effects of the Death of Christ," p. 30, "The Success of Christianity as Evidence of its Truth," p. 29, MS Bend Sermons, MdBD; and *Private Devotions Preparatory to the Sacrament* (Baltimore: Dobbins, 1802).

41. John P. K. Henshaw, *The Communicant's Guide; or An Introduction to the Sacrament of the Lord's Supper* (Baltimore: J. D. Toy and W. R. Lucas, 1831), pp. 88–89, 102–64.

42. John C. Backus, *Revivals of Religion in the Presbyterian Churches of Baltimore* (Philadelphia: J. M. Wilson, 1858), pp. 10–11.

43. Holdcraft, "The Old Otterbein Story," pp. 47–50.

44. In regard to preaching, American Methodists followed the example of their spiritual father, John Wesley: "I desire plain truth for plain people. Therefore, of set purpose, I abstain from all nice and philosophical speculations; from all perplexed and intricate reasonings; and as far as possible, from even the show of learning...." Quoted in Coleman, "Factors," p. 327n.

45. George Roberts, *The Substance of a Sermon (But Now More Enlarged) Preached to, and at the Request of the Conference of the Methodist Episcopal Church, Held in Baltimore, March, 1807* (Baltimore: J. West Butler, 1807), p. 72; Coleman, "Factors," p. 332.

46. Holland, *Memoirs*, pp. 423–26. For samples of sermon outlines prepared by Methodist itinerants serving on occasion in Baltimore, see the manuscript notebooks of William Ryland and Nelson Reed, MdBL.

47. Holland, *Memoirs*, pp. 445–48.

48. Minutes of Leaders Meeting, 20 December 1820, Methodist Episcopal Church Book, Baltimore City Station, 1818–23, MdBL, p. 17. See also Holland, *Memoirs*, pp. 313–14.

49. An average sermon by Joseph Bend or James Kemp was about 2,800 words. See their collection of sermons at MdBD.

50. Joseph Bend to William Duke, 11 August, 1802; J. E. Snodgrass, *Sketches of the Baltimore Pulpit* (Baltimore: Knight & Colburn, 1843), p. 27.

51. An average sermon by James Inglis or William Nevins was about 4,200 words. Inglis, *Sermons*; William Nevins, *Sermons by the Late Rev. William Nevins* (New York: John S. Taylor, 1837).

52. The only exception to this rule was Patrick Allison, who received the following criticism by a visitor to Baltimore: "... I think him a ... gentleman, but a great many Presbyterians about you would not think so, for he reads his sermons...." Gardner, *First Presbyterian*, p. 19.

53. "Second Presbyterian Church Records, Baltimore," vol. 2, MdHi; Sprague, *Annals*, 4: 278–84, 629–40, 645–51.

54. For comments on the delivery of Baltimore preachers see Snodgrass, *Sketches*, pp. 17, 27, 32, 69, 75, 107, 116–17. See also Raphael Semmes, *Baltimore as Seen by Visitors* (Baltimore: Maryland Historical Society, 1953), p. 86.

55. James Kemp, "The Ordination of the Apostles," and "Sermon on Church Government," MdBD; James Kemp, *Sermon on the Manner in which the Gospel Was Established and the Christian Church Organized: Preached Before the General Convention of the Protestant Episcopal Church in USA, on October 31, 1821* (Philadelphia: S. Potter & Co., 1821), and *A Sermon on the Nature and Object of a Gospel Ministry* (Baltimore: Sower & Cole, 1803); Wyatt, *Sermon Exhibiting Some of the Principal Doctrines.*.

56. Joseph Bend, "On Confirmation No. 1," "On Confirmation No. 2," "On the Liturgy No. 1," "On the Liturgy No. 2," "On the Introduction of the Book of Common Prayer, Ratified by the Convention of October, 1789," MS Bend Sermons, MdBD; John P. K. Henshaw, *The Minister's Instruction to the People on the Subject of Confirmation* (Baltimore, 1818).

57. Wyatt, *Sermon Exhibiting Some of the Principal Doctrines*, p. 9.

58. See Inglis, *Sermons*, and Nevins, *Sermons*, passim.

59. See the collection of sermons of Joseph Bend and James Kemp, MdBD.

60. For examples of this assertion, see Joseph Bend, "The Friendship of the World Enmity with God," "The Christian Race," "The Gospel Redeems Man from the Bondage of Sin," and

"The Impossibility of Serving God and Mammon," MS Bend Sermons, MdBD.

61. Joseph Bend, "Not to be Slothful in Business, Yet to be Fervent in Spirit, Serving the Lord," p. 25. See also "Working," and "Fruits Required from Men are Proportioned to Their Advantages," MS Bend Sermons, MdBD.

62. James Kemp, *A Sermon on the Christian Warfare Preached at the Funeral of the Rt. Rev. Dr. Claggett, Late Bishop of the Protestant Episcopal Church in Maryland, with a Sketch of his Character and a Short Account of his Life* (Baltimore: J. Robinson, 1817), pp. 2–5.

63. Joseph Bend, "On Prayer, No. 2," MS Bend Sermons, MdBD.

64. Joseph Bend, "Overrighteousness," MS Bend Sermons, MdBD, p. 7.

65. William E. Wyatt, ed., *The Monument: A Small Selection from the Sermons of the Late Rt. Rev. James Kemp, D. D. Rector of St. Paul's Parish, Baltimore and Bishop of the Protestant Episcopal Church of Maryland, Together with the Address Delivered at the Time of his Interment by W. E. Wyatt. To Which are Prefixed Brief Biographical Notices of the Bishop* (Baltimore: J. Robinson, 1833), pp. 156–57.

66. James Kemp, "Character of Alexander C. Hanson," 25 April 1819, MdBD.

67. Summerfield, *Sermons*, pp. 406–7.

68. Ibid., p. 387.

69. Nevins, *Sermons*, pp. 14–15.

70. Ibid., pp. 9–21, 101–12, 197–206, 251–60; Inglis, *Sermons*, pp. 9–21, 113–24, 125–32, 141–52.

71. Ibid., pp. 113–24.

72. Ibid., pp. 309–18. See also Nevins, *Sermons*, pp. 223–28, 231–33, 310–12; Nevins, *Select Remains*, pp. 119–20, 139, 147–49; and W. C. Walton, *Narrative of a Revival of Religion in the Third Presbyterian Church in Baltimore* (Northampton, 1826), pp. 2–24.

73. See Summerfield, *Sermons*; Inglis, *Sermons*; Nevins, *Sermons*; and Wyatt, *The Monument* MS Bend Sermons, MdBD.

74. Inglis, *Sermons*, pp. 297–308.

75. Nevins, *Sermons*, p. 305.

76. Ibid., pp. 218–19, 235–39, 331; Nevins, *Select Remains*, pp. 86, 119–20, 242; Frederick Beasley, *A Sermon Delivered Before the Convention of the Protestant Episcopal Church in the State of Pennsylvania Held in St. James's Church, Philadelphia, May 3, 1815* (Philadelphia: Edward Earle, printed by William Fry, 1815), pp. 4–7; William Wyatt, *The Gospel Preached to the Poor. A Sermon Preached at the Ordination Held by the Rt. Rev. James Kemp, D.D. in Trinity Chapel, St. James Parish, Baltimore Co., September 17, 1823* (Baltimore: J. Robinson, 1823), p. 3.

77. Inglis, *Sermons*, p. 227. See also Roberts, *The Substance of a Sermon*, pp. 21–23; Wyatt, *The Monument*, pp. 91, 110–11; Summerfield, *Sermons*, pp. 280–86.

78. Inglis, *Sermons*, p. 227.

79. George Lemmon, *A Sermon on the Following Words. "This is a Faithful Saying, and Worthy of All Acceptation, that Christ Jesus Came into the World to Save Sinners"* (Baltimore: A. Mittenberger, 1810), pp. 9–11. See also Joseph Bend, "The Atonement of Christ with its Moral Designs," "Christ a Propitiation for the Sins of the World," "On the Satisfaction Made by Christ," "On the Sacrifice Made by Christ," and "Nature, Ends, and Effects of the Death of Christ," MS Bend Sermons, MdBD; Wyatt, *The Monument*, pp. 91–105; Nevins, *Sermons*, pp. 213–16; Nevins, *Select Remains*, p. 137; Inglis, *Sermons*, pp. 187–96, 197–206.

80. Joseph Bend, "On the Sacrifice Made By Christ," "The Atonement of Christ with its Moral Designs," and "The Fallacy of Certain Specious Doctrines Detected," MS Bend Sermons, MdBD; Inglis, *Sermons*, pp. 47–60; Summerfield, *Sermons*, pp. 281–86.

81. Inglis, *Sermons*, pp. 35–46, 125–32, 169–78, 271–80; Nevins, *Sermons*, pp. 108–10; William Nevins, *Practical Thoughts* (New York: 1836), p. 217; Summerfield, *Sermons*, pp. 185–88; John Hargrove, *Sermon on the True Nature of the Resurrection of Man, Delivered February 11, 1816 in the New Jerusalem Temple in the City of Baltimore on a Funeral Occasion* (Baltimore: William Warner, 1816), pp. 14–15; Joseph Bend, "The Safety and Security of Upright Walking," MS Bend Sermons, MdBD.

82. Nevins, *Select Remains*, pp. 354–55; Nevins, *Sermons,* pp. 148–49, 369–70, 377–78; Wyatt, *The Monument,* pp. 88, 154, 161–62; Frederick Beasley, *A Sermon on Duelling, Delivered in Christ Church, Baltimore, April 28, 1811* (Baltimore: J. Robinson, 1811), p. 39; Joseph Bend, *A Discourse Delivered in St. Paul's Church Baltimore, on Sunday June 19, 1791, Recognizing the Relationship Subsisting Between the Congregation and the Author, in Consequence of his Recent Election to the Office of Rector of Said Church* (Baltimore: Graham, 1790), pp. 19–20, and "Redeeming the Time," "On Conscience," "Incentives to Holiness," "Summary of the Arguments in Favor of Christianity," MS Bend Sermons, MdBD.

83. Inglis, *Sermons*, pp. 150–52, 241–43; Nevins, *Sermons*, pp. 239–41, 248–50, 401–5; Wyatt, *Gospel Preached to the Poor*, p. 33; Joseph Bend, "State of the Unrighteous," "The Fate of the Wicked Considered," and "On the Certainty of Future Happiness," MS Bend Sermons, MdBD.

84. Kemp, *Sermon on the Christian Warfare*, and "On the Death of Gen. Alexander Hamilton," July 1804, and "A Commentary on the Burial of the Dead," MdBD; Joseph Bend, *A Discourse Delivered in Christ Church Baltimore, 1798* (Baltimore: Dobblin, 1798), "Counsel of God and Future Glory," and "On Walking With God," MS Bend Sermons, MdBD; Jared Sparks, *A Sermon Preached in the Hall of the House of Representatives in Congress, Washington City, March 3, 1822, Occasioned by the Death of the Hon. William Pickney, Late Member of the Senate of the U.S.* (Washington: Davis & Force, 1822).

85. William Nevins, however, did preach occasional apologetical sermons that argued the reasonableness of a merciful God sentencing the impenitent to eternal damnation. Nevins, *Sermons*, pp. 34–41, 231–34.

86. Joseph Bend, "Occasioned by the Third Visitation of Baltimore by the Yellow Fever," MS Bend Sermons, MdBD, p. 3.

87. Joseph Bend, "For the Fast on Account of the Malignant Fever Prevailing in Philadelphia in 1793," "Occasioned by the Third Visitation of Baltimore by the Yellow Fever," "For the Thanksgiving on February 19, 1795," "For the Fast Observed May 9, 1798," MS Bend Sermons, MdBD; *A Form of Prayer, Compiled for the Use of the Congregations of St. Paul's and Christ Church, Baltimore, on Wednesday May 9, being the Day Recommended by the President of the US to be Offered as a Day of Solemn Humiliation, Fasting, and Prayer* (Baltimore: Hayes, 1798); Inglis, *A Sermon Delivered ... September 8, 1808*; James Inglis, *A Discourse Delivered in the First Presbyterian Church, October 2, 1814, Before the Lt. Col., the Officers, and Soldiers, of the First Regiment of Artillery* (Baltimore: J. Robinson for Neal, Willis, & Cole, 1814); Hargrove, *Sermon Delivered ... October 20, 1814*; John Claggett, "Order for Thanksgiving Worship," April 1815, MdBD; [Riordan], *Cathedral Records*, p. 45.

88. 2 Chronicles 7: 13, 14. See Asbury, *Journals*, 2: 175.

89. Inglis, *Sermon Delivered ... September 8, 1808*, pp. 5–6.

90. Ibid., p. 11.

91. Inglis, *Discourse Delivered ... October 2, 1814*, p. 21; Hargrove, *Sermon Delivered ... October 20, 1814*, p. 9.

92. Frederick Beasley, *An Inaugural Discourse Delivered in Christ Church, Baltimore on December 31, 1809 at the Time in which the Author was Instituted as Associate Pastor into St. Paul's Parish* (Baltimore: Coale & Thomas, 1810), p. 10.

Chapter 6. Revivalism

1. Whitney R. Cross, *The Burned-Over District: The Social and Intellectual History of Enthusiastic Religion in Western New York, 1800–1850* (Ithaca: Cornell University Press, 1950); Charles R. Keller, *The Second Great Awakening in Connecticut* (New Haven: Yale University Press, 1942); Charles A. Johnson, *A Frontier Camp Meeting: Religion's Harvest Time* (Dallas: Southern Methodist University Press, 1955); Dickson Bruce, Jr., *And They All Sang Hallelujah: Plain Folk Camp-Meeting Religion, 1800–1845* (Knoxville: The University of Tennessee Press,

1974); John B. Boles, *The Great Revival, 1787–1805* (Lexington: University of Kentucky Press, 1972); Charles I. Foster, *An Errand of Mercy: The Evangelical United Front, 1790–1837* (Chapel Hill: University of North Carolina Press, 1960); Clifford S. Griffin, *Their Brother's Keepers: Moral Stewardship in the United States, 1800–1865* (New Brunswick: Rutgers University Press, 1960); T. Scott Miyakawa, *Protestants and Pioneers* (Chicago: University of Chicago Press, 1964).

2. See William G. McLoughlin, Jr., *Modern Revivalism: Charles Grandison Finney to Billy Graham* (New York: the Ronald Press Company, 1959), pp. 11–165, passim; Bernard A. Weisberger, *They Gathered at the River* (Boston: Little Brown, & Co., 1958), pp. 86–148, passim; Paul E. Johnson, *A Shopkeeper's Millennium: Society and Revivals in Rochester, N.Y. 1815–1837* (New York: Hill & Wang, 1978); Marion L. Bell, *Crusade in the City; Revivalism in Nineteenth-Century Philadelphia* (Lewisburg, Pa: Bucknell University Press, 1977), pp. 23–77.

3. See David Lovejoy, *Religious Enthusiasm and the Great Awakening* (Englewood Cliffs, N.J.: Prentice-Hall, Inc., 1969), pp. 1–22, for a discussion on the meaning of the conversion experience.

4. Joseph Bend to James Kemp, 3 June 1796, MdBD.

5. Joseph Bend to William Duke, 3 November 1798, MdBD.

6. Joseph Bend to William Duke, 8 July 1799. For similar expressions, see Joseph Bend to William Duke, 21 April 1795; Joseph Bend to Bishop Claggett, 19 July 1795; 6 December 1795; May 1796; Joseph Bend to James Kemp, 4 February 1800, MdBD.

7. Duke, *Observations on the Present State*, pp. 6–53, passim.

8. Anna Braithwaite Thomas, *The Story of the Baltimore Yearly Meeting from 1672–1938* (Baltimore: Weant Press, Inc., 1938), p. 49.

9. Joseph T. Smith, *Eighty Years Embracing a History of Presbyterianism in Baltimore, with an Appendix* (Philadelphia: Westminster Press, 1899), p. 15.

10. These figures are based upon a study of the Baltimore titles listed in the Evans and Shaw-Shoemaker Early American Imprints. The results are summarized in Table 16.

11. See Table 1.

12. Lester B. Scherer, "Ezekiel Cooper, 1767–1847, An Early American Methodist Leader" (Ph.D. diss., Northwestern University, 1965), pp. 50–51. See also Lee, *Life of John Lee*, p. 123.

13. Baltimore City and Fells Points membership statistics after 1805 may be found in *Minutes of the Annual Conferences of the Methodist Episcopal Church*, vols. I and II. For statistics before 1805, see "Baltimore City Station Methodist Episcopal Records," Microfilm reel M 408, and "Annual Register for the Methodist Episcopal Church on Fells Point," Microfilm reel M 409, MdHR.

14. For typical explanations of Methodist expansion, see W. M. Gewehr, "Some Factors in the Expansion of Frontier Methodism," *Journal of Religion* 8 (8 January 1928): 79–120; W. W. Sweet, *The Rise of Methodism in the West* (Dallas: Smith & Lamar, 1820), pp. 1–70, *Religion on the American Frontier, 1783–1840: The Methodists, A Collection of Source Materials* (Chicago: University of Chicago Press, 1946), 4: 51–70; Coleman, "Factors;" and N. E. Hughes, Jr., "The Methodist Christmas Conference," *Maryland Historical Magazine* (1959), pp. 272–92.

15. O'Brien, *The American Revolution and Religion*, p. 201.

16. Johnson, *A Frontier Camp Meeting*, p. viii.

17. Bruce, *And They All Sang Hallelujah*, p. 136.

18. *Mutual Rights and Christian Intelligencer* 1 (20 September 1828): 6; (20 June 1829): 79; 2 (6 July 1830): 176; (5 October 1830): 187.

19. Ibid. (20 June 1829): 799.

20. Ibid. (20 June 1829): 79; (August 6, 1829): 92.

21. *Extracts of Letters Containing Some Account of the Work of God Since 1800* (New York: Totten for Cooper & Wilson, 1805), pp. 109–11, 114–18.

22. *Wesleyan Repository* 2 (August 1822): 138–43. For a similar account from a citizen of Baltimore, see *A Short Reply to Burk and Guy*, pp. 13–14; *The Methodist Magazine* 9 (December 1826): 475–76.

23. *Mutual Rights and Christian Intelligencer* 1 (6 October 1828): 10.

24. *Extracts of Letters*, pp. 85–86, 88–91, 114–18.

25. Ibid., p. 116.

26. Ibid., p. 86.

27. Ibid., pp. 88–91.

28. Gordon Pratt Baker, ed., *Those Incredible Methodists, A History of the Baltimore Conference of the United Methodist Church* (Nashville: The Parthenon Press, 1972), pp. 94–95.

29. *The Methodist Magazine* 9 (December 1826): 475–76.

30. Ibid., 8 (December 1825): 486–87; (February 1818): 73–74; *Mutual Rights and Christian Intelligencer* 3 (5 October 1829): 107.

31. Scherer, "Ezekiel Cooper," p. 51.

32. *Minutes of the Baltimore Baptist Association Held by Appointment in the Meetinghouse of the First Baltimore Church, May 18–20, 1820* (Alexandria: S. H. Davis, 1820), p. 6; *Minutes of the Baltimore Baptist Association Held in the Meetinghouse of the Ebenezar Church in the City of Baltimore, May 13–15, 1824* (Baltimore: R. J. Matchett, 1824), p. 5; "Journal of the Baltimore Annual Conference Methodist Episcopal Church, 1800–1833," typescript located at DWyT, p. 107.

33. Henry Boehm, *Reminiscences, Historical and Biographical, of Sixty-four Years in the Ministry*, ed. J. B. Wakeley (New York: Carlton & Porter, 1866), p. 30. For another account of the Conference revival of 1800, see Baker, *Those Incredible Methodists*, p. 88–89.

34. *Wesleyan Repository* 2 (July 1822): 89.

35. "Journal of the Baltimore Annual Conference, Methodist Episcopal Church, 1800–1833," typescript located at DWyT, pp. 47–48. Also see pp. 38, 79, 90, 126, and 207.

36. *The Methodist Magazine* 1 (February 1818): 73–74; (April 1818): 154–59.

37. Fielder Israel Papers, MS 488, Box, MdHi.

38. Alfred Z. Hartman, "History of Methodism in Maryland," typescript at MdHi; "Baltimore City Station Methodist Episcopal Records," Microfilm reel M408, MdHR; [Isaac Cook], *Early History of Methodist Sabbath Schools in Baltimore County and Vicinity; and Other Interesting Facts Concerned Therewith, Compiled by a Sabbath School Scholar of 1817* (Baltimore: Henry F. Cook, 1877), p. 7.

39. The only areas in the city beyond a half-mile radius of a Methodist house were portions of Wards 1, 8, and 12. No more than 10,000 of the 62,000 city residents lived in these regions.

40. About 80% of the churchgoers identified in city directories lived within one-half mile of their church.

41. "Proceedings and Accounts for Building Caroline Street Methodist Episcopal Church, February 24, 1818," MdBL; *The Second Annual Report Sinking Fund* (Baltimore: n.p., 1833).

42. Local church histories generally provide the cost and square footage or pew numbers of the meeting house. To estimate the seating capacity for each house, I either multiplied the number of pews by 12, or divided the square footage by 4 feet/seat for small houses and by 5.6 feet/seat for larger houses. Next, I ascertained the cost per seat by dividing the cost of the building and interior by the seating capacity. The above figures are based upon estimates from five Catholic, four Episcopal, Methodist, and Presbyterian, three Baptist, two Friend, and one Lutheran, Unitarian, and Swedenborgian houses.

43. Robertson, "Christian Newcomer," p. 120n.

44. See Table 17.

45. *The Methodist Magazine* 1 (April 1818): 159.

46. Quoted in Beirne, *St. Paul's Parish*, pp. 54–55.

47. *A Short Reply to Burk and Guy*, p. 14.

48. Scherer, "Ezekiel Cooper," p. 50.

49. "Journal of the Baltimore Annual Conference Minutes, 1800–1833," typescript located at DWyT, p. 54.

50. Ibid., pp. 102, 103, 106.

51. In addition to censuring Krebs, a resolution was passed disapproving "any official members or members of our Society attending D. Coker's meetings." Fielder Israel Papers, MS 488, Box 13, MdHi.

52. Leaders Meeting Minutes, 15 March 1820, "Methodist Episcopal Church Book, Baltimore City Station, 1818–1823," MdBL, pp. 4–5.

53. *The Methodist Magazine* 1 (April 1818): 158.

54. Ibid. (February 1818): 73–74.

55. Ibid. (December 1825): 487. For similar accounts of Methodist reporters emphasizing the orderliness of camp meetings, see *Wesleyan Repository* 3 (January 1823): 360; and *Mutual Rights and Christian Intelligencer* 3 (20 October 1829): 112.

56. See Table 17.

57. Walton, *Narrative*, pp. 2–3; Backus, *Revivals of Religion*, pp. 7–12; "Episcopalian" to the Reverend J.P.K. Henshaw, 17 February 1822, MdBD.

58. Walton, *Narrative*, p. 2.

59. Ibid., pp. 2–3; Backus, *Revivals of Religion*, pp. 7–12.

60. Ibid., pp. 10–11; Nevins, *Select Remains*, p. 15.

61. Backus, *Revivals of Religion*, pp. 10–11.

62. "Second Presbyterian Church Records, Baltimore, Volume 2," MdHi.

63. Backus, *Revivals of Religion*, p. 12.

64. Ibid.

65. Ibid.

66. Ibid., pp. 7–14.

67. Walton, *Narrative*, pp. 17–18.

68. Ibid., p. 21.

69. Nevins, Select Remains, p. 15.

70. For Nevins's attitude toward the new measure controversy, see Nevins, *Practical Thoughts*, pp. 91, 96.

71. In 1834, New York, with a population of 230,000, had 132 churches. Philadelphia, with 200,000, had 83 churches.

72. See Table 1.

73. "Baltimore City Station Methodist Episcopal Records," Microfilm real M 408, and "Annual Register for the Methodist Episcopal Church on Fells Point," Microfilm reel M 411, MdHR. See also chapter 1 above.

74. Annie Burns, "First Presbyterian Church Records," typescript located at DLC.

75. *The Methodist Magazine* 1 (April 1818): 159.

76. For the relationship between the rise of millennial expectations and interdenominational missionary associations, see chapter 7.

77. Bruce G. Laurie, "The Working People of Philadelphia, 1827–1853" (Ph.D. diss., University of Pittsburg, 1971), pp. 104–5; Russell E. Francis, "The Religious Revival of 1858 in Philadelphia," *The Pennsylvania Magazine of History and Biography* (January 1946), pp. 52–77; Handy, *History of the Church*, p. 195.

78. Johnson, *Shopkeeper's Millennium*, pp. 102–8.

79. James Kemp to William Duke, 26 June 1817. For optimistic reports on the spiritual health of St. Paul's parish, see also James Kemp to Joseph Jackson, 2 April 1813; 20 March 1815, MdBD.

Chapter 7. Ecumenism

1. Heiner, *Centenary Sermon*, pp. 23–24; Scharf, *History of Baltimore*, p. 43; Beirne, *St. Paul's Parish*, pp. 39–40.

2. Wills, *Historical Sketch*, pp. 40–42; Scharf, *History of Baltimore*, pp. 534–36; *Sesquicentennial St. Patrick's*, pp. 21–22.

3. Dennis Clark, "Baltimore, 1729–1829: The Genesis of a Community" (Ph.D. diss., The Catholic University, 1976), pp. iv–v, 382–88. See also Sam Bass Warner, *The Private City: Philadelphia in Three Periods of its Growth* (Philadelphia: University of Pennsylvania Press, 1968).

4. See Table 16.

5. *Federal Gazette* (15 November 1805); *Constitution of the Society for the Relief of the Poor Attached to the Methodist Episcopal Church of the City and Precincts of Baltimore, Baltimore, 1815,* pasted on "Minute and Account Book of Baltimore City Station, 1814–1815," Fielder Israel Papers, MS 488, MdHi; *Baltimore American* (12, 28, & 31 January 1817; 1 & 5 February 1817).

6. *Rules and Orders to be Observed by the Baltimore Benevolent Society Established in Order to Raise a Fund for the Members in Case of Sickness or Infirmity, and for Any Other Charitable Purposes to which the Members of Said Society May Hereafter Agree* (Baltimore: Sowers, 1796), pp. 3–15.

7. Methodist Episcopal Church Book, Baltimore City Station, 1818–23, MdBL, pp. 16–19.

8. For accounts of Baltimore Friends' association with American Indians, see *A Brief Account of the Proceedings of the Committee Appointed by the Yearly Meeting of Friends, Held in Baltimore, for Promoting the Improvement and Civilization of the Indian Natives* (Baltimore: Cole & Hewes, 1805); *Mission to the Indians: A Sketch of the Further Proceedings of the Committees Appointed by the Yearly Meeting of Friends of Pennsylvania and Maryland, for Promoting the Improvement and General Civilization of the Indian Natives in Some parts of North America* (London: W. Philips & George Yard, 1812), pp. 29–35; and Dunlap, *Quaker Education,* pp. 367–430.

9. *Constitution of the Maryland Society for Promoting the Abolition of Slavery* (Baltimore: Goddard & Angell, 1789), pp. 3–8; Tyson, *Life of Elisha Tyson,* pp. 19–36; *Letter from Granville Sharp, Esq. of London to the Maryland Society for Promoting the Abolition of Slavery and the Relief of Free Negroes and Others, Unlawfully Held in Bondage* (Baltimore: Yundt & Patton, 1793), pp. 3–11.

10. Ibid., pp. 461–58; *At A Meeting of the Maryland Society for Promoting the Abolition of Slavery Held at Baltimore, February 4, 1792* (Baltimore: Goddard & Angell, 1792), pp. 1–8.

11. Tyson, *Life of Elisha Tyson,* pp. 96–102; Bliss Forbush, *Moses Sheppard, Quaker Philanthropist of Baltimore* (Philadelphia: J. B. Lippincott Co., 1968), p. 62.

12. Maring, "Denominational History," p. 56; *Fourth Annual Report of the Baltimore Conference Missionary Society, Auxiliary to the Missionary Society of the Methodist Episcopal Church* (Baltimore: n.p., 1824); *Constitution of the Society for the Advancement of Christianity in the Diocese of Maryland* (Baltimore: J. Robinson, 1818), pp. 3–8.

13. *The Constitution of the Bible Society of Baltimore, Adopted at a Meeting of a Number of the Citizens Convened in the First Presbyterian Church on Monday, August 20, 1810* (Baltimore: B. W. Sower & Co., 1810), pp. 3–5; *The Ninth and Tenth Annual Reports of the Board of Managers of the Bible Society of Baltimore, for the Years 1819 and 1820* (Baltimore: J. Robinson, 1820), p. 11.

14. See Table 21.

15. *The First Annual Report of the Female Auxiliary Bible Society of Baltimore, Presented and Read at the Anniversary Meeting Held in First Presbyterian Church, April 3, 1815, with a Constitution and List of Subscribers and Benefactors* (Baltimore: R. W. Pomeroy, 1815), pp. 3–24.

16. Ibid.; *Report of the Board of Managers of the Bible Society of Baltimore, Presented at the Fifth Annual Meeting of the Society, September 15, 1815* (Baltimore: J. Robinson, 1815), pp. 3–4; *The Sixth Annual Report of the Bible Society of Baltimore, Presented at the Anniversary Meeting Held in the First Presbyterian Church on the Fourth Monday in September, 1816* (Baltimore: Schaeffer & Maund, 1817), pp. 3–6.

17. *The First Annual Report of the Female Auxiliary Bible Society,* pp. 3–24.

18. See the complete listing of the annual reports of these societies in the bibliography.

19. *The Sixth Annual Report of the Bible Society,* pp. 6–9; *Constitution of the Maryland Auxiliary Bible Society with an Address to the People of the State* (Baltimore: John D. Toy, 1821), pp. 7–12.

20. *Report of the Board of Managers of the Bible Society of Baltimore, Presented at the Eighth Anniversary of the Society, May 5, 1818* (Baltimore: J. Robinson, 1818), pp. 4–7; *The Ninth and Tenth Annual Reports of the Board of Managers of the Bible Society,* pp. 4–5.

21. *The Second Report of the Young Men's Bible Society of Baltimore, Auxiliary to the American Bible Society, Including the First Reports of the Ladies Branch of the Young Men's Bible Society, Presented to the Subscribers at Their Annual Meeting December 27, 1821, to which is Added a List of Subscribers* (Baltimore: William O. Niles, 1822), pp. 3–28.

22. Ibid., pp. 16–17; *Constitution, By-laws, and Rules of Order of the Ladies Branch Bible Society of Baltimore* (Baltimore: John D. Toy, 1821), pp. 3–12; *Constitution of the Maryland Auxiliary Bible Society,* pp. 1–6; *One Hundred and Ten Years of Bible Society Works in Maryland, 1810–1920* (Baltimore: Maryland Bible Society, 1921), pp. 21–25.

23. *The Ninth Report of the Young Men's Bible Society of Baltimore, Auxiliary to the American Bible Society, Including an Account of the Operation of the Bible Societies Throughout the State of Maryland, Also The Eighth Report of the Ladies Branch Bible Society, Presented at Their Annual Meeting, December 4, 1828* (Baltimore: John D. Toy, 1829), pp. 5–14.

24. *Journal of a Protestant Episcopal Convention 1828 Held in St. Anne's Annapolis, June 4–6, 1828* (Baltimore: J. Robinson, 1828), pp. 2–3; "Journal of the Baltimore Annual Conference, Methodist Episcopal Church, 1800–1833," typescript located at DwyT, p. 223; *The Ninth Report of the Young Men's Bible Society,* pp. 19–21.

25. *The Twelfth Report of the Young Men's Bible Society of Baltimore, Auxiliary to the American Bible Society, Also The Eleventh Report of the Ladies Branch Bible Society Presented at Their Annual Meeting, November 1831* (Baltimore: Lucas & Deaver, 1831).

26. *The First Annual Report of the Religious Tract Society of Baltimore for the Year Ending May 1817* (Baltimore: Richard J. Matchett, 1817), p. 4.

27. *Third Annual Report of the Religious Tract Society of Baltimore 1819 with the Constitution, an Appendix, and a List of Subscribers* (Baltimore: William Warner, 1819), p. 10.

28. Ibid., pp. 20–24.

29. Cook, *Early History of Methodist Sabbath Schools,* p. 7.

30. Ibid., pp. 11, 16.

31. Ibid., p. 16; *The First and Second Annual Reports of the Board of Delegates from the Male Sunday Schools of Baltimore* (Baltimore: J. Robinson, 1820), pp. 3–4; Gardner, *First Presbyterian,* p. 61.

32. *Constitution and Rules of the Baltimore Female Union Society for the Promotion of Sunday Schools* (Baltimore: John D. Toy, 1820), pp. 1–14.

33. *The First and Second Annual Reports of the Board of Delegates,* pp. 3–10; "Federal Hill Male Sunday School Minute Book, 1819–1827," MS 1108, MdHi; "Trinity Protestant Episcopal Church Register, 1815–1836," MS 850, MdHi.

34. The following descriptions are principally based upon the constitutions and annual reports of the Male and Female Sunday School Unions of Baltimore. A complete listing of the published annual reports is found in the bibliography.

35. *The Annual Report of the Asbury Sunday School Society, Presented at Their Annual Meeting Held in Light St. Church* (Baltimore: William Woody, 1823), p. 21.

36. *Third Annual Report of the Female Union Society for the Promotion of Sabbath Schools* (Baltimore: J. Robinson, 1820), p. 19.

37. These conclusions are based on a statistical study of attendance patterns obtained from the published annual reports. The persistence percentages were obtained by dividing the total number of children admitted each year by the number listed as regulars at the end of each year.

38. *The Fourth Report of the Baltimore Female Union Society for the Promotion of Sunday Schools, Read at Their Annual Meeting, November 5, 1821, to which is Annexed An Address Delivered on the Occasion by the Rev. Mr. Dashiell, Rector of St. John's Church, Baltimore* (Baltimore: Benjamin Edes, 1821), pp. 3–12.

39. *The Second Annual Report of the Female Union Society for the Promotion of Sunday Schools, Read at Their Annual Meeting, November 5, 1821, to which is Annexed An Address Delivered on the Occasion by the Rev. Mr. Dashiell, Rector of St. John's Church, Baltimore* (Baltimore: Benjamin Edes, 1821), pp. 3–12.

40. *The First and Second Annual Reports of the Board of Delegates,* p. 8.

41. *Third Annual Report of the Female Union Society,* p. 25.

42. See Tables 19–20.

43. *Report of the Directors of the Baltimore Female Mite Society for the Education of Heathen Children in India* (Baltimore: Benjamin Edes, 1818), pp. 3–14; *Final Report of the Baltimore Female Mite Society* [n.d.], MdHi, pp. 1–4.

44. Sharf, *History of Baltimore*, p. 577.

45. J. P. K. Henshaw, *A Plea for Seamen. A Sermon Preached on the Occasion of a Collection in Aid of Funds of the Seamen's Union Bethel Society in St. Peter's Church, Baltimore on the Evening of February 19, 1826* (Baltimore: William Woody, 1826), pp. 15, 27–28.

46. *Eighth Annual Report of the Seamen's Union Bethel Society of Baltimore, May 3, 1831* (Baltimore: John D. Toy, 1831), p. 2.

47. *Report of the Board of Managers of the Protestant Episcopal Female Society of Baltimore for the Dissemination of Religious Knowledge, Presented at the Annual Meeting of the Society, May 9, 1818* (Baltimore: J. Robinson, 1818), pp. 3–20; *First Annual Report of the Prayer Book and Homily Society of Maryland, 1819. With the Constitution, and a List of Subscribers and Benefactors . . .* (Baltimore: Wm. Warner, 1819), pp. 2–16; *Sixth Annual Report of the Board of Managers of the Protestant Episcopal Female Tract Society of Baltimore. Including the Constitution, By-Laws, etc., of the Juvenile Male Auxiliary Tract Society of Baltimore* (Baltimore: J. D. Toy, 1823), pp. 3–36.

48. Ibid., *First Annual Report of the Juvenile Female Auxiliary Tract Society of St. Paul's Church, Baltimore, April 5, 1823* (Baltimore: John D. Toy, 1823), pp. 3–5; "Trinity Church, Baltimore, Constitution of the Juvenile Prayer Book Society," 18 June 1822, MdBD; *Tenth Annual Report of the Protestant Episcopal Female Tract Society of Baltimore* [Baltimore: 1828]; *Fifteenth Annual Report of the Board of Managers of the Protestant Episcopal Female Tract Society of Baltimore, Including the Constitution and Bylaws* (Baltimore: J. D. Toy, 1830).

49. Clark, "Baltimore," p. 450.

50. Adams, *Life and Writings*, 1: 176–82.

51. *Constitution for the Government of the Maryland Auxiliary Society for Colonizing the Free People of Color of the United States* [Baltimore: 1817], Broadside.

52. Jared Sparks, *A Historical Outline of the American Colonization Society and Remarks on the Advantages and Practicability of Colonizing in Africa for the Free People of Color from the United States* (Boston: O. Everett, 1824), pp. 24, 26; also see Tyson, *Life of Elisha Tyson*, pp. 110–11.

53. Quote in Daniel Coker's *Journal*, pp. 45–46.

54. *Proceedings of a Meeting of the Friends of African Colonization Held in the City of Baltimore on the 17th of October, 1827* (Baltimore: n.p., 1827), pp. 5–17; *Address of the Board of Managers of the Maryland State Colonization Society* [n.p., n.d.], Rare Book Room, DLC, pp. 3–11.

55. *Constitution of the Temperance Societies Attached to the Methodist Episcopal Church of Baltimore City Station, Auxiliary to the Baltimore Temperance Society, with a List of Members* (Baltimore: John Toy, 1831), pp. 1–17; "MS Proceedings of the Baltimore Temperance Society," MdHi.

56. Sydney Ahlstrom, *A Religious History of the American People* (New Haven: Yale University Press, 1972), p. 385; Handy, *History of the Churches*; Winthrop S. Hudson, *Religion in America* (New York: Charles Scribner's Sons, 1973), p. 180.

57. See Griffin, *Their Brother's Keepers*; Foster, *An Errand of Mercy*; Lois W. Banner, "Religious Benevolence as Social Control: A Critique of an Interpretation," *Journal of American History* 60 (June 1973): 23–42; and Keller, *Second Great Awakening*.

58. See Table 21.

59. Foster, *An Errand of Mercy*, p. 115.

60. *Second Report of the Young Men's Bible Society*, p. 14.

61. Henshaw, *A Plea for Seamen*, pp. 11–12, 15.

62. *Report of Bible Society 1818*, p. 17.

63. *Social and Camp Meeting Songs*, p. 52.

64. *The Christian Orator, or a Collection of Speeches Delivered on Public Occasions before*

Religious Benevolent Societies (Baltimore: Lincoln & Edmounds for Cushing & Jewett, 1818), p. i.

65. *Second Annual Report of the Female Union Society*, p. 7.

66. Henshaw, *A Plea for Seamen*, pp. 5–6. Also see *The Ninth and Tenth Annual Reports . . . of the Bible Society*.

67. John George Schmucker, *The Prophetic History of the Christian Religion Explained, or A Brief Exposition of the Revelation of St. John, According to a New Discovery of Prophetic Times, by Which the Whole Chain of Prophecies is Arranged, and Their Certain Completion Proved from History Down to the Present, with Summary Views of Those not Yet Accomplished*, vol. 1 (Baltimore: Schaeffer & Mauns, 1817–21).

68. Markus M. Carll, *Discourse . . . at New Jerusalem Temple . . . August 4, 1816* (Baltimore, 1816). For other contemporary works on the coming kingdom, see Joseph Sutcliffe, *An Introduction to Christianity, Designed to Preserve Young People from Irreligion and Vice* (Baltimore: Edes, 1816); Robert Hawker, *Zion Pilgrims* (Baltimore: Toy for Martin, 1818), p. 197; *Return of the Jews and the Second Advent. Proved in Scripture by a Citizen of Baltimore* (Baltimore, 1817).

69. Mary Goddard, *Proposals to Amend and Perfect the Policy of the Government of the U.S.A., or the Fulfilling of the Prophecies in the Latter Days Commenced by the Independence of America . . .* (Baltimore, 1782), pp. 11, 15–16, 31–36; *Second Report of Young Men's Bible Society*, p. 12; *Minutes of the Baltimore Baptist Association Held by Appointment at Pleasant Valley, Washington Co., Maryland, September 6–8, 1816* (Baltimore, 1816); Hatch, *The Sacred Cause*.

Chapter 8. Schism

1. Joseph Bend, "The Necessity of Revelation," "The Success of Christianity and Evidence of its Truth," "The Argument from the Life and Character of Jesus," "The Argument from the Excellent Effects of Christianity," "The Argument from the Excellent Nature of Christianity," "The Objection from the Number, the Abilities, the Virtue of Infidels Refuted," "Objection against Christianity, from the Delay to its Publication, its Want of Universality, Removed," MS Bend Sermons, MdBD. See also *The Convention of the Protestant Episcopal Church in the State of Maryland to the Vestries and Other Members of Said Church* [Baltimore: 1794], pp. 1, 8.

2. James Jones Wilmer, *Consolation: Being a Replication to Thomas Paine and Others on Theologics* (Philadelphia: Woodward, 1794). See also James Muir, *Examination of the Principles Contained in the Age of Reason* (Baltimore: Adams, 1795).

3. *The Temple of Truth*, no. 5 (22 August 1801), pp. 90–91.

4. Ibid., no. 11 (17 October, 1801), pp. 174–75.

5. See *Journal of a Convention of the Protestant Episcopal Church 1803* (Baltimore: Sower, 1803), p. 6; *Christianity Displayed: or a Rational View of the Great Scripture Doctrine of Redemption and Salvation through Jesus Christ, Together with Some Practical Observations by a Citizen of Baltimore* (Baltimore: Craig, Engles, & Co., 1806), pp. 9–54; John B. Colvin, *An Essay Towards an Exposition of the Futility of Thomas Paine's Objections to the Christian Religion* (Baltimore: Fryer & Rider, 1807), pp. 3–48.

6. David Simpson, *A Plea for Religion and the Sacred Writings, Address to the Disciples of Thomas Paine and to Wavering Christians of Every Denomination* (Baltimore: Dobbin & Murphy for John Hagerty, 1807).

7. See chapter 7 above.

8. Wyatt, *The Monument*, pp. 64–65.

9. James Jones Wilmer, *A Sermon on the Doctrine of the New Jerusalem Church: Being the First Promulgated Within the United States of America. Delivered on the First Sunday in April, 1792, in the Court-house of Baltimore-Town, by James Wilmer, Examined and Approved for the Ministerial Office, by the Late Dr. Terrick, Bishop of London* (Baltimore: Goddard & Angell, 1792), pp. 8–15, 18–20; John Hargrove, *The Substance of a Sermon* (Baltimore: Warner & Hanna, 1803), pp. 11–12, 16; *A Compendious View and Brief Defense of the Peculiar and Leading*

Doctrines of the New Jerusalem Church (Baltimore: Samuel Sower, 1798), pp. xiv–xv, xxv.

10. Wilmer, *A Sermon*, p. 16; Block, *The New Church in the New World*, pp. 90–93.

11. For the unseemly side of the debate, see *An Investigation of the Doctrine of Baron Swedenborg, or of the Church Called New Jerusalem, in Two Letters Addressed to the Rev. Mr. H.*--- (Baltimore: Samuel Sower, 1799), pp. 3–46, passim; *A Short Reply to Burk and Guy*, pp. 5–23; *The War Dance*, pp. 5–12; *The War Dance, No. 2*, pp. 1–24.

12. Funk, *A Heritage to Hold*, pp. 6–7.

13. Edward Hinkley to Jared Sparks, 20 December 1816, quoted in Adams, *Life and Writings*, 1: 126.

14. Funk, *A Heritage to Hold*, pp. 6–7.

15. Edward Hinkley to Jared Sparks, 19 April 1817, quoted in Adams, *Life and Writings*, 1: 127–29.

16. Jared Sparks to Miss Storrow, 15 January 1819, quoted in ibid., pp. 136–37.

17. William E. Channing, *A Sermon Delivered at the Ordination of the Rev. Jared Sparks to the Pastoral Care of the First Independent Church of Baltimore, May 5, 1819* (Baltimore: J. Robinson, 1819).

18. Jared Sparks to Miss Storrow, 6 June 1819, quoted in Adams, *Life and Writings*, 1: 148.

19. Ibid., pp. 154, 176.

20. Samuel Miller, *The Difficulties and Temptations which Attended the Preaching of the Gospel in Great Cities: A Sermon Preached in the First Presbyterian Church, Baltimore, October 19, 1820 at the Ordination and Installation of Rev. William Nevins as Pastor of Said Church* (Baltimore: n.p., 1820).

21. Jared Sparks, *An Inquiry into the Comparative Moral Tendency of Trinitarian & Unitarian Doctrines; in a Series of Letters to the Rev. Dr. Miller of Princeton* (Boston: Wells & Lilly, 1823); Samuel Miller, *Letters on Unitarianism Addressed to the Members of the First Presbyterian Church, Baltimore* (Lexington, Ky.: T. T. Skillman, 1823).

22. Ibid., pp. 11–16.

23. Edward Everett to Jared Sparks, 13 April 1821, quoted in Adams, *Life and Writings*, pp. 180–81.

24. Wyatt, *Sermon Exhibiting Some of the Principal Doctrines*; George Weller, *A Reply to the Review of Dr. Wyatt's Sermon and Mr. Sparks Letters on the Protestant Episcopal Church which Originally Appeared in the Christian Disciple at Boston, and Subsequently in a Separate Form at Baltimore: in which it is Attempted to Vindicate the Church from the Charges of that Review by a Protestant Episcopalian* (Boston: R. P. & C. Williams, 1821); *An Address to the Ministers of the Unitarian Society By a Citizen of Baltimore* (Baltimore: T. R. Lusby, 1821); *An Affectionate Address to Trinitarians and Unitarians on the True and Only Object of Christian Worship, By a Layman of the New Jerusalem Church of Baltimore* (Baltimore: Lusby & Dornin, 1821).

25. Jared Sparks to the Reverend Charles Briggs, 22 August 1821, quoted in Adams, *Life & Writings*, 1: 185.

26. Jared Sparks to Miss Storrow, 29 October 1821, quoted in ibid., pp. 186–87.

27. Ibid., p. 182.

28. Funk, *A Heritage to Hold*, p. 17.

29. G. W. Burnap, *Lectures on the Doctrines of Christianity* (Boston: James Munroe & Co., 1848), p. iii.

30. G. W. Musgrave, *A Vindication of Religious Liberty, or the Nature and Efficiency of Christian Weapons* (Baltimore: Woods, 1834), p. 3. See also William Nevins, *Thoughts on Poperty* (New York, 1836).

31. *Strictures on the Establishment of Colleges; Pastoral Letter of the Ministers, Bishops, etc. of the Presbytery of Baltimore* (Baltimore, 1811); Joseph Bend to William Duke, 17 May 1806, MdBD; [Dubourg], *St. Mary's Seminary*.

32. See Joseph Agonito, "Ecumenical Stirrings: Catholic-Protestant Relations During the Episcopacy of John Carroll," *Church History* (Spring 1976).

33. *An Address from the Dissenting Brethen* (Baltimore: Hayes, 1804), pp. 1–20; *Minutes of the Baltimore Baptist Association Held . . . 1807*, pp. 6–8.

34. Wills, *Historical Sketch*, p. 57; Scharf, *History of Baltimore*, p. 559; *Minutes of the Baltimore Baptist Association, Held May 18, 1826 at Harford Church* (Rockville, Md.: n.p., 1826), p. 4.

35. Holdcraft, "Old Otterbein," typescript at MdHi; Table 1.

36. Hofmann, *History of Zion Church*, pp. 9–29; Wust, *Zion in Baltimore*, pp. 19–22.

37. Ibid., p. 51.

38. Ibid., p. 42.

39. Ibid., pp. 45–50, 52–53; "Record of Proceedings of the First English Evangelical Lutheran Church, Baltimore," typescript located at MdHi, pp. 2–9, 55.

40. For an in-depth account of Reuter's escapades in Baltimore before 1802, see Vincent J. Feecher, *A Study of the Movement for German National Parishes in Philadelphia and Baltimore, 1787–1802* (Romae: Apud Aedes Universitatis Gregorianae, 1955), pp. 58–87.

41. Ibid., p. 96.

42. *The State of Maryland Against the Vestry of St. Peter's*, pp. 59–67.

43. *A Correct Narrative*, pp. 5–22; *The State of Maryland Against the Vestry of St. Peter's*, pp. 67–72.

44. Feecher, *A Study*, pp. 276–77.

45. Heiner, *Centenary Sermon*, pp. 30–34.

46. Ibid., pp. 35–37.

47. For a discussion of the fundamental theological differences between the high- and low-church factions, see Rightmyer, "The Episcopate of Bishop Kemp," pp. 66–84.

48. Joseph Bend to William Duke, 9 June 1802, 27 July 1804, 22 February 1810; Joseph Bend to James Kemp, 2 July 1802, Elijah Rattoone to Bishop Claggett, 9 December 1803, MdBD.

49. Joseph Bend to William Duke, 27 December 1798; 27 January 1806; 14 May 1810; 3 September 1810; James Kemp, "Remarks Upon a 'Protest,'" MdBD.

50. Joseph Bend to Bishop Claggett, 28 July 1808, MdBD.

51. *To the Vestries of the Parishes of the Episcopal Church of Maryland* (Baltimore: J. Kingston, 1813); *Letter of the Rev. Mr. Jackson to Gregory Nazianzen, in Vindication of Himself Against the Aspersions Cast upon Him by the Vestry of St. Peter's Church* (Baltimore: J. Robinson, 1813), pp. 3–12; Dashiell, *An Address*, pp. 3–6.

52. *Journal of a Protestant Episcopal Convention 1812 Held in St. Paul's, Baltimore, May 20–23, 1812* (Baltimore: J. Robinson, 1812), pp. 8–10.

53. James Kemp to Joseph Jackson, 1 May 1813; 17 July 1813, MdBD; *Journal of a Protestant Episcopal Convention 1813, Held at St. Paul's Baltimore, June 9, 1813* (Baltimore: J. Robinson, 1813), p. 6; *Journal of a Protestant Episcopal Convention 1814, Held at St. Paul's, Baltimore, June 1–4, 1814* (Baltimore: J. Robinson, 1814), p. 9.

54. Dashiell, *An Address*, pp. 3–11; *A Letter in Answer to the Objections Offered to the Consecration of a Suffragan Bishop for the Diocese of Maryland, with Preliminary Remarks and Notes. By Bishop White, Bishop Hobart, and Bishop Moore* (Baltimore: J. Robinson, 1816), pp. 5–12.

55. Dashiell, *An Address*, p. 16; George Dashiell to Bishop Claggett, 14 September 1814.

56. For the details of the trial and aftermath, see chapter 3.

57. Dashiell, *An Address*, p. 24.

58. James Kemp to Joseph Jackson, 20 February 1816; 15 April 1816; 24 April 1817; James Kemp to Bishop Claggett, 15 April 1816; 23 April 1816; 13 July 1816; James Kemp to William Duke, 25 March 1817, MdBD.

59. J. P. K. Henshaw to Bishop Kemp, 5 January 1818, MdBD.

60. *Journal of a Protestant Episcopal Convention 1821, Held at St. Paul's, Baltimore, June 20–22, 1821* (Baltimore: J. Robinson, 1821), p. 27; *Address of the Board of Trustees of the Protestant Episcopal Theological Seminary of Maryland to Members of the Church in this Diocese* (Georgetown: J. C. Dunn, 1822); pp. 3–25; Kemp, *A Pastoral Letter*, pp. 3–28. See also James Kemp to Tench Tilghman, 19 November 1822; 3 December 1822, MdBD.

61. *Journal of a Protestant Episcopal Convention 1827*, pp. 31–34.

62. "Resolutions on the Death of Bishop Kemp, Minutes of a Meeting of Protestant Episcopal

Clergy in Baltimore on Tuesday, November 6, 1827," MdBD.

63. *Journal of a Protestant Episcopal Convention 1828*, pp. 12–13; *An Address to the Members of the Protestant Episcopal Church in Maryland on the Condition of the Diocese. By a Layman of Maryland* (Baltimore: Lucas & Deaver, 1829), pp. 3–37; *Journal of a Protestant Episcopal Convention 1829 Held in St. Paul's, Baltimore, June 17–20, 1829* (Baltimore: J. Robinson, 1829), pp. 7–9, 17; *Journal of a Protestant Episcopal Convention 1830, Held in St. Paul's, Baltimore, June 9–12, 1830* (Baltimore, 1830), pp. 7, 15, 17, 19, 20.

64. John M. Duncan, *A Plea for Ministerial Liberty. A Discourse Addressed by Appointment to the Directors and Students of the Theological Seminary of the Presbyterian Church at Princeton on the 17th of May 1824* (Baltimore: Cushing & Jewett, 1824), pp. 43–44.

65. Ibid., pp. 49–68, passim.

66. Samuel Miller, *The Utility and Importance of Creeds and Confessions: An Introductory Lecture Delivered at the Opening of the Summer Session of the Theological Seminary of the Presbyterian Church, Princeton, July 2, 1824* (Princeton: Borrestein, 1824).

67. John M. Duncan, *Remarks on the Rise, Use, and Unlawfulness of Creeds and Confessions of Faith in the Church of God* (Baltimore: Cushing & Jewett, 1825).

68. Samuel Miller, *A Letter to a Gentleman of Baltimore in Reference to the Case of the Rev. Mr. Duncan* (Baltimore: n.p. 1826); John M. Duncan, *A Reply to Dr. Miller's Letter to a Gentleman of Baltimore in Reference to the Case of Rev. Mr. Duncan* (Baltimore: Cushing & Jewett, 1826), and *Lectures on the General Principles of Moral Goverment as They Are Exhibited in the First Three Chapters of Genesis* (Baltimore: Cushing & Sons, 1832).

69. Duncan, *A Reply to Dr. Miller's Letter*, pp. 95–101.

70. Ibid., pp. 102–20.

71. Oliver Huckel, *The Faith of the Fathers and the Faith of the Future: Two Addresses Delivered at the One Hundredth Anniversary of the Associate Reformed Church of Baltimore* (Baltimore: The Arundel Press, 1897), pp. 12–21.

72. "Diary of R. H. Townshend," typescript located at Enoch Pratt Public Library, Baltimore, pp. 125–28; Phebe R. Jacobsen, *Quaker Records in Maryland* (Annapolis: Hall of Records Commission, Maryland, 1966), pp. 85–86; Bliss Forbush, *A History of Baltimore Yearly Meeting of Friends: 300 Years of Quakerism in Maryland, Virginia, D.C., and Central Pennsylvania* (Sandy Spring, Md.: Baltimore Yearly Society of Friends, 1972), pp. 64–70; Thomas, *Story of Baltimore Yearly Meeting*, pp. 51–55.

73. For the arguments of Methodist Episcopal reformers before 1824, see the pro-reform periodical *Wesleyan Repository*, 1821–24.

74. *Mutual Rights* 1 (August 1824): 3–10, 20–22.

75. "Journal of the Baltimore Annual Conference Methodist Episcopal Church, 1800–1833," typescript located at DWyT; *Mutual Rights* 3 (May 1827): 248–52.

76. Alexander McCaine, *The History and Mystery of the Methodist Episcopacy; or a Glance at the Institutions of the Church* (Baltimore: n.p., 1827); Thomas E. Bond, *Appeal to the Methodists in Opposition to the Changes Proposed in the Church Government* (Baltimore: Armstrong & Plaskit, 1827), pp. 2–69.

Conclusion. The Baltimore Awakening in Perspective

1. Among the numerous studies that adhere to this view are Robert Baird, *Religion in the United States of America* (1844; New York: Arno Press, 1969); Leonard Woolsey Bacon, *A History of American Christianity* (New York: The Christian Literature Co., 1897); William Warren Sweet, *The Story of Religion in America* (New York: Harper & Bros., 1930); Kenneth Scott Latourette, *A History of Christianity*, vol. 2 (New York: Harper & Row, Publishers, 1975); Winthrop Hudson, *Religion in America*, 3d ed. (New York: Charles Scribner's Sons, 1980); and Sydney E. Ahlstrom, *A Religious History of the American People*, 2 vols. (Garden City, N.Y.: Doubleday & Co., Inc., 1975). For the discussion of the development and limitations of this

historiography, see Douglas H. Sweet, "Church Vitality and the American Revolution: Historiographical Consensus and Thoughts Towards a New Perspective," *Church History* 45 (1976): 341–59.

2. Standard treatments of the eastern phase of the awakening include Charles Keller, *The Second Great Awakening in Connecticut* (New Haven: Yale University Press, 1942); David M. Ludlum, *Social Ferment in Vermont, 1791–1850* (New York: Columbia University Press, 1939); Sidney E. Mead, *Nathaniel William Taylor, 1786–1859: A Connecticut Liberal* (Chicago: University of Chicago Press, 1942); and Kenneth Silverman, *Timothy Dwight* (New York: Twayne Publishers, 1969). For western-style revivalism, see Catharine C. Cleveland, *The Great Revival in the West, 1797–1805* (Chicago: University of Chicago Press, 1916); John B. Boles, *The Great Revival, 1787–1805* (Lexington: University of Kentucky Press, 1972); Charles A. Johnson, *The Frontier Camp Meeting* (Dallas: Southern Methodist University Press, 1955); and Dickson D. Bruce, Jr., *And They All Sang Hallelujah* (Knoxville: University of Tennessee Press, 1974).

3. For the role of Charles Finney in shaping nineteenth-century revivalism, see William G. McLoughlin, Jr., *Modern Revivalism: Charles Grandison Finney to Billy Graham* (New York: Ronald Press Co., 1959); Bernard A. Weisberger, *They Gathered at the River* (Boston: Little, Brown and Co., 1958); Whitney R. Cross, *The Burned-Over District* (Ithaca: Cornell University Press, 1950); and Marian L. Bell, *Crusade in the City* (Lewisburg: Bucknell University Press, 1977).

4. See Keller, *Awakening in Connecticut*; McLoughlin, *Modern Revivalism*; Weisberger, *They Gathered at the River*; Ronald E. Osborn, *The Spirit of American Christianity* (New York: Harper Brothers, 1959); William W. Sweet, *Religion in the Development of American Culture, 1765–1840* (New York: Charles Scribner's Sons, 1952); Perry Miller, "From the Covenant to the Revival," in *The Shaping of American Religion*, vol. I, ed. James Ward Smith and A. Leland Jamison (Princeton: Princeton University Press, 1961).

5. Donald G. Mathews, "The Second Great Awakening as an Organizing Process, 1780–1830," *American Quarterly* 21 (Spring 1969): 23–43. Also see T. Scott Miyakawa, *Protestants and Pioneers: Individualism and Conformity on the American Frontier* (Chicago: University of Chicago Press, 1964).

6. Paul E. Johnson, *A Shopkeeper's Millennium: Society and Revivals in Rochester, New York, 1815–1837* (New York: Hill and Wang, 1978). For a related interpretation, see Bruce Laurie, *Working People of Philadelphia, 1800–1850* (Philadelphia: Temple University Press, 1980).

7. Mary Ryan, *Cradle of the Middle Class: The Family in Oneida County, New York, 1790–1865* (New York: Cambridge University Press, 1981).

8. Nancy F. Cott, "Young Women in the Second Great Awakening," *Feminist Studies* 3 (Fall 1975): 15–29, and *The Bonds of Womanhood* (New Haven: Yale University Press, 1977). Other provoking recent analyses include Lois W. Banner, "Religion and Reform in the Early Republic: The Role of Youth," *American Quarterly* 23 (December 1971): 677–95; Joan Jacobs Brumberg, *Mission for Life: The Story of the Family of Adoniram Judson* (New York: The Free Press, 1980); Anne C. Loveland, *Southern Evangelicals and the Social Order, 1800–1860* (Baton Rouge: Louisiana State University Press, 1980); and Donald G. Mathews, *Religion in the Old South* (Chicago: University of Chicago Press, 1977).

9. See John R. Bodo, *The Protestant Clergy and Public Issues, 1812–1848* (Princeton: Princeton University Press, 1954); Charles C. Cole, Jr., *The Social Ideas of the Northern Evangelists, 1820–1860* (New York: Columbia University, 1954); Charles I. Foster, *An Errand of Mercy: The Evangelical United Front, 1790–1837* (Chapel Hill: University of North Carolina Press, 1960); Clifford S. Griffin, *Their Brothers' Keepers: Moral Stewardship in the United States, 1800–1865* (New Brunswick: Rutgers University Press, 1960). For critiques of this interpretation, see Lois W. Banner, "Religious Benevolence as Social Control: A Critique of an Interpretation," *Journal of American History* 60 (June 1973): 23–42; and Lawrence F. Kohl, "The Social Control Concept and Jacksonian America," paper delivered at the Sixth Annual Meeting of the Society for Historians of the Early American Republic, Indianapolis, 1984.

10. Barbara Welter, "The Cult of True Womanhood: 1820–1860," *American Quarterly* 18, no.

2, pt. 1 (Summer 1966): 151–74.

11. Donald G. Mathews, "Women's History: Everyone's History," in *Women in the New World,* vol. 1 (Nashville: Abingdon Press, 1981); Timothy L. Smith, *Revivalism and Social Reform in Mid-Nineteenth Century America* (Nashville: Abingdon Press, 1957), and "Righteousness and Hope: Christian Holiness and the Millennial Vision of America, 1800–1900," *America Quarterly* 31 (Winter 1979): 21–45; Carroll Smith Rosenberg, *Religion and the Rise of the American City: The New York City Mission Movement, 1812–1870* (Ithaca: Cornell University Press, 1971), and "Beauty, the Beast, and the Militant Woman," *American Quarterly* 23 (1971): 562–84; Winthrop Hudson, "Early Nineteenth-Century Evangelical Religion and Women's Liberation," *Foundations* 23 (Spring 1980): 151–85; Page Putname Miller, "Women in the Vanguard of the Sunday School Movement," *Journal of Presbyterian History* 58 (Fall 1980): 311–25; Ann Firor Scott, "The Ever Widening Circle: The Diffusion of Feminist Values from Troy Female Seminary, 1822–1872," *History of Education Quarterly* 19 (Winter 1979): 3–25; Joe L. Kincheloe, Jr., "Transcending Role Restrictions: Women at Camp Meetings and Political Rallies," *Tennessee Historical Quarterly* 40 (Spring 1981): 158–69; Nancy A. Hardesty, *Women Called to Witness: Evangelical Feminism in the Nineteenth Century* (Nashville: Abingdon Press, 1984).

12. Cott, *Bonds of Womanhood*; Mary P. Ryan, "A Woman's Awakening: Evangelical Religion and the Families of Utica, New York, 1800–1840," *American Quarterly* 30 (Winter 1978): 602–23, and "Power of Women Networks," *Feminist Studies* 5 (Spring 1979); Ann Douglas, *The Feminization of American Culture* (New York: Alfred A. Knopf, 1977); Barbara Welter, "The Feminization of American Religion, 1800–1860," in Mary Hartman and Lois W. Banner, eds., *Clio's Consciousness Raised: New Perspectives on the History of Women* (New York, 1974); and Barbara L. Epstein, *The Politics of Domesticity* (Middletown: Wesleyan University Press, 1981); and Leonard I. Sweet, *The Minister's Wife: Her Role in Nineteenth-Century American Evangelicalism* (Philadelphia: Temple University Press, 1983).

13. For a critique of Finney's role in early-nineteenth-century revivalism, see Richard Carwardine, "The Second Great Awakening in the Urban Centers: An Examination of Methodism and the 'New Measures,'" *Journal of American History* 59 (September 1972): 327–40.

14. Richard Shiels, "The Myth of the Second Great Awakening," paper delivered at the meeting of the American Historical Association, Dallas, December 1977.

15. For an account of the shifting theological focus within mid-nineteenth-century Protestantism, see Douglas, *Feminization of American Culture*; and James Turner, *Without God, Without Creed: The Origins of Unbelief in America* (Baltimore: Johns Hopkins University Press, 1985).

Appendix A

1. For example, the U.S. Census of 1790 indicates that 41% of the population of Baltimore City was under age 16. Therefore, in order to account for children under this age within a particular denomination, multiply the number of adult members by 1.69. See *Century of Population Growth*, p. 214.

2. One illustration of a relatively low percentage of adult communicants is St. Paul's parish, which in 1809 listed 1,100 adult members and only 160 communicants. See *Journal of a Convention of the Protestant Episcopal Church, Maryland Diocese, in St. Paul's Church, Baltimore, June 13–16, 1810* (Baltimore: Robinson, 1810), p. 19.

3. Specifically, the average yearly adult mortality rate among members of First Baptist between 1796 and 1822 was 2.2%. The averages for Second Baptist between 1808 and 1830 and for Ebenzer and Third Baptist between 1819 and 1830 were 1.7% and 1.9% respectively. The aggregate average for all Baptist congregations was 2.0%. See the minutes of the Baltimore Baptist Association between 1796 and 1830. Also see Class Lists of 1803, Baltimore City Station Methodist Episcopal Records, Microfilm reel M 408, MdHR.

4. For figures regarding the total reported deaths in Baltimore, see Griffith, *Annals*, p. 294; and *A Series of Letters and Other Documents Relating to the Late Epidemic of Yellow Fever*

(Baltimore: published by the authority of the mayor, printed by William Warner, 1820).

5. A study comparing Cathedral pew holders with Catholic households baptizing infants produced the expected results: namely, that pew holders were more than twice as likely to be found in the upper occupational ranks as the parents of baptized children.

6. Data sources located at MdHi: First Methodist Episcopal Church Records, vol. 1, Baltimore City 14, pp. 213–64; St. Paul's Protestant Episcopal Parish, Register, vol. 1, 1790–1808, Baltimore City 27, pp. 382–437; St. Paul's Parish, Register, 1776–1837, Baltimore City 28, pp. 476–89, 545–46, 586–98; Trinity Church Register, 1805–17, Baltimore City 39, pp. 24–31, 56–59; St. Peter's Protestant Episcopal Church, Register, 1803–85, Baltimore City 35, pp. 20–26; First Presbyterian Church, 1767–1879, Baltimore City 20, pp. 16–95, 97–99, 111–16, 129–134; Second Presbyterian Church Records, pp. 74–81; First German Reformed Church, vol. 2, Baltimore City 12, pp. 3–11, 50–63, 89–97; German Evangelical Reformed (Old Otterbein) Church, 1798–1850, Baltimore City 23, pp. 74–84, 97–103, 114–118; Register of the Associate Reformed Congregation, 1812–65, Baltimore City 1, pp. 110–12, 125–28; New Jerusalem (Swedenborgian) Church, Register, Baltimore City 22, p. 21; First Unitarian Church Papers; Register of the Marriages performed by the Rev. Lewis Richard, 1784–1820, MS 690; Hofmann, *Zion church*, pp. 31–34. Data sources located at MdHR: Baltimore Monthly Meeting Marriages, 1794–1817, M 577; Baltimore City Station Methodist Episcopal Class Records, 1789–1813, M 408, Class Records, 1803–19, M 408, Class Register, 1825–30, M 409; East Baltimore Station Church Register, 1800–18, M 411, Church Register, 1818–36, M 411; Ebenezer Baptist Church Minutes, M 159; Cathedral of the Assumption of the Virgin Mary Register.

7. "Occupation and Ethnicity in Five Nineteenth-Century Cities: A Collaborative Inquiry," *Historical Methods Newsletter* 7 (June 1974): 174–216.

8. See Alan Pred, "Manufacturing in the American Mercantile City," *Asso. of American Geographers* 56 (June 1966): 307–38.

9. The Spearman coefficient is a rank-difference method of measuring correlation. In this case, the congregations are ranked first, second, third, etc., according to the percentages in Rank 3, and again according to the percentages in the category Not Listed. The differences in ranks for each congregation are squared, and the sums of the squares calculated. The coefficient rho is computed by the formula

$$\rho = 1 - \frac{6 \sum D^2}{N (N^2 - 1)}$$

where D^2 = the sum of squared differences between ranks, and N = the number of congregations. For the six congregations with sample sizes above 30, the Spearman rho coefficient is 0.83. When the German Lutheran congregation is omitted owing to an assumed language rather than economic bias, the Spearman rho coefficient is a perfect 1.00. The figures are indicative of a direct correspondence between the percentage not listed and the percentage listed as unskilled laborers. See J. P. Guilford, *Fundamental Statistics in Psychology and Education* (New York: McGraw-Hill Book Co., 1942), pp. 227–30.

SELECT BIBLIOGRAPHY

Part I
Primary Sources

NONPUBLISHED MATERIAL
Enoch Pratt Free Library, Baltimore
Diary of Richard H. Townsend

Hall of Records, Annapolis
African Methodist Episcopal Church Membership Roll.
Baltimore City Station Methodist Episcopal Records.
Baltimore City Tax Assessment List for 1804 and 1813.
Baltimore Monthly Meeting Minutes.
Baltimore Preparation Meeting Minutes.
Basilica of the Assumption of the Virgin Mary Burial Records.
East Baltimore Station Methodist Episcopal Records.
Ebenezer Baptist Church Papers.
First United Presbyterian Church Records.
Otterbein Evangelical Reformed Church Records.
St. Paul's Parish Records.
Trinity Episcopal Church Records.
Zion Lutheran Church Records.

Library of Congress, Washington, D.C.
Burns, Annie. Burial Records of the Light Street Methodist Episcopal Church.
———. Cathedral of the Assumption of the Virgin Mary Burial Records.
———. East Baltimore Station Methodist Episcopal Church Records.
———. First Presbyterian Church Records.
———. Index to Register of the Associate Reformed Congregation.
———. Index to Register of the First German Reformed Congregation.
———. Index to Register of St. Paul's Parish.
———. Index to Register of Zion German Lutheran.

———. Register of First English Lutheran Church.

Lovely Lane Methodist Museum, Baltimore
Isaac P. Cook Manuscripts.
Methodist Episcopal Church Book for Baltimore City Station, 1818–23, 1823–32.
Methodist Episcopal Trials and Judgments, 1816–22, City Station.
Minutes Quarterly Conference, East Baltimore Station 1801–07, 1816–19.
Proceedings and Accounts for Building Caroline Street Methodist Episcopal Church,
    24 February 1818.
Proceeds and Accounts for Building Eastern Avenue Methodist Episcopal Church.

Maryland Diocesan Archives, Baltimore
Account of Rev. William West with St. Paul's Parish, 1790.
Consecration of Churches and Establishment of Parishes, 1792–1898.
Constitution of the Juvenile Prayer Book Society of Trinity Church.
Ethan Allan Collection of Letters of Maryland Clergymen.
Inventory of Rev. William West, 1791.
James Kemp Lectures and Sermons.
Joseph Bend Sermons.
Maryland Society for Promoting Useful & Ornamental Knowledge Records.
Minutes of the Philokrisean Society.
Protest Against the Appointment of a Suffragan Bishop.
St. Paul's Church Communicant and Confirmation Records.
St. Paul's Church Sunday School Records.
William Duke Manuscripts.

Maryland Historical Society, Baltimore
Associate Reformed Congregation Register.
Baltimore City Tax Assessment List for 1815.
Christ Protestant Episcopal Church Register.
English Lutheran Church Proceedings.
Federal Hill Male Sunday School Minute Book.
Fielder Israel Papers.
First German Reformed Church Register.
First Independent Church Records.
First Methodist Episcopal Church Records.
First Presbyterian Church Register.
First Unitarian Church Papers.
German Evangelical Reformed (Old Otterbein) Church Register.
Maryland State Colonization Society Papers.
Methodist Burial Grounds in the Southern Precinct.

New Jerusalem (Swedenborgian) Church Register.

Plans of the First or "Old Round Top" Baptist Church.

Proceedings of the Baltimore Temperance Society.

Register of the Marriages Performed by the Rev. Lewis Richard.

St. Paul's Protestant Episcopal Church Register.

St. Peter's Protestant Episcopal Church Register.

Second Presbyterian Church Register.

Society for the Attainment of Useful Knowledge, Papers.

Society for the Relief of the Poor of the Methodist Episcopal Church, Records.

Trinity Protestant Episcopal Church Register.

Wesley Theological Seminary, Washington, D.C.

Journal of the Baltimore Annual Conference Methodist Episcopal Church, 1800–33.

PUBLISHED MATERIAL

Baltimore City Directories

The Baltimore Town and Fells Point Directory. The First Edition. By (William) Thompson and (James L.) Walker. Baltimore: printed for the Proprietors, by Pechin & Co., 1796.

The Baltimore Directory for 1799, Containing the Names, Occupations, and Places of Abode of the Citizens, Arranged in Alphabetical Order. By John Mullin. [Baltimore]: printed for the Editor, by Warner & Hanna, 1799.

The New Baltimore Directory, and Annual Register, for 1800 and 1801. [Baltimore]: by Warner & Hanna, Printers & Booksellers, 1800–01.

The Baltimore Directory for 1802. By Cornelius William Stafford. Baltimore: printed for the Editor, by John W. Butler, 1802.

The Baltimore Directory for 1803. By Cornelius William Stafford. Baltimore: printed for the Author, by John W. Butler, 1803.

The Baltimore Directory for 1804. By James Robinson. [Baltimore]: printed for the Publisher, by Warner & Hanna, at the Bible & Heart Printing Office, 1804.

The Baltimore Directory and Citizens Register for 1807. By James M'Henry. [Baltimore]: printed by Warner & Hanna, 1807.

The Baltimore Directory and Citizens Register for 1808, Containing the Names, Occupations, and Places of Abode, of the Inhabitants, Arranged in Alphabetical Order. To which Are Added, a Supplement and Several Useful Tables. Baltimore: printed for the Proprietor, 1808.

The Baltimore Directory for 1810. By William Fry. Baltimore: printed for the Publisher, G. Dobbin & Murphy, 1810.

Fry's Baltimore Directory for 1812. Baltimore: printed by B. W. Sower & Co. for the Publisher, 1812.

The Baltimore Directory and Register for 1814–15. By James Lakin. Baltimore: printed by J. C. O'Reilly, 1814.

The Baltimore Directory and Register for 1816. By Edward Matchett. Baltimore: printed and sold at the Wanderer Office, 1816.

The Baltimore Directory for 1817–18. Corrected Up to the First of April. To be Con-

tinued Annually in May. Baltimore: printed by James Kennedy, 1817.

The Baltimore Directory for 1819. Corrected Up to June 1819. Compiled by Samuel Jackson. Baltimore: printed by Richard J. Matchett, 1819.

The Baltimore Directory for 1822 & '23. Compiled by C. Keenan. Baltimore: printed by Richard J. Matchett, 1822.

Matchett's Baltimore Directory for 1824. Corrected Up to the First of February. Baltimore: printed and published by R. J. Matchett, 1824.

Matchett's Baltimore Directory for 1827. Baltimore: printed and published by R. J. Matchett, 1827.

Matchett's Baltimore Director [sic]. *Corrected Up to June 1829. Containing an Engraved Plan of the City.* Baltimore, 1829.

Matchett's Baltimore Director [sic]. Corrected Up to June 1831. Containing with (or without) A Plan of the City. Baltimore, 1831.

Matchett's Baltimore Director [sic]. *Corrected Up to May 1833. Containing with (or without) A Plan of the City, with References to Public Buildings.* Baltimore, 1837.

Denominational Publications

Baltimore Baptist Association. *Minutes of the Baltimore Baptist Association Held at Baltimore Town, August 8–10, 1795.* [Baltimore, 1795].

————. *Minutes of the Baltimore Baptist Association Held at Old Seneca, Montgomery Co., October 8–10, 1802.* Baltimore, 1802.

————. *Minutes of the Baltimore Baptist Association Held at the Meeting House, Sideling Hill, Bedford Co., Pa., October 12–14, 1804.* Baltimore, 1804.

————. *Minutes of the Baltimore Baptist Association Held at House of Jacob Dean, Trough Creek Valley, Huntington Co., Pa., October 11–13, 1805.* Baltimore, 1805.

————. *Minutes of The Baltimore Baptist Association Held at the Meeting House Condoway, Bedford Co., Pa., October 10–12, 1806.* Baltimore, 1806.

————. *Minutes of the Baltimore Baptist Association Held at Pleasant Valley, Wash. Co., Maryland, on October 16–18, 1807.* Baltimore, 1807.

————. *Minutes of the Baltimore Baptist Association Held in City of Washington, D.C., on October 14–17, 1808.* [Baltimore, 1808].

————. *Minutes of the Baltimore Baptist Association Held at First Baptist Meeting House, Baltimore City, October 12–15, 1809.* [Baltimore, 1809].

————. *Minutes of the Baltimore Baptist Association Held in the Brick Meeting House, Forks of Winter's Run, Harford County, State of Maryland, October 18–21, 1810.* Baltimore, 1810.

————. *Minutes of the Baltimore Baptist Association Held in the Baptist Meeting House Gunpowder, Baltimore Co., Maryland, October 17–20, 1811.* Baltimore, 1811.

————. *Minutes of the Baltimore Baptist Association Held at Sater's Meeting House, Baltimore County, Maryland, July 31–August 2, 1812.* Baltimore, 1812.

————. *Minutes of the Baltimore Baptist Association Held in the Second Baptist Meeting House in the City of Baltimore, on September 10–13, 1813.* Frederick Town, 1813.

————. *Minutes of the Baltimore Baptist Association Held in the Baptist Meeting House at Upper Seneca, Montgomery County, Maryland, on September 9–11, 1814.* Baltimore, 1814.

————. *Minutes of the Baltimore Baptist Association Held by Appointment, in the Baptist Meeting House at Old Seneca, Montgomery County, Maryland, September 8–10, 1815.* Baltimore, 1815.

————. *Minutes of the Baltimore Baptist Association Held by Appointment at Pleasant Valley, Washington Co., Maryland, September 6–8, 1816.* Baltimore, 1816.

————. *Minutes of the Baltimore Baptist Association Held by Appointment at Patapsco Meeting House, Baltimore Co., Maryland, September 10–12, 1818.* Baltimore, 1818.

————. *Minutes of the Baltimore Baptist Association Held by Appointment at Alexandria, District of Columbia, May 13–15, 1819.* Alexandria, 1819.

————. *Minutes of the Baltimore Baptist Association held by Appointment in the Meeting House of the First Baltimore Church, May 18–20, 1820.* Alexandria, 1820.

————. *Minutes of the Baltimore Baptist Association Held by Appointment in the Warren Meeting House, Baltimore Co., Maryland, May 17–19, 1821.* Baltimore, 1821.

————. *Minutes of the Baltimore Baptist Association Held by Appointment at Pleasant Valley, Washington Co., Maryland, May 16–18, 1822.* Washington City, 1822.

————. *Minutes of the Baltimore Baptist Association, Held by Appointment at Taneytown, Maryland, on May 16–18, 1823.* Baltimore, 1823.

————. *Minutes of the Baltimore Baptist Association Held in the Meeting House of the Ebenezar Church in the City of Baltimore, May 13–15, 1824.* Baltimore, 1824.

————. *Minutes of the Baltimore Baptist Association Held by Appointment at the Meeting House of the Bethel Church, Near Poolsville, Montgomery Co., Maryland, May 12–14, 1825.* Baltimore, 1825.

————. *Minutes of the Baltimore Baptist Association Held May 18, 1826 at Harford Church.* Rockville, Md., 1826.

————. *Minutes of the Baltimore Baptist Association Held by Appointment in Pleasant Valley, Washington Co., Maryland, May 17–20, 1827.* Rockville, Md., 1827.

————. *Minutes of the Baltimore Baptist Association, Held by Appointment at Black Rock, Maryland, May 15–17, 1828.* Washington City, 1828.

————. *Minutes of the Baltimore Baptist Association Held by Appointment in the Meeting House of the Second Church, Washington City, May 14–16, 1829.* Washington, 1829.

————. *Minutes of the Baltimore Baptist Association Held by Appointment in the Meeting House of the Church at Upper Seneca, Montgomery Co., Maryland, May 13–15, 1830.* [Baltimore, 1830].

————. *Minutes of the Baltimore Baptist Association Held by Appointment, with the Ebenezar Baptist Church, Baltimore May 14–16, 1835.* Rockville, 1835.

————. *Minutes of the Baltimore Baptist Association Held by Appointment at the Second Baptist Church, Baltimore, May 15–17, 1840.* Washington, 1840.

Baltimore Yearly Meeting Society of Friends. *The Revised Discipline.* Baltimore, 1794.

————. *A Brief Account of the Proceedings of the Committee Appointed by the Yearly Meeting of Friends, Held in Baltimore, for Promoting the Improvement and Civilization of the Indian Natives.* Baltimore, 1805.

————. *Discipline of the Yearly Meeting of Friends Held in Baltimore, 1806.* Baltimore, 1806.

————. *A Sketch of the Further Proceedings of the Committees Appointed by the Yearly Meeting of Friends of Pennsylvania & Maryland, for Promoting the Improvement and Gradual Civilization of the Indian Natives in Some Parts of North America.* London, 1812.

———. *Extracts from the Minutes of Baltimore Yearly Meeting, 1833.* [Baltimore, 1833].

———. *Memorials Concerning Several Ministers and Others, Deceased, of the Religious Society of Friends, Baltimore Yearly Meeting.* Baltimore, 1833.

Catholic Church in the U.S. Baltimore. *Pastoral Letter of the Most Rev. the Archbishop of Baltimore . . . in Council Assembled at Baltimore, in October, 1829, to the Roman Catholic Laity of the U.S.A.* Baltimore, 1829.

Minutes of the Annual Conferences of the Methodist Episcopal Church. vols. 1 & 2. New York, 1840.

Minutes of the Several Conversations between the Rev. Thomas Coke, LL.D., the Rev. Francis Asbury, and Others at a Conference begun in Baltimore, in the year 1784. Composing a Form of Discipline for the Minister, Preacher, and Other Members of the Methodist Episcopal Church in America. Philadelphia, 1785.

Protestant Episcopal Church Maryland Diocese. *Notices and Journals and Remains of Journals of the Two Preliminary Conventions of the Clergy and the First Five Annual Conventions and Two Adjourned Conventions of the Clergy and Laity of the Protestant Episcopal Church in the Diocese of Maryland in the Years 1783, 1784, 1785, 1786, 1787, 1788.* [Baltimore, 1788].

———. *At a Meeting or Convention of Clergy and Lay Delegates of the Protestant Episcopal Church of Maryland, at Baltimore, May 29, 1788.* [Baltimore, 1788].

———. *Journal of a Protestant Episcopal Convention, 1789, Held in St. Paul's, Baltimore, Tuesday June 2–Friday June 5, 1789.* Baltimore, 1789.

———. *Journal of a Protestant Episcopal Convention 1790, Held at Easton, May 27–31, 1790.* Wilmington, 1790.

———. *Journal of the Proceedings of a Convention of the Protestant Episcopal Church in Maryland, Held in Baltimore, June 16–18, 1791.* Baltimore, 1791.

———. *Journal of a Protestant Episcopal Convention 1793, Held at Easton, May 23–25, 1795.* Baltimore, 1793.

———. *Journal of the Proceedings of a Convention of the Protestant Episcopal Church in Maryland, Held in Baltimore, June 12–14, 1794.* Baltimore, 1794.

———. *The Convention of the Protestant Episcopal Church in the State of Maryland to the Vestries and Members of Said Church.* Baltimore, 1794.

———. *Journal of a Convention of the Protestant Episcopal Church, Held in Baltimore Town, May 28–30, 1795.* Baltimore, 1795.

———. *Journal of a Protestant Episcopal Convention 1796, Held at Easton, May 19–21, 1796.* Baltimore, 1797.

———. *Journal of a Convention of the Protestant Episcopal Church, Held in Baltimore, June 8–10, 1797.* Baltimore, 1797.

———. *Journal of a Protestant Episcopal Convention 1798, Held in Baltimore, May 31–June 2, 1798.* Baltimore, 1798.

———. *Journal of a Protestant Episcopal Convention 1799, Held at Easton, in Whitsun Week.* Easton, 1799.

———. *Journal of a Protestant Episcopal Convention 1800, Held at Baltimore, June 4–7, 1800.* [Baltimore, 1800].

———. *Journal of a Convention in Baltimore . . . May 27–29, 1801.* [Baltimore], 1801.

————. *Constitution and Canons of the Protestant Episcopal Church, Maryland.* Easton, 1802.

————. *Journal of a Convention in Easton, in Whitsun Week, 1802.* Easton, 1802.

————. *Journal of a Convention in Baltimore June 1–3, 1803.* Baltimore, 1803.

————. *Journal of a Protestant Episcopal Convention, 1804, Held in Baltimore, May 23–25, 1804.* Baltimore: Cole & Hewes, 1804.

————. *Articles of Religion of the Protestant Episcopal Church of Maryland Published at Easton, June 5, 1805.* Baltimore, 1805.

————. *Journal of a Convention at Easton . . . June, 1805.* Baltimore, 1805.

————. *Journal of the Protestant Episcopal Convention 1806, Held in St. Paul's, Baltimore, May 28–31, 1806.* Baltimore, 1806.

————. *Journal of a Protestant Episcopal Convention 1807 in St. Paul's Church, Baltimore, May 20–24, 1807.* Baltimore, 1807.

————. *Journal of a Protestant Episcopal Convention 1808, Held in Christ Church, Easton, June 8–10, 1808.* Baltimore, 1808.

————. *Rules and Regulations for the Conduct of the Society Formed at the Meeting of the Convention of the Protestant Episcopal Church in Maryland, which Assembled in Baltimore, May 20, 1807.* Baltimore, 1808.

————. *Constitution and Canons.* Baltimore, 1809.

————. *Journal of a Convention . . . Baltimore, May 24–27, 1809.* Baltimore, 1809.

————. *Journal of a Convention of the Protestant Episcopal Church, Maryland Diocese, in St. Paul's Church, Baltimore, June 13–16, 1810.* Baltimore, 1810.

————. *Journal of a Protestant Episcopal Convention 1811, Held at St. Paul's, Baltimore, June 19–21, 1811.* Baltimore, 1811.

————. *Journal of a Protestant Episcopal Convention 1812, Held in St. Paul's, Baltimore, May 20–23, 1812.* Baltimore, 1812.

————. *Journal of a Protestant Episcopal Convention 1813, Held at St. Paul's, Baltimore, June 9, 1813.* Baltimore, 1813.

————. *To the Vestries of the Parishes of the Episcopal Church of Maryland.* Baltimore, 1813.

————. *Journal of a Protestant Episcopal Convention 1814, Held at St. Paul's, Baltimore, June 1–4, 1814.* Baltimore, 1814.

————. *Journal of a Convention of Protestant Episcopal Church of Maryland, Held in Christ Church, Easton, May 17–19, 1815.* Baltimore, 1815.

————. *Journal of a Convention of the Protestant Episcopal Church 1816, Held in St. Anne's Church, Annapolis, June 12–14, 1816.* Annapolis, 1816.

————. *Journal of a Convention of Protestant Episcopal Church, June 4–6, 1817, Held in All Saints, Frederick Town.* Annapolis, 1817.

————. *Journal of a Convention of Protestant Episcopal Church, Held at St. Paul's, Baltimore, May 20–22, 1818.* Annapolis, 1818.

————. *Journal of a Protestant Episcopal Convention 1819, Held in St. Paul's, Baltimore, June 9–11, 1819.* Annapolis, 1819.

————. *Journal of a Protestant Episcopal Convention 1820, Held in St. Paul's, Baltimore, May 31–June 2, 1820.* Baltimore, 1820.

————. *Journal of a Protestant Episcopal Convention 1821, Held at St. Paul's, Baltimore, June 20–22, 1821.* Baltimore, 1821.

————. *A Compilation for the Use of the Members of the Protestant Episcopal Church in Maryland, Consisting of the Constitution and Canons of the Church in the United States*. Baltimore, 1822.

————. *Journal of a Protestant Episcopal Convention 1822, Held in St. John Church, City of Washington, June 5–8, 1822*. Washington, 1822.

————. *Journal of a Protestant Episcopal Convention, 1823, Held in St. Paul's Baltimore, May 28–30, 1823*. Baltimore, 1823.

————. *Journal of a Protestant Episcopal Convention 1824, Held in St. Paul's, Baltimore, June 16–18, 1824*. Baltimore, 1824.

————. *Journal of a Protestant Episcopal Convention 1825, Held in St. Paul's, Baltimore, June 1–3, 1825*. Baltimore, 1825.

————. *Journal of a Protestant Episcopal Convention 1826, Held in St. Paul's, Baltimore, May 24–26, 1826*. Baltimore, 1826.

————. *Journal of a Protestant Episcopal Convention 1827, Held in ChesterTown, Kent Co., June 13–15, 1827*. Baltimore, 1827.

————. *Journal of a Protestant Episcopal Convention 1828, Held in St. Ann's, Annapolis, June 4–6, 1828*. Baltimore, 1828.

————. *Journal of a Protestant Episcopal Convention 1829, Held in St. Paul's, Baltimore, June 17–20, 1829*. Baltimore, 1829.

————. *Journal of a Protestant Episcopal Convention 1830, Held in St. Paul's Baltimore, June 9–12, 1830*. Baltimore, 1830.

Protestant Episcopal Church of the U.S.A. *Journal of the Protestant Episcopal Church General Convention 1808, in Baltimore, May 17–26, 1808*. New York, 1808.

————. *The New Week's Preparation for a Worthy Receiving of the Lord's Supper, Recommended to the Devout in General, and Particularly to the Members of the Protestant Episcopal Church of the U.S.A.* Baltimore, 1803.

Books, Pamphlets, and Sermons of Baltimore Religious Leaders

Allison, Patrick. *Candid Animadversions on a Petition, Presented to the General Assembly of Maryland by the Rev. Dr. William Smith and the Rev. Thomas Gates, First Published in 1783, Together with a Series of Papers Addressed to the Citizens of Maryland*. Baltimore, 1793.

————. *A Discourse Delivered in the Presbyterian Church in the City of Baltimore, February 22, 1800, the Day Dedicated to the Memory of Gen. George Washington*. Baltimore, 1800.

————. *Thoughts on the Examination and Trials of Candidates for the Sacred Ministry*. Philadelphia, 1766.

Annan, Robert. *A Concise and Faithful Narrative of the Various Steps in which Led to the Unhappy Division which Hath Taken Place among the Members of the Associated Body in the U.S.* Philadelphia, 1789.

————. *Some Animadversions on Doctrines of Universal Salvation*. Philadelphia, 1787.

Annan, Robert, et al. *The Address and Petition of a Number of the Clergy of Various Denominations in the City of Philadelphia to the Senate and House of Representatives of the State of Pennsylvania Relative to the Passing of a Law against Vice and Immorality*. Philadelphia, 1793.

Asbury, Francis. *The Journal and Letters of Francis Asbury*. 3 vols. London, 1958.

Beasley, Frederick. *American Dialogues of the Dead and Dialogues of the American Dead*. Philadelphia, 1814.

————. *An Inaugural Discourse Delivered in Christ Church, Baltimore on December 31, 1809 at the Time in which the Author was Instituted as Associate Pastor into St. Paul's Parish.* Baltimore, 1810.

————. *A Search of Truth in the Science of the Human Mind.* Philadelphia, 1822.

————. *A Sermon Delivered at the Request of the Ladies Society Instituted for the Relief of Distressed Women and Children in the City of Albany, January 10, 1808.* Albany, 1808.

————. *A Sermon Delivered Before the Convention of the Protestant Episcopal Church in the State of New York, October 4, 1808.* New York, 1808.

————. *A Sermon Delivered Before the Convention of the Protestant Episcopal Church in the State of Pennsylvania, Held in St. James's Church, Philadelphia, May 3, 1815.* Philadelphia, 1815.

————. *A Sermon on Duelling, Delivered in Christ Church, Baltimore, April 28, 1811.* Baltimore, 1811.

Bend, Joseph. *A Discourse Delivered in Christ Church Baltimore, 1798.* Baltimore, 1798.

————. *A Discourse Delivered in St. Paul's Church Baltimore, on Sunday June 19, 1791, Recognizing the Relationship Subsisting Between the Congregation and the Author, in Consequence of his Recent Election to the Office of Rector of Said Church.* Baltimore, 1790.

————. *A Discourse Delivered in St. Paul's Church, Philadelphia, July 25, 1790 on Occasion of the Death of Mrs. Lucia Magaw, Wife of Rev. Samuel Magow.* Philadelphia, 1790.

————. *The Past History and Present Condition of the Institution of St. Paul's Parish.* Baltimore, 1860.

————. *Private Devotions Preparatory to the Sacrament.* Baltimore, 1802.

Bond, Thomas E. *Appeal to the Methodists in Opposition to the Changes Proposed in the Church Government.* Baltimore, 1827.

————. *The Economy of Methodism Illustrated and Defended in a Series of Papers.* New York, 1852.

————. *Methodism, Not a Human Contrivance; But a Providential Arrangement.* Baltimore, 1839.

Bourne, George. *Remarks Upon a Pamphlet Entitled 'An Inquiry into the Validity of Methodist Episcopacy.'* Baltimore, 1807.

Burnap, George W. *An Address Delivered At the Funeral of Henry Payson, on Sunday, December 28, 1845.* Baltimore, 1846.

————. *Lectures on the Doctrines of Christianity.* Boston, 1848.

————. *The Sphere and Duties of Women: A Course of Lectures.* Baltimore, 1848.

Carll, Markus M. *Discourse Delivered at the New Jerusalem Temple in Baltimore, on Sunday, August 4, 1816.* Baltimore, 1816.

Carroll, John. *A Discourse on General Washington Delivered in the Catholic Church of St. Peter's, in Baltimore, February 22, 1800.* Baltimore, 1800.

————. *John Carroll Bishop of Baltimore, to My Beloved Brethren ... February 22, 1797.* Baltimore, 1797.

Claggett, Thomas J. and Kemp, James. *A Pastoral Letter Address to the Members of the Protestant Episcopal Church, Maryland.* Baltimore, 1816.

Coate, Samuel. *The Beauties and Excellencies of True Religion.* Baltimore, 1808.

Coker, Daniel. *A Dialogue Between a Virginian and an African Minister*. Baltimore, 1810.

———. *Journal of Daniel Coker, A Descendant of Africa, From the Time of Leaving New York, in the Ship Elizabeth, Capt. Sebor, on a Voyage for Sherbro, in Africa in Company with Three Agents and about Ninety Persons of Color. With an Appendix*. Baltimore, 1820.

Cole, John. *The Divine Harmonist*. Baltimore, 1808.

———. *The Rudiments of Music, or an Introduction to the Art of Singing, Compiled for the Use of Schools*. Baltimore, 1810.

Colvin, John B. *An Essay Towards an Exposition of the Futility of Thomas Paine's Objections to the Christian Religion*. Baltimore, 1807.

Dashiell, George. *Address of the Vestry to the Members of the Protestant Episcopal Church of St. Peter's, in the City of Baltimore*. Baltimore, 1806.

———. *An Address to the Protestant Episcopal Church in Maryland*. [Baltimore, 1816].

———. *An Ordination Sermon Delivered on the 29th of April, 1821, in St. John's Church, Baltimore*. Baltimore, 1821.

———. *A Sermon Occasioned by the Burning of the Theatre in the City of Richmond, Virginia, on the 26th of December, 1811, Delivered in St. Peter's Church, Baltimore, January 12, 1812*. Baltimore, [1812].

Dreyer, John H. *Concord and Religion; the Principle Sources of Civil Prosperity: A Discourse Delivered in the German Reformed Church in the City of New York, on Sunday Succeeding the 36th Anniversary of the Independence of the U.S.* New York, 1812.

[Dubourg, William V.] *St. Mary's Seminary and Catholics at large Vindicated against the Pastoral Letter of the Ministers, Bishops, &c. of the Presbytery of Baltimore*. Baltimore, 1811.

Duke, William. *A Letter Addressed to the Rev. George Dashiell, Occasioned by a Pamphlet Entitled An Address to the Protestant Episcopal Church in Maryland*. Baltimore, 1816.

———. *Observations on the Present State of Religion in Maryland*. Baltimore, 1795.

Duncan, John, M. *A Discourse on the Official Relations of New Testament Elders*. 2d ed. Baltimore, 1853.

———. *The Eunuch's Confession; or Scriptural Views of the Sonship of Jesus Christ*. 2d ed. Baltimore, 1853.

———. *Lectures on the General Principles of Moral Government as They are Exhibited in the First Three Chapters of Genesis*. Baltimore, 1832.

———. *A Plea for Ministerial Liberty. A Discourse Addressed by Appointment to the Directors and Students of the Theological Seminary of the Presbyterian Church at Princeton, on the 17th of May, 1824*. Baltimore, 1824.

———. *Remarks on the Rise, Use, and Unlawfulness of Creeds and Confessions of Faith in the Church of God*. Baltimore, 1825.

———. *A Reply to Dr. Miller's Letter to a Gentleman of Baltimore in Reference to the Case of Rev. Mr. Duncan*. Baltimore, 1826.

Emory, John. *A Defense of 'Our Fathers' and of the Original Organization of the Methodist Episcopal Church against the Rev. Alexander McCaine, and Others*. New York, 1827.

————. *A Farther Reply to the 'Objections Against the Position of a Personal Assurance of the Pardon of Sin by a Direct Communication of the Holy Spirit' which Were First Published in the Christian Register, under the Signature of W. W. and Have Been Republished in 'An Essay, with Notes' by William White, D.D., Bishop of the Protestant Episcopal Church in Commonwealth of Pennsylvania*. Philadelphia, 1818.

Eyton, John. *The Lord Jesus Christ Sermon on the Mount, with a Course of Questions and Answers, Explaining that Valuable Position of Scripture, and Intended Chiefly for the Instruction of Young Persons*. Baltimore, 1808.

Finley, E. L. *An Address Delivered by Request of the Managers of the Sunday School Union, for the State of Maryland, at Their Annual Meeting, Held on the 30th Day of November 1830 in the First Presbyterian Church*. Baltimore, 1831.

Glendy, John. *An Oration on the Death of Lieut. Gen. George Washington Composed on the Special Request of the Commandant and His Brother Officers, of the Cantonment in the Vicinity, and Delivered at Staunton, on the 22nd Day of February, 1800*. Baltimore, 1835.

Griffith, Alfred, et al. *To the Members of the Baltimore Annual Conference*. Baltimore, 1824.

Hargrove, John. *Sermon Delivered in the City of Baltimore at the New Jerusalem Temple, October 20, 1814, the Day Appointed and Set Apart for Public Thanksgiving; for the Late Deliverance of that City and Its Inhabitants from the United & Formidable Attack of the British Fleet and Army*. Baltimore, 1814.

————. *A Sermon on the Object and Nature of Christian Worship; Delivered at the Opening of the New Jerusalem Temple, in Baltimore City, January 5, 1800*. Baltimore, 1800.

————. *A Sermon, on the Second Coming of Christ, and on the Last Judgment, Delivered December 25, 1804 Before Both Houses of Congress at the Capital in the City of Washington D.C.* Baltimore, 1805.

————. *Sermon on the True Nature of the Resurrection of Man, Delivered February 11, 1816 in the New Jerusalem Temple in the City of Baltimore on a Funeral Occasion*. Baltimore, 1816.

————. *The Substance of a Sermon of the Leading Doctrine of the New Jerusalem Church, Delivered December 26, 1802, Before the President of the United States, and Several Members of Congress at the Capital in the City of Washington*. Baltimore, 1803.

Helffenstein, Albert Sr. *Christian Baptism, According to the Authority of the Scriptures, Both in Relation to its Subjects and Mode*. Hagerstown, 1838.

Henshaw, John P. K. *Address of the Trustees of St. Peter's School to the Congregation of St. Peter's Church and To the Public*. [Baltimore, 1822].

————. *The Apostolic Ministry: Views of Calvin and the Early Presbyterians, Wesley, Clarke, and Others Upon the Apostolic Succession*. New York, n.d.

————. *Bishops Seabury and Porteus on Confirmation*. Annapolis, 1816.

————. *The Communicant's Guide; or An Introduction to the Sacrament of the Lord's Supper*. Baltimore, 1831.

————. *An Inquiry into the Meaning of the Prophecies Relating to the Second Advent of Our Lord Jesus Christ. Lecture, Delivered in St. Peter's Church, Baltimore*. Baltimore, 1842.

————. *The Minister's Instruction to the People on the Subject of Confirmation*. Baltimore, 1818.

————. *A Plea for Seamen. A Sermon Preached on the Occasion of a Collection in-aid of Funds of the Seamen's Union Bethel Society in St. Peter's Church, Baltimore on the Evening of February 19, 1826.* Baltimore, 1826.

————. *A Sermon Preached Before the Society for the Education of Pious Young Men for the Ministry of the Protestant Episcopal Church at the Fifth Annual Meeting, Held in Christ Church, Alexandria, on October 30, 1823.* Baltimore, 1823.

————. *Theology for the People: in a Series of Discourses on the Catechism of the Protestant Episcopal Church.* Baltimore, 1840.

————. *The Usefulness of Sunday Schools; A Sermon Preached at the Request of the American Sunday School Union, in St. Andrews Church, Philadelphia, May 20, 1833.* Philadelphia, 1833.

Holland, John. *Memoirs of the Life and Ministry of the Rev. John Summerfield, AM.* New York, 1846.

Hopkins, Gerard T. *A Mission to the Indians from the Indian Committee of Baltimore Yearly Meeting to Fort Wayne, in 1804.* Philadelphia, 1862.

Inglis, James. *A Discourse Delivered in the First Presbyterian Church, Baltimore, October 2, 1814, Before the Lt. Col., the Officers, and Soldiers, of the First Regiment of Artillery, 3D.B.M.M.* Baltimore, 1814.

————. *A Missionary Sermon, Delivered in Philadelphia, May 25, 1812 Before the General Assembly of the Presbyterian Church.* Baltimore, 1812.

————. *A Sermon Delivered in the First Presbyterian Church, Baltimore, on Thursday, September 8, 1808, Being a Day of Fasting, Humiliation, and Prayer Appointed by the General Assembly of the Presbyterian Church in the U.S.A.* Baltimore, 1808.

————. *Sermons of the Late Dr. James Inglis, Pastor of the First Presbyterian Church in Baltimore, With Some of His Forms of Prayer.* Baltimore, 1820.

Ireland, John. *Funeral Panegyric of George Washington, Pronounced February 22, 1800 in the United Churches of St. Paul's and Christ Church, Baltimore, State of Maryland.* London, 1802.

Jennings, Samuel K. *An Exposition of the Late Controversy in the Methodist Episcopal Church, of the True Objections of the Parties Concerned therein, and of the Proceedings by which Reformers were Expelled, in Baltimore, Cincinnati and Other Places . . . By a Layman.* Baltimore, 1831.

————. *Remarks Upon the Subject of Education to which Are Added the General Rules of the School Under the Appellation of the Asbury College.* Baltimore, 1824.

Johns, John. *An Address Delivered Before the American Whig & Cliosophic Societies of the College of New Jersey, September 29, 1840.* Princeton, 1840.

————. *The Annual Sermon Before the Bishops, Clergy and Laity Constituting the Board of Missions of the Protestant Episcopal Church in the U.S.A., Preached in St. Paul's, Boston, June 20, 1838.* New York, 1838.

————. *A Tract on Confirmation, Issued by the Executive Committee of the Mission & Tract Society of the Diocese of Virginia, 1848.* Richmond, 1848.

————. *Valedictory Discourse Delivered at Christ Church, Baltimore, October 3, 1832.* Baltimore, 1842.

Kemp, James. *An Address at Laying the Cornerstone of the New St. Paul's, May 4, 1814.* Baltimore, 1814.

————. *An Address Delivered at the Commencement of the General Theological Seminary of the Protestant Episcopal Church in the U.S., Held in Christ Church, N.Y., July 29, 1825.* New York, 1825.

————. *Address Delivered at the Opening of the Late Convention of the Protestant*

Episcopal Church in Maryland. Baltimore, 1823.

————. *An Address to Christians: To Which is Added the Evil of a Late Attendance on Divine Worship.* Baltimore, 1808.

————. *An Address to the Clergy and Laity of the Protestant Episcopal Church in Maryland.* Baltimore, 1816.

————. *A Charge Delivered to the Clergy of the Protestant Episcopal Church in the Diocese of Maryland at a Convention Held in the City of Washington, on June 5, 1822.* Washington, 1822.

————. *Episcopacy Vindicated: In a Series of Letters to the Rev. Dr. Miller.* New Haven, Conn., 1808.

————. *Familiar and Easy Guide to the Understanding of the Church Catechism, in Question and Answer, for the Use of Children.* Baltimore, 1818.

————. *Meditations, Resolutions, and Prayers Preparatory to Confirmation by a Father to a Beloved Daughter.* Baltimore, 1817.

————. *A Pastoral Letter Addressed to the Members of the Protestant Episcopal Church in the Diocese of Maryland.* Baltimore, 1822.

————. *A Pastoral Letter Address to the Members of the Protestant Episcopal Church in the Diocese of Maryland.* Baltimore, 1824.

————. *A Serious Caution Against Trusting to a Death-Bed Repentance. A Sermon.* Baltimore, 1815.

————. *A Sermon, Delivered in Christ Church, Cambridge, Maryland, February 22, 1800, Being the Day of Mourning Appointed by Congress for the Death of Gen. George Washington, Late President of U.S.* Easton, Md., 1800.

————. *A Sermon on the Christian Warfare Preached at the Funeral of the Rt. Rev. Dr. Claggett, Late Bishop of the Protestant Episcopal Church in Maryland, with a Sketch of His Character and a Short Account of His Life.* Baltimore, 1817.

————. *A Sermon on Loving One Another, Preached on the Anniversary of St. John the Evangelist, December 27, 1806, Before the Brethren of the Jerusalem Lodge.* Easton, Maryland, 1807.

————. *Sermon on the Manner in which the Gospel Was Established and the Christian Church Organized: Preached Before the General Convention of the Protestant Episcopal Church in U.S.A., on October 31, 1821.* Philadelphia: 1821.

————. *A Sermon on the Nature and Object of a Gospel Ministry.* Baltimore, 1803.

————. *Sermon Preached at the Institution of the Rev. James Kemp D.D. into the Rectorship of St. Paul's Church, Baltimore on February 7, 1813.* [Baltimore], 1813.

————. *Three Essays: On the Constitution of the Christian Church; the Succession in the Ministry; and Schism. With Notes.* Easton, Md., 1812.

————. *A Tract Upon Conversion with an Appendix Containing Six Important Questions with Answers on the Knowledge of the Forgiveness of Sins.* Baltimore, 1807.

Kemp, James and Brice, Nicolas. *To the Members of the Congregation of St. Paul's Church in the City of Baltimore. July 22, 1819.* Baltimore, 1819.

Lemmon, George. *A Sermon on the Following Words, "This is a Faithful Saying, and Worthy of All Acceptation, that Christ Jesus Came into the World to Save Sinners."* Baltimore, 1810.

Levington, William. *The Rector and Vestry of St. James' First African Protestant Episcopal Church in the City of Baltimore Would Most Respectfully Solicit the Attention of the Christian Public.* Broadside. Baltimore, 1829.

McCaine, Alexander. *The History and Mystery of the Methodist Episcopacy; or a*

Glance at the Institutions of the Church. Baltimore, 1827.

Morris, John G. *Fifty Years in the Lutheran Ministry.* Baltimore, 1878.

———. *Life Reminiscences of an Old Lutheran Minister.* Philadelphia, 1896.

Musgrave, George Washington. *A Vindication of Religious Liberty, or the Nature and Efficiency of Christian Weapons.* Baltimore, 1834.

Nevins, William. *Practical Thoughts.* New York, 1836.

———. *Select Remains of the Rev. William Nevins with a Memoir.* New York, 1836.

———. *Sermons by the Late Rev. William Nevins.* New York, 1837.

———. *Thoughts on Popery.* New York, 1836.

Osbourn, James. *Divine Communications, or Spiritual Letters to Faithful Men.* Baltimore, 1822.

———. *A Fac Simile, or the Religion of New England Portrayed, to which is Added a Journal of Facts.* Baltimore, 1836.

———. *A Glimpse of the Building of Mercy, or an Outline of the Mystical Building of Christ and a Sketch of the Ancient House of the Hagarenes, or the Tabernacle of Anti-Christ Portrayed.* Baltimore, 1831.

———. *The Lawful Captive Delivered, or the Life of the Author.* Baltimore, 1835.

———. *A Review of the Base Conduct of William Parkinson, Pastor of the First Baptist Church, New York City, as Exhibited in a Work Published against Him Last Fall Entitled "Imposture and Deception Detected and Exposed."* Baltimore, 1830.

———. *Spiritual Gleanings, or Celestial Fruit from the Tree of Life. Intended for the Use and Benefit of Sin-Sick Souls.* Baltimore, 1845.

———. *Strictures on a Piece Entitled "Zion's Call" Written by a Layman and Inserted in the Boston Recorder of January 26, 1825.* Baltimore, 1826.

———. *Thoughts of Peace in Time of War; or God's Goodness to Israel in the Worst of Times.* Baltimore, 1822.

Pissee, Thomas. *The Beauty of Holiness in the Common Prayer, as Set Forth in Four Sermons Preached at the Rolls Chapel in 1816, Adapted to the Protestant Episcopal Church in the U.S. with an Introduction by James Kemp.* Baltimore, 1817.

Reese, David, M. *A Letter to the Rev. G. W. Musgrave, "Bishop!" of the Third Presbyterian Church of Baltimore, Being a Reply to His Late Work Entitled "Polity of the Methodist Episcopal Church in the U.S.," &c.* Baltimore, 1843.

Reis, Edmund. *A Short Account of the Life, Conversion, and Death of Michael M'Comb.* Newburyport, 1815.

Roberts, George. *Strictures on a Sermon, Delivered by Nathan Williams, in Tolland on the Public Fast, April 17, 1793; with Some Observations on Dr. Huntington's Letters, Annexed to Said Sermon, in a Letter by George Roberts.* Philadelphia, 1794.

———. *The Substance of a Sermon (But Now More Enlarged) Preached to, and at the Request of the Conference of the Methodist Episcopal Church, Held in Baltimore, March, 1807.* Baltimore, 1807.

Sparks, Jared. *A Historical Outline of the American Colonization Society and Remarks on the Advantages and Practicability of Colonizing in Africa for the Free People of Color from the U.S.* Boston, 1824.

———. *An Inquiry into the Comparative Moral Tendency of Trinitarian and Unitarian Doctrines; in a Series of Letters to the Rev. Dr. Miller of Princeton.* Boston, 1823.

———. *Review of the Maryland Report on the Appropriation of Public Lands for*

Schools, as Drawn Up and Reported to the Senate of Maryland, January 30, 1821. Baltimore, 1821.

———. *A Sermon Preached in the Hall of the House of Representatives in Congress, Washington City, March 3, 1822, Occasioned by the Death of the Hon. William Pinkney, Late Member of the Senate of the U.S.* Washington, 1822.

Stockton, Thomas H. *A Discourse on the Life and Character of the Rev. Samuel K. Jennings, M.D., Delivered at St. John's Church, Liberty St., Baltimore, Sabbath evening, March 11, 1855.* Baltimore, 1855.

Stokes, Robert. *A Petition to the General Government from the People of Color. Also an Address to the Children of Israel.* Baltimore, 1833.

Summerfield, John. *Sermons and Sketches of Sermons by the Rev. John Summerfield with an Introduction by the Rev. Thomas E. Bond.* New York, 1845.

Walton, W. C. *Narrative of a Revival of Religion in the Third Presbyterian Church in Baltimore.* Northampton, 1826.

Wilmer, James Jones. *An Address to the Citizens of the U.S. on National Representation with a Sketch of the Origin of Government, and the State of Public Affairs.* Baltimore, 1796.

———. *The American Nepos: A Collection of the Lives of the Most Remarkable and the Most Eminent Men who Have Contributed to the Discovery, the Settlement, and the Independence of America, Calculated for the Use of Schools.* Baltimore, 1811.

———. *Consolation: Being a Replication to Thomas Paine and Others on Theologics.* Philadelphia, 1794.

———. *Man as He Is, and the World as It Goes.* Baltimore, 1803.

———. *Memoirs by James Wilmer.* Baltimore, 1792.

———. *Narrative Respecting the Conduct of the British from Their First Landing on Spesutia Island, till Their Progress to Harve de Grace.* Baltimore, 1813.

———. *A Sermon on the Doctrine of the New-Jerusalem Church: Being the First Promulgated within the United States of America, Delivered on the First Sunday of April, 1792, in the Courthouse of Baltimore-Town.* Baltimore, 1792.

Wyatt, William E. *An Address by the Rev. Dr. Wyatt Delivered Before the Protestant Episcopal Female Tract Society of Baltimore, 1821.* Baltimore, 1821.

———. *Christian Offices, for the Use of Families and Individuals; Compiled from the Liturgy of the Protestant Episcopal Church and from the Devotional Writings of Various Authors.* New York, 1850.

———. *A Discourse on Christian Education Delivered Before the Association of the Alumni of Columbia College at Their Anniversary, October 9, 1833.* Baltimore, 1833.

———. *The Gospel Preached to the Poor. A Sermon Preached at the Ordination Held by the Rt. Rev. James Kemp, D.D. in Trinity Chapel, St. James Parish, Baltimore Co., Sept. 17, 1823.* Baltimore, 1823.

———. *Sermon Exhibiting Some of the Principal Doctrines of the Protestant Episcopal Church of U.S. by which that Church is Distinguished from Other Denominations of Christians.* Baltimore, 1820.

Wyatt, William E., ed. *The Monument: A Small Selection from the Sermons of the Late Rt. Rev. James Kemp, D. D. Rector of St. Paul's Parish, Baltimore and Bishop of the Protestant Episcopal Church of Maryland, Together with the Address Delivered at the Time of his Interment by W. E. Wyatt. To Which are Prefixed Brief Biographical Notices of the Bishop.* Baltimore, 1833.

Publications of Voluntary Associations

BENEVOLENT SOCIETIES

Baltimore Benevolent Society. *Rules and Orders to be Observed by the Baltimore Benevolent Society Established in Order to Raise a Fund for the Mutual Relief for the Members Thereof in Case of Sickness or Infirmity, and for Any Other Charitable Purposes to Which the Members of Said Society May Hereafter Agree*. Baltimore, 1796.

Baltimore Charitable Marine Society. *Rules and Bylaws*. Baltimore, 1798.

———. *Rules and Bylaws*. Fells Point, Md., 1810.

Baltimore Female Humane Association. *A Brief Account of the Baltimore Female Humane Association Charity School of the City of Baltimore*. Baltimore, 1803.

Baltimore General Dispensary. *Rules and Bylaws of the Baltimore General Dispensary*. Baltimore, 1803.

Baltimore Vaccine Society for Exterminating the Small Pox. *The Constitution*. Baltimore, 1822.

Female Humane Association. *A Plan of the Female Humane Association Charity School*. Broadside. Baltimore, 1800.

Impartial Humane Society of Baltimore. *Acts Incorporating the Impartial Humane Society of Baltimore; Also the Bylaws for the Regulation of Said Society*. Baltimore, 1830.

Library Company of Baltimore. *A Catalogue of the Books, etc. Belonging to the Library Company of Baltimore, to which Are Prefixed the Act for the Incorporation of the Company, Their Constitution, Their Bylaws, and an Alphabetical List of the Members*. Baltimore, 1809.

Maryland Society for Promoting the Abolition of Slavery. *Constitution of the Maryland Society for Promoting the Abolition of Slavery*. Baltimore, 1789.

———. *At a Meeting of the Maryland Society for Promoting the Abolition of Slavery Held at Baltimore, February 4, 1792*. Baltimore, 1792.

Methodist Preacher's Aid Society of Baltimore. *Constitution and Bylaws of the Methodist Preacher's Aid Society of Baltimore, Incorporated February, 1827*. Baltimore, 1827.

St. Andrew's Society. *The Constitution and Rules of the St. Andrew's Society of Baltimore in the State of Maryland*. Baltimore, 1825.

Sandy Spring Boarding School Association. *Articles for the Government of the Sandy Spring Boarding School Association*. Baltimore, 1803.

Society for the Relief of the Indigent Sick. *Constitution and Bylaws of the Society for the Relief of the Indigent Sick*. Baltimore, 1834.

Society for the Relief of the Poor. *Constitution of the Society for the Relief of the Poor Attached to the Methodist Episcopal Church of the City and Precincts of Baltimore, Baltimore, 1815*. [Baltimore, 1815].

Society of St. George, in Maryland. *Rules and Constitution of the Society of St. George, in Maryland*. Baltimore, 1799.

Tammany Society. *Constitution of the Tammany Society, or Columbian Order, Established at Baltimore, in the Month of Corn, and Year of Discovery 314*. Baltimore, 1806.

Temperance Societies. *Constitution of the Temperance Societies Attached to the*

Methodist Episcopal Church of Baltimore City Station, Auxiliary to the Baltimore Temperance Society, with a List of Members. Baltimore, 1831.

Washington Society of Maryland. *The Constitution*. Baltimore, 1810.

Young Men's Society of Baltimore. *An Address to the Young Men of Baltimore: With the Constitution, Bylaws, and Standing Rules of the Young Men's Society of Baltimore, Instituted May, 1832*. Baltimore, 1832.

MISSIONARY SOCIETIES

Asbury Sunday School Society. *The Annual Report of the Asbury Sunday School Society, Presented at Their Annual Meeting Held in Light Street Church*. Baltimore, 1823.

Baltimore Conference Missionary Societies. *Fourth Annual Report of the Baltimore Conference Missionary Society, Auxiliary to the Missionary Society of the Methodist Episcopal Church*. Baltimore, 1824.

Baltimore Female Mite Society. *Report of the Directors of the Baltimore Female Mite Society for the Education of Heathen Children in India*. Baltimore, 1818.

———. *Final Report of the Baltimore Female Mite Society*. N. p., n.d.

Baltimore Female Union Society. *Constitution and Rules of the Baltimore Female Union Society for the Promotion of Sunday Schools*. Baltimore, 1820.

Bible Society of Baltimore. *An Address to the Public by the Board of Managers of the Bible Society of Baltimore, with the Constitution of the Society Annexed*. Baltimore, 1815.

———. *Communication Relative to the Progress of Bible Societies in the U.S., with Other Articles of Information Exhibiting the Progress of Similar Institutions*. Baltimore, 1813.

———. *The Constitution of the Bible Society of Baltimore, Adopted at a Meeting of a Number of the Citizens Convened in the First Presbyterian Church on Monday, August 20, 1810*. Baltimore, 1810.

———. *Report of the Board of Managers of the Bible Society of Baltimore, Presented at the Fifth Annual Meeting of the Society, September 25, 1815*. Baltimore, 1815.

———. *The Sixth Annual Report of the Bible Society of Baltimore, Presented at the Anniversary Meeting Held in the First Presbyterian Church on the Fourth Monday in September, 1816*. Baltimore, 1817.

———. *Report of the Board of Managers of the Bible Society of Baltimore, Presented at the Seventh Annual Meeting of the Society. September 25, 1817*. Baltimore, 1817.

———. *Report of the Board of Managers of the Bible Society of Baltimore, Presented at the Eighth Anniversary of the Society, May 5, 1818*. Baltimore, 1818.

———. *The Ninth and Tenth Annual Reports of the Board of Managers of the Bible Society of Baltimore, for the Years 1819 and 1820*. Baltimore, 1820.

Board of Delegates from the Male Sunday Schools of Baltimore. *The First and Second Annual Reports of the Board of Delegates from the Male Sunday Schools of Baltimore*. Baltimore, 1820.

Book Society of the Protestant Episcopal Church. *The Good Old Way, or the Religion of Our Forefathers as Explained in the Articles, Liturgy, and Homilies of the Church*. Annapolis, 1816.

Female Auxiliary Bible Society. *The First Annual Report of the Female Auxiliary Bible Society of Baltimore, Presented and Read at the Anniversary Meeting Held in First Presbyterian Church, April 3, 1815, with a Constitution and List of Subscribers and*

Benefactors. Baltimore, 1815.

————. *The Second Annual Report of the Female Auxiliary Bible Society of Baltimore, Presented at the Anniversary Meeting Held in the First Presbyterian Church, April 1, 1816.* Baltimore, 1816.

————. *The Third Annual Report of the Female Auxiliary Bible Society of Baltimore, Presented and Read at the Anniversary Meeting Held in the First Presbyterian Church, April 3, 1817.* Baltimore, 1817.

Female Union Society. *Constitution and Rules of the Baltimore Female Union Society for the Promotion of Sunday Schools. Baltimore, 1820.*

————. *Second Annual Report of the Female Union Society for the Promotion of Sabbath Schools, November 1819.* Baltimore, 1819.

————. *Third Annual Report of the Female Union Society for the Promotion of Sabbath Schools.* Baltimore, 1820.

————. *The Fourth Report of the Baltimore Female Union Society for the Promotion of Sabbath Schools, Read at Their Annual Meeting, November 5, 1821, to which is Annexed an Address Delivered on the Occasion by the Rev. Mr. Dashiell, Rector of St. John's Church, Baltimore.* Baltimore, 1821.

First Philosophical and Evangelical Association of Baltimore. *Constitution of the First Philosophical and Evangelical Association of Baltimore.* Baltimore, 1825.

Juvenile Female Auxiliary Tract Society of St. Paul's Church. *First Annual Report of the Juvenile Female Auxiliary Tract Society of St. Paul's Church, Baltimore, April 5, 1823.* Baltimore, 1823.

Ladies Branch Bible Society of Baltimore. *Constitution, Bylaws, and Rules of Order of the Ladies Branch Bible Society of Baltimore.* Baltimore, 1821.

Maryland Auxiliary Bible Society. *Constitution of the Maryland Auxiliary Bible Society with an Address to the People of the State.* Baltimore, 1821.

Maryland Auxiliary Society. *Constitution for the Government of the Maryland Auxiliary Society for Colonizing the Free People of Color of the U.S.* Broadside. [Baltimore, 1817].

Maryland Colonization Society. *Proceedings of a Meeting of the Friends of African Colonization Held in the City of Baltimore, on the 17th of October, 1827.* Baltimore, 1827.

Maryland State Colonization Society. *Address of the Board of Managers of the Maryland State Colonization Society.* [Baltimore, 1833].

————. *Address of the Maryland State Colonization Society, to the People of Maryland; with the Constitution of the Society, and an Appendix.* Baltimore, 1831.

Prayer Book and Homily Society of Maryland. *The Constitution of the Prayer Book and Homily Society for Maryland.* Baltimore, 1818.

————. *First Annual Report on the Prayer Book and Homily Society of Maryland, 1819, with the Constitution and a List of Subscribers and Benefactors.* Baltimore, 1819.

————. *The Fifth Annual Report of the Prayer Book and Homily Society of Maryland, 1823, with the Constitution and List of Officers.* Baltimore, 1823.

Protestant Episcopal Church Society for the Education of Pious Young Men for the Ministry of the Protestant Episcopal Church. *Circular of the Education Society, to its Members and Auxiliaries, October, 1825.* [Baltimore, 1825].

Protestant Episcopal Female Society of Baltimore. *Report of the Board of Managers of the Protestant Episcopal Female Society of Baltimore for the Dissemination of Reli-*

gious Knowledge, Presented at the Annual Meeting of the Society, May 9, 1818. Baltimore, 1818.

Protestant Episcopal Female Tract Society of Baltimore. *Sixth Annual Report of the Board of Managers of the Protestant Episcopal Female Tract Society of Baltimore, Including the Constitution, By-Laws, etc., of the Juvenile Male Auxiliary Tract Society of Baltimore.* Baltimore, 1823.

———. *Tenth Annual Report of the Protestant Episcopal Female Tract Society of Baltimore.* [Baltimore, 1828].

———. *Fifteenth Annual Report of the Board of Managers of the Protestant Episcopal Female Tract Society of Baltimore, Including the Constitution and Bylaws.* Baltimore, 1830.

———. *Seventeenth Annual Report of the Board of Managers of the Protestant Episcopal Female Tract Society of Baltimore, with an Address by the Rev. Dr. Wyatt.* Baltimore: 1832.

———. *Series of Tracts Nos. 33, 34.* Baltimore, n.d.

———. *Series of Tracts Nos. 35, 36, 37, 38, 40.* Baltimore, 1822.

———. *Series of Tracts Nos. 41, 42, 43, 44, 45, 49, 50.* Baltimore, 1823.

———. *Series of Tracts Nos. 53, 54, 55, 56, 57, 58, 59.* Baltimore, 1824.

Religious Tract Society of Baltimore. *The First Annual Report of the Religious Tract Society of Baltimore for the Year Ending May, 1817.* Baltimore, [1817].

———. *Third Annual Report of the Religious Tract Society of Baltimore 1819 with the Constitution, an Appendix, and a List of Subscribers.* Baltimore, 1819.

Seamen's Union Bethel Society. *Eighth Annual Report of the Seamen's Union Bethel Society of Baltimore, May 3, 1831.* Baltimore, 1831.

Society for the Advancement of Christianity. *Constitution of the Society for the Advancement of Christianity in the Diocese of Maryland.* Baltimore, 1818.

Young Men's Bible Society and Ladies Branch Bible Society. *The Second Report of the Young Men's Bible Society of Baltimore, Auxiliary to the American Bible Society, Including the First Reports of the Ladies Branch of the Young Men's Bible Society, Presented to the Subscribers at Their Annual Meeting December 27, 1821, to which is Added a List of Subscribers.* Baltimore, 1822.

———. *The Ninth Report of the Young Men's Bible Society of Baltimore, Auxiliary to the American Bible Society, Including an Account of the Operations of Bible Societies Throughout the State of Maryland, Also the Eighth Report of the Ladies Branch Bible Society, Presented at Their Annual Meeting, December 4, 1828.* Baltimore, 1829.

———. *The Twelfth Report of the Young Men's Bible Society of Baltimore, Auxiliary to the American Bible Society, Also the Eleventh Report of the Ladies Branch Bible Society, Presented at Their Annual Meeting, November 1831.* Baltimore, 1831.

Local Congregations

Associate Reformed Presbyterian Church. *The Baltimore Collection of Sacred Musik, Selected and Compiled Under the Direction of a Committee of the Associate Reformed Presbyterian Church of Baltimore.* Baltimore, 1819.

Baltimore City Station Methodist Episcopal Church. *Address of the Male Members of the Methodist Episcopal Church in Baltimore to Their Brethren Throughout the United States.* [Baltimore, 1827].

———. *Local Preachers Plan of Appointments for the Country for 1832 & 3.* Broadside. [Baltimore], 1881.

———. *Regulations Adopted to Carry More Fully into Effect in this Station, the Spirit and Design of the Discipline of the Methodist Episcopal Church.* Broadside. [Baltimore, n.d.].

First Baptist Church, Baltimore. *An Address from the Dissenting Brethren.* [Baltimore, 1804].

———. *A Church Covenant; Including a Summary of the Fundamental Doctrines of the Gospel, Compiled by Elkanah Holmes, and Unanimously Adopted by the First Baptist Church, Baltimore.* Baltimore, 1818.

———. *The Members' Manual of the First Baptist Church in Baltimore.* Baltimore, 1836.

New Jerusalem Church, Baltimore. *A Copy of the Incorporated Constitution of the New Jerusalem Church.* Baltimore, 1804.

St. James African Protestant Episcopal Church, Baltimore. *Origination, Constitution, and By-Laws of St. James First African Protestant Episcopal Church in the City of Baltimore, Adopted April 23, 1829.* Baltimore, 1829.

St. John's Methodist Protestant Church, Baltimore. *Amended Charter of Incorporation of St. John's Methodist Protestant Church, Liberty ST., Baltimore,* 1829.

St. Patrick's Church, Baltimore, Cantiques Francais, A L'Usage du Catechisme de L'Eglise de Saint-Patrick de Baltimore. Baltimore, 1798.

St. Paul's Church, Baltimore. *A Form of Prayer, Compiled for the Use of the Congregations of St. Paul's and Christ Church, Baltimore, on Wednesday, May 9, Being the Day Recommended by the President of the U.S., to be Offered as a Day of Solemn Humiliation, Fasting, and Prayer.* Baltimore, 1798.

———. *To the Pewholders and Other Contributors of St. Paul's Parish in Baltimore County.* Baltimore, 1804.

NEWSPAPERS AND PERIODICALS

Baltimore American and Daily Commercial Advertiser

Baltimore Daily Intelligencer

Baltimore Federal Intelligencer

Federal Republican and Baltimore Telegraph

Maryland Gazette or Baltimore Advertiser

Maryland Journal and Baltimore Advertiser

Methodist Magazine and Quarterly Review

Mutual Rights

Mutual Rights and Christian Intelligencer

Temple of Truth

Unitarian Miscellany

Wesleyan Repository

MISCELLANEOUS PUBLICATIONS

Address to the Clergy of the U.S. on the Theological Writings of the Hon. Emanuel Swedenborg, by a Member of the New Jerusalem Church. Bedford, Pa., 1824.

An Address to the Members of the Protestant Episcopal Church in Maryland on the

Condition of the Diocese, by a Layman of Maryland. Baltimore, 1829.

An Address to the Ministers of the Unitarian Society, by a Citizen of Baltimore. Baltimore, 1821.

Affectionate Address to Trinitarians and Unitarians on the True and Only Object of Christian Worship, by a Layman of the New Jerusalem Church of Baltimore. Baltimore, 1821.

Barnes, Robert, comp. *Marriages & Deaths from the Maryland Gazette, 1727–1839.* Baltimore, 1973.

Boehm, Henry. *Reminiscences, Historical and Biographical, of Sixty-four Years in the Ministry.* Edited by J. B. Wakeley. New York, 1866.

Bushnell, Horace. *Christian Nurture. Introduction by Luther A. Weigle.* New Haven, 1950.

Channing, William E. *A Sermon Delivered at the Ordination of the Rev. Jared Sparks to the Pastoral Care of the First Independent Church of Baltimore, May 5, 1819.* Baltimore, 1819.

Christianity Displayed: or a Rational View of the Great Scripture Doctrine of Redemption and Salvation through Jesus Christ, Together with Some Practical Observations, by a Citizen of Baltimore. Baltimore, 1806.

A Collection of Religious Tracts from Different Authors, Republished for the Information and Serious Perusal of All Sober Inquirers. Baltimore, 1799.

Colvin, John B. *An Essay Towards an Exposition of the Futility of Thomas Paine's Objections to the Christian Religion.* Baltimore, 1807.

A Compendious View and Brief Defense of the Peculiar and Leading Doctrines of the New Jerusalem Church. Baltimore, 1798.

[Cook, Isaac]. *Early History of Methodist Sabbath Schools in Baltimore City and Vicinity; and Other Interesting Facts Concerned Therewith, compiled by a Sabbath Scholar of 1817.* Baltimore, 1877.

A Correct Narrative of the Rise and Progress of the Religious Fracas which Took Place in the German Roman Catholic Church of St. John in Baltimore on Wednesday the 30th of May, 1804. Baltimore, 1804.

Darton, William. *A Present for a Little Girl.* Baltimore, 1806.

A Defense of the Pastoral Letter. Baltimore, [1811].

de Tocqueville, Alexis. *Democracy in America.* Vol. 1. The Henry Reeve Text. Revised by Francis Bowen. Edited by Philips Bradley. New York, 1956.

Extracts of Letters Containing Some Account of the Work of God Since 1800. New York, 1805.

F---L---, esq. *The Female Friend; or the Duties of Christian Virgins; to which is Added Advice to a Young Married Lady.* Baltimore, 1809.

Finley, James B. *Selected Chapters from the History of the Wyandot Mission at Upper Sandusky, Ohio.* Cincinnati, 1840.

Grellett, Stephen. *Memoirs of the Life and Gospel Labours of Stephen Grellett.* 2 vols. Edited by Benjamin Seabohm. Philadelphia: 1860.

Griffith, Thomas W. *Annals of Baltimore.* Baltimore: 1833.

———. *Sketches of the Early History of Maryland.* Baltimore: 1821.

Hawley, William. *A Letter to the Rt. Rev. Bishop Kemp of the Protestant Episcopal Church in the Diocese of Maryland, and an Address to the Congregation of St. John's Church, in the City of Washington; Occasioned by the Appointment of a Unitarian*

Chaplain to Congress, on Sunday, December 9, 1821. Washington: 1822.

Head of Families at the First Census of the United States Taken in the Year 1790: Maryland. Baltimore: 1952.

Hollingsworth, Francis. *Explanation of the Reasons and Motives for the Advice Given on a Late Occasion*. Baltimore: 1815.

An Investigation of the Doctrine of Baron Swedenborg, or of the Church called New Jerusalem, in Two Letters Addressed to the Rev. Mr. H---, by a Inhabitant of Baltimore County. Baltimore, 1799.

Jennings, William. *An Address to the Catholic Voters of Baltimore*. Baltimore, 1828.

The Key of Paradise, Opening the Gate to Eternal Salvation. Baltimore, 1804.

Latrobe, John H. B. *Picture of Baltimore Containing a Description of All Objects of Interest in the City; and Embellished with Views of the Principal Public Buildings*. Baltimore, 1832.

A Letter in Answer to the Objections Offered to the Consecration of a Suffragan Bishop for the Diocese of Maryland, with Preliminary Remarks and Notes. Baltimore, 1816.

Letter of the Rev. Mr. Jackson to Gregory Nazianzen, in Vindication of Himself Against the Aspersions Cast Upon Him by the Vestry of St. Peter's Church. Baltimore, 1813.

Letter to a Deist in Baltimore Showing the Futility of His Arguments Against the Scriptures in His Address to the Unitarian Ministers. Frederick, Maryland, 1822.

McElhiney, Rev. Mr. *Address Before the Female Tract Society of Baltimore, May 10, 1826*. Baltimore, 1826.

Maryland Tax List, Baltimore County 1783. Baltimore, 1970.

Miller, Samuel. *Christian Weapons Not Carnal, But Spiritual: A Sermon Delivered in the Second Presbyterian Church, Baltimore, October 13, 1826, at the Installation of Rev. John Breckinridge, as Colleague with the Rev. John Glendy in the Pastoral Charge of the Said Church*. Princeton, 1826.

———. *The Difficulties and Temptations which Attended the Preaching of the Gospel in Great Cities; A Sermon Preached in the First Presbyterian Church, Baltimore, October 19, 1820 at the Ordination and Installation of Rev. William Nevins as Pastor of Said Church*. Baltimore, 1820.

———. *A Letter to a Gentleman of Baltimore in Reference to the Case of the Rev. Mr. Duncan*. Baltimore, 1826.

———. *Letters on Unitarianism Addressed to the Members of the First Presbyterian Church, Baltimore*. Lexington, Ky., 1823.

———. *The Life of Samuel Miller*. vol. 2. Philadelphia, 1869.

———. *The Utility and Importance of Creeds and Confessions: an Introductory Lecture Delivered at the Opening of the Summer Session of the Theological Seminary of the Presbyterian Church, Princeton, July 2, 1824*. Princeton, 1824.

A Portrait of the Evils of Democracy Submitted to the Consideration of the People of Maryland. Baltimore, 1816.

[Pratt, John Horace]. *An Authentic Account of All the Proceedings on the Fourth of July, 1815, with Regard to Laying the Cornerstone of the Washington Monument, Now Erecting in the City of Baltimore, Accompanied by an Engraving of the Monument*. Baltimore, 1815.

The Prodigal Daughter. Baltimore, 1822.

Prophetic Conjectures on the French Revolution and Other Recent and Shortly Ex-

pected Events, Extracted from Archbishop Brown, 1551, Rev. J. Knox, 1572 (and others). Baltimore, 1794.

Protestant Episcopal Theological Seminary. *Address of the Board of Trustees of the Protestant Episcopal Theological Seminary of Maryland to Members of the Church in This Diocese*. Georgetown, 1822.

Review of the Rev. Jared Sparks' Letters on the Protestant Episcopal Church in Reply to the Rev. Dr. Wyatt's Sermon. Baltimore, 1820.

A Rod for Dr. Kemp; or An Examination of His Tract Upon Conversion; Proving that He Is at Variance with the Scriptures, His Own Church, and Himself, by a Layman. Baltimore, 1807.

St. Mary's Seminary, Baltimore. List of the Superiors, Professors, and Students Ordained, 1791–1916. New York, 1917.

A Series of Letters and Other Documents Relating to the Late Epidemic of Yellow Fever. Baltimore, 1820.

A Short Reply to Burk and Guy with Some Ripe Fruit for a Friend to Truth, by a Layman of the New Jerusalem Church. Baltimore, [1804].

Simpson, David. *A Plea for Religion and the Sacred Writings Addressed to the Disciples of Thomas Paine and to Wavering Christians of Every Denomination*. Baltimore, 1807.

Snodgrass, J. E. *Sketches of the Baltimore Pulpit*. Baltimore, 1843.

The State of Maryland Against the Vestry of St. Peter's Church, in which a Portion of the Members of the Church Prayed for a Mandamus to be Directed to the Vestry. Baltimore, 1817.

Stephens, Daniel. *The Character of a Faithful and Evangelical Ministry; A Sermon Preached at the Opening of the Convention of the Diocese of Maryland, on May 20, 1818*. Baltimore, 1818.

Steuart, John. *An Address Delivered at Rev. Mr. Duncan's Church on the Anniversary of the Infant School Society of Baltimore, at the Request of the Managers*. Baltimore, 1831.

Strictures on the Establishment of Colleges, Particularly that of St. Mary, in the Precincts of Baltimore, as Formerly Published in the Evening Post and Telegraph. Baltimore, 1806.

To the Citizens of Baltimore. Baltimore, 1822.

Tocsin! or Another Alarm Addressed to the Members of the Episcopal Church in the U.S., Respecting the Character and Views of the Self-Styled Evangelical Clergy, Designed as a Supplement to a Recent 'Letter' by 'Monitor,' by a Friend of Ecclesiastical Unity and Order. Baltimore, 1824.

Tyng, Stephen H. *Attachment to the Redeemer's Kingdom. A Sermon Preached Before the Prayer Book and Homily Society in Christ Church, Baltimore, June 2, 1825*. Georgetown, 1825.

Tyson, John S. *Life of Elisha Tyson the Philanthropist, by a Citizen of Baltimore*. Baltimore, 1825.

U.S. Bureau of the Census. *A Century of Population Growth*. Washington, D.C., 1909.

———. *Negro Population in the United States 1790–1815*. Washington, D.C., 1918.

———. *Return of the Whole Number of Persons Within the Several Districts of the United States, According to "An Act Providing for the Second Census or Enumeration of the Inhabitants of the United States." Passed February the twenty-eighth, one thousand eight hundred. Printed by Order of the House of Representatives.* Washington, 1802.

————. *U.S. Bureau of the Census, Fifth Census, or Enumeration of the Inhabitants of the United States, as Corrected at the Department of State, 1830.* Washington, D.C., 1832.

Varle, Charles. *A Complete View of Baltimore with a Statistical Sketch.* Baltimore, 1833.

The War Dance No War Whoop: Being a Reply to a Letter from the Rev. George Dashiell to an Invisible Clergyman, alias the Rev. on the Subject of the War Dance as Lately Exhibited in Baltimore, by the Chiefs and Warriors of the Osage Tribe of Indians, in a Series of Letters, by a Layman. [Baltimore, 1804].

The War Dance No War Whoop.... No. 2. Baltimore, 1804.

[Weller, George]. A Reply to the Review of Dr. Wyatt's Sermon and Mr. Sparks' Letters on the Protestant Episcopal Church, which Originally Appeared in the Christian Disciple at Boston, and Subsequently in a Separate Form at Baltimore: in which It Is Attempted to Vindicate the Church from the Charges of that Review by a Protestant Episcopalian. Boston, 1821.

Wirt, William. *Address to the People of Maryland.* Baltimore, 1833.

Worthington, Charles. *Reply to the Circular of the Vestry of St. Peter's Church.* Baltimore, 1815.

Part II
Secondary Sources

CHURCH HISTORIES

Allen, Ethan. *The Garrison Church, Sketches of the History of St. Thomas' Parish.* New York: James Pott & Co., 1898.

Armstrong, James E. *History of the Old Baltimore Conference from the Planting of Methodism in 1773 to the Division of the Conference in 1851.* Baltimore: King Brothers, 1907.

Backus, John C. *An Historical Discourse: on Taking Leave of the Old Edifice of the First Presbyterian Congregation in Baltimore.* Baltimore: J. W. Woods, 1860.

————. *Revivals of Religion in the Presbyterian Churches of Baltimore.* Philadelphia: J. M. Wilson, 1858.

Baker, Gordon Pratt, ed. *Those Incredible Methodists, History of the Baltimore Conference of the United Methodist Church.* Nashville: The Parthenon Press, 1972.

Baltimore Methodism and the General Conference of 1908. Baltimore: Baltimore City Missionary and Church Extension Society, 1908.

Beirne, Francis F. *St. Paul's Parish: A Chronicle of the Mother Church.* Baltimore: Horn-Shafer Co., 1967.

Boulden, James E. P. *The Presbyterians of Baltimore; Their Churches and Historic Grave Yards.* Baltimore: William K. Boyle & Son, 1875.

Brief Sketch of the History of Christ Church Baltimore; Prepared on the Occasion of the Celebration of the 26th Anniversary, Sunday, January 9, 1898 of the First Services Held in the Present Christ Church. [Baltimore, 1898].

[Buck, George]. *Christ Protestant Episcopal Church, Baltimore, Maryland.* [Baltimore]: Meyer & Thalheimer, 1937.

Evans, Hugh Davey. *The Future of St. Paul's Parish, Baltimore*. Baltimore: n.p., 1878.

Fein, Isaac M. *The Making of an American Jewish Community*. Philadelphia: Jewish Publication Society, 1971.

Forbush, Bliss. *A History of Baltimore Yearly Meeting of Friends: 300 Years of Quakerism in Maryland, Virginia, D.C., and Central Pennsylvania*. Sandy Spring, Maryland: Baltimore Yearly Society of Friends, 1972.

Funk, Rebecca. *A Heritage to Hold in Fee 1817–1917, First Unitarian Church of Baltimore*. Baltimore: Garamond Press, 1962.

Gardner, John H., Jr. *The First Presbyterian Church of Baltimore: A Two Century Chronicle*. Baltimore: First Presbyterian Church, 1962.

Grammer, Julius E. *Statistics of St. Peter's Protestant Episcopal Church, Baltimore*. Baltimore: J. B. Rose & Co., 1868.

Guttmacher, Adolf. *A History of the Baltimore Hebrew Congregation, 1830–1905*. Baltimore: The Lord Baltimore Press, 1905.

Heiner, Elias. *Centenary Sermon Delivered in the Second Street Church on Sabbath Morning December 8, 1850 on the Occasion of the Centenary Celebration of the First German Reformed Congregation of Baltimore*. Baltimore: Sherwood & Co., 1850.

Historical Souvenir of the Fourteenth Triennial Sessions of the General Synod of the Reformed Church in the U.S. Published and Presented with the Compliments of the Fourteen Reformed Churches of Baltimore, Maryland. Baltimore: Stonebraker Bros., [1902].

Hodges, J. S. B. *The Future of St. Paul's Parish, Baltimore, A Sermon Preached in St. Paul's Church, Septuagesima Sunday, January 27, 1878*. Baltimore: St. Paul's Vestry, 1878.

Hofmann, Julius. *A History of Zion Church of the City of Baltimore 1755–1897*. Baltimore: C. W. Schneidereith & Sons, 1905.

Holdcraft, Paul E. "The Old Otterbein Church Story." (August 1959). Translated by August C. Wagner. Typescript located at the Maryland Historical Society, Baltimore, Md.

Huckel, Oliver. *The Faith of the Fathers and the Faith of the Future: Two Addresses Delivered at the One Hundredth Anniversary of the Associated Reformed Church of Baltimore*. Baltimore: The Arundel Press, 1897.

Kates, Frederick W., comp. *Bridge Across Four Centuries: The Clergy of St. Paul's Parish Baltimore, Maryland 1692–1957*. Baltimore: St. Paul's Parish, 1957.

Kinsolving, Arthur B. *A Short History of St. Paul's Parish, Baltimore, Maryland, 1692–1939*. Baltimore: n.p., 1939.

Manual of the First Presbyterian Church, Baltimore, 1877. Baltimore: William K. Boyle & Son, 1877.

Memorial Volume of the Centenary of St. Mary's Seminary of St. Sulpice, Baltimore, Maryland, 1791–1891. Baltimore: John Murphy & Co., 1891.

150th Anniversary of the East Baltimore Station Methodist Episcopal Church, Souvenir Program and Historical Sketch. Baltimore: n.p., 1923.

Poultney, James W., and Sinclair, James E. *A Short History of St. Paul's Parish, Baltimore, Maryland*. Baltimore: Fosnot & Williams Co., 1934.

Ridgely, Helen West. *The Old Brick Churches of Maryland*. New York: Anson D. F. Randolph & Co., 1894.

[Riordan, Michael J., comp.]. *Cathedral Records: From the Beginning of Catholicity in*

Baltimore to the Present Time. Baltimore: The Catholic Mirror Publishing Co., 1906.

Savage, Frederick A. *A Brief History of Christ Church, Baltimore*. Baltimore: n.p., 1944.

Sesquicentennial Saint Patrick's Parish, Baltimore, Maryland, 1792–1942. Baltimore: St. Mary's Industrial School, 1942.

Smith, Joseph T. *Eighty Years Embracing a History of Presbyterianism in Baltimore, with an Appendix*. Philadelphia: Westminster Press, 1899.

Society of Friends, Baltimore Monthly Meeting. *A Sketch of 'Old Town' Meeting House, Baltimore, and Some Account of Its Occupants, as Read on Its 100th Anniversary*. Baltimore: J. W. Woods, 1881.

Thomas, Anna Braithwaite. *The Story of the Baltimore Yearly Meeting from 1672 to 1938*. Baltimore: Weant Press Inc., 1938.

Thompson, Henry F. *Sketch of the Early History of St. Paul's Parish, Baltimore*. Baltimore: John S. Bridges & Co., 1906.

Walker, Thomas H. *One Hundred Years of History, 1802–1902: Second Presbyterian Church, Baltimore, Maryland*. Baltimore: Sun Printing Office, 1902.

Warren, Paul C. *One Hundred Fifty Years, 1803–1953. The Second Presbyterian Church of Baltimore*. Baltimore: Horn-Shafer Co., 1953.

Weishampel, J. F., Jr. *History of Baptist Churches in Maryland Connected with the Maryland Baptist Union Association*. Baltimore: published by Weishampel, 1885.

Wheeler, Robert C. *135th Anniversary Caroline Street Methodist Church*. Baltimore: Hamilton Printing Co., 1953.

Wills, Joshua. *Historical Sketch of the Second Baptist Church of Baltimore, Maryland*. Philadelphia: George F. Lasher, 1911.

Wood, Joseph R. *A Historical Sketch of Exeter Street Methodist Episcopal Church, Baltimore, Maryland*. Baltimore: Thomas & Evans, 1902.

Wust. Klans. G. *Zion in Baltimore 1755–1955: The Bicentennial History of the Earliest German-American Church in Baltimore, Maryland*. Baltimore: published by Zion Church of the City of Baltimore, 1955.

GENERAL

Adams, Herbert B. *The Life and Writings of Jared Sparks*. Boston: Houghton, Mifflin & Co., 1893.

Ahlstrom, Sidney. *A Religious History of the American People*. New Haven: Yale University Press, 1972.

Allen, Ethan. *Clergy in Maryland of the Protestant Episcopal Church Since the Independence of 1783*. Baltimore: James S. Waters, 1860.

Bell, Marion L. *Crusade in the City: Revivalism in Nineteenth-Century Philadelphia*. Lewisburg, Pa: Bucknell University Press, 1977.

Block, Marguerite Beck. *The New Church in the New World: A Study of Swedenborgians in America*. New York: Henry Holt & Co., 1932.

Boles, John B. *The Great Revival, 1787–1805*. Lexington: University of Kentucky Press, 1972.

Browne, Gary L. *Baltimore in the Nation, 1789–1861*. Chapel Hill: University of North Carolina Press, 1980.

Bruce, Dickson, Jr. *And They All Sang Hallelujah: Plain Folk Camp-Meeting Religion, 1800–1845.* Knoxville: University of Tennessee Press, 1974.

Bucke, Emory S., ed. *The History of American Methodism.* 3 vols. New York: Abingdon Press, 1964.

Carroll, Kenneth Lane. *Quakerism on the Eastern Shore.* Baltimore: Maryland Historical Society, 1970.

The Catholic Encyclopedia. vol. 2. New York: Encyclopedia Press, Inc., 1913.

Colhouer, Thomas H. *Sketches of the Founders of the Methodist Protestant Church, and its Bibliography.* Pittsburgh: Methodist Protestant Book Concern, 1880.

Cott, Nancy. *The Bonds of Womanhood.* New Haven: Yale University Press, 1977.

Cross, Whitney R. *The Burned-Over District: The Social and Intellectual History of Enthusiastic Religion in Western New York, 1800–1850.* Ithaca: Cornell University Press, 1950.

Cunz, Dieter. *The Maryland Germans, A History.* Port Washington, Kennikat Press, 1972.

Douglas, Ann. *The Feminization of American Culture.* New York: Alfred A. Knopf, 1977.

Drake, Thomas E. *Quakers and Slavery in America.* New Haven: Yale University Press, 1950.

Drinkhouse, Edward. *History of Methodism Reform.* Norwood, Mass.: J. S. Cushing & Co., 1899.

Dunlap, William C. *Quaker Education in Baltimore and Virginia Yearly Meetings with an Account of Certain Meetings of Delaware and the Eastern Shore Affiliated with Philadelphia.* Philadelphia: University of Pennsylvania, 1936.

Ellis, John Tracy. *American Catholicism.* 2d ed., rev. Chicago: University of Chicago Press, 1969.

Epstein, Barbara. *The Politics of Domesticity: Women, Evangelicalism, and Temperance in Nineteenth Century America.* Middletown: Wesleyan University Press, 1981.

Feecher, Vincent J. *A Study of the Movement for German National Parishes in Philadelphia and Baltimore, 1787–1802.* Romae: Apud Aedes Universitatis Gregorianae, 1955.

Forbush, Bliss. *Moses Sheppard, Quaker Philanthropist of Baltimore.* Philadelphia: J. B. Lippincott Co., 1968.

Foster, Charles T. *An Errand of Mercy: The Evangelical United Front, 1790–1837.* Chapel Hill: University of North Carolina Press, 1960.

Gaustad, Edwin S., ed. *The Rise of Adventism: Religion and Society in Mid-Nineteenth-Century America.* New York: Harper & Row, 1974.

Gilchrist, David, ed. *The Growth of Seaport Cities: 1790–1825.* Charlottesville: University of Virginia, 1967.

Goss, Charles C. *Statistical History of the First Century of American Methodism.* New York: Carlton & Porter, 1866.

Griffin, Clifford S. *Their Brother's Keepers: Moral Stewardship in the United States, 1800–1865.* New Brunswick: Rutgers University Press, 1960.

Gross, John O. *Methodist Beginnings in Higher Education.* Nashville: Board of Education, Methodist Church, 1959.

Hatch, Nathan. *The Sacred Cause of Liberty: Republican Thought and the Millennium.* New Haven: Yale University Press, 1976.

Jacobsen, Phebe R. *Quaker Records in Maryland*. Annapolis: Hall of Records Commission, Maryland, 1966.

Johnson, Charles A. *A Frontier Camp Meeting: Religion's Harvest Time*. Dallas: Southern Methodist University Press, 1955.

Johnson, Paul E. *A Shopkeeper's Millennium: Society and Revivals in Rochester, New York, 1815–1837*. New York: Hill and Wang, 1978.

Keller, Charles R. *The Second Great Awakening in Connecticut*. New Haven: Yale University Press, 1942.

Laurie, Bruce. *Working People of Philadelphia, 1800–1850*. Philadelphia: Temple University Press, 1980.

Loveland, Anne C. *Southern Evangelicals and the Social Order, 1800–1860*. Baton Rouge: Louisiana University Press, 1980.

McLoughlin, William G. *Modern Revivalism: Charles Grandison Finney to Billy Graham*. New York: The Ronald Press Company, 1959.

———. *Revivals, Awakenings, and Reform*. Chicago: University of Chicago Press, 1978.

Mathews, Donald G. *Religion in the Old South*. Chicago: University of Chicago Press, 1977.

———. *Slavery and Methodism: A Chapter in American Morality, 1780–1845*. Princeton: Princeton University Press, 1965.

Melton, Julius. *Presbyterian Worship in America: Changing Patterns Since 1787*. Richmond: John Knox Press, 1967.

Miyakawa, T. Scott. *Protestants and Pioneers: Individualism and Conformity on the American Frontier*. Chicago: University of Chicago Press, 1964.

Nash, Gary B. *The Urban Crucible: Social Change, Political Consciousness, and the Origins of the Revolution*. Cambridge: Harvard University Press, 1979.

Olson, Sherry H. *Baltimore: The Building of an American City*. Baltimore: Johns Hopkins University Press, 1980.

One Hundred and Ten Years of Bible Society Works in Maryland, 1810–1920. Baltimore: Maryland Bible Society, 1921.

Richardson, Harry V. *Dark Salvation: The Story of Methodism as It Developed Among Blacks in America*. Garden City, N.Y.: Anchor Press, 1976.

Ridgway, Whitman H. *Community Leadership in Maryland, 1790–1840: A Comparative Analysis of Power in Society*. Chapel Hill: University of North Carolina Press, 1979.

Rightmyer, Nelson W. *Parishes of the Diocese of Maryland*. Reisterstown, Md.: Education Research Assoc., 1960.

Rosenberg, Carroll Smith. *Religion and the Rise of the American City: The New York City Mission Movement, 1817–1870*. Ithaca: Cornell University Press, 1971.

Ryan, Mary P. *Cradle of the Middle Class: The Family in Oneida County, New York, 1790–1865*. New York: Cambridge University Press, 1981.

Scharf, J. Thomas. *History of Baltimore City and County with a New Introduction by Edward G. Howard*. Baltimore: Regional Publishing Co., 1971.

Scott, Donald. *From Office to Profession: The New England Ministry, 1750–1850*. Philadelphia: University of Pennsylvania Press, 1978.

Sprague, William Buell. *Annals of the American Pulpit*. 9 vols. New York: Robert Carter & Brothers, 1857–[69].

Steffen, Charles G. *The Mechanics of Baltimore: Workers and Politics in the Age of Revolution, 1763–1812*. Urbana: University of Illinois Press, 1984.

Steiner, Bernard C. *One Hundred and Ten Years of Bible Society Work in Maryland, 1810–1920*. Baltimore: Maryland Bible Society, 1921.

Sweet, W. W. *Religion in the Development of American Culture*. New York: Charles Scribner's Sons, 1952.

————. *Revivalism in America: Its Origins, Growth, and Decline*. New York: Charles Scribner's Sons, 1944.

Turner, James. *Without God, Without Creed: The Origins of Unbelief in America*. Baltimore: Johns Hopkins University Press, 1985.

Vexler, Robert I., comp. and ed. *Baltimore: A Chronological and Documentary History 1632–1970*. Dobbs Ferry, N.Y.: Oceana Publications Inc., 1975.

Weisberger, Bernard A. *They Gathered at the River*. Boston: Little, Brown, & Co., 1958.

Welter, Barbara. *Dimity Convictions*. Athens: Ohio University Press, 1976.

ARTICLES

Banner, Lois W. "Religious Benevolence as Social Control: A Critique of an Interpretation." *Journal of American History* 60 (June 1973): 23–42.

Bernard, Richard M. "A Portrait of Baltimore 1800: Economic and Occupational Patterns." *Maryland Historical Magazine* 69 (Winter 1974): 341.

Blumin, Stuart. "The Historical Study of Vertical Mobility." *Historical Methods Newsletter* 1 (September 1968): 1–13.

Carwardine, Richard. "The Second Great Awakening in the Urban Centers: An Examination of Methodism and the 'New Measures.'" *The Journal of American History* 59 (September 1972): 327–40.

Cott, Nancy F. "Young Women in the Second Great Awakening," *Feminist Studies* 3 (1975): 15–29.

Ellis, John Tracy. "A Guide to the Baltimore Cathedral Archives." *Catholic Historical Review* 32 (October 1946): 341–60.

Ervin, Spencer. "The Established Church of Colonial Maryland." *Historical Magazine of the Protestant Episcopal Church* 24 (1955): 232–92.

Goen, C. C. "The 'Methodist Age' in American Church History." *Religion in Life* (Autumn 1965), pp. 562–72.

Hershberg, Theodore; Katz, Michael; Blumin, Stuart; Glasco, Lawrence; and Griffen, Clyde. "Occupation and Ethnicity in Five Nineteenth Century Cities: A Collaborative Inquiry." *Historical Methods Newsletter* 7 (June 1974): 174–216.

Katz, Michael. "Occupational Classification in History." *Journal of Interdisciplinary History* 3 (Summer 1972): 63–88.

Mathews, Donald G. "The Second Great Awakening as an Organizing Process, 1780–1830: An Hypothesis." *American Quarterly* 21 (Spring 1969): 23–43.

Nash, Gary. "Urban Wealth and Poverty in Pre-Revolutionary America." *Journal of Interdisciplinary History* 4, no. 4 (Spring 1976): 545–84.

Rightmyer, Nelson W. "The Episcopate of Bishop Kemp of Maryland." *Historical Magazine of the Protestant Episcopal Church* 28, no. 1 (1959): 66–84.

Ryan, Mary P. "A Women's Awakening: Evangelical Religion and the Families of Utica, New York, 1800–1840." *American Quarterly* 30 (Winter 1978): 602–23.

Schwartz, Hillel. "Adolescence and Revivals in Ante-Bellum Boston." *Journal of Religious History* 8 (December 1974): 144–58.

Shiels, Richard D. "The Second Great Awakening in Connecticut: A Critique of the Traditional Interpretation." *Church History* 49 (December 1980): 401–15.

Thomas, John L. "Romantic Reform in America, 1815–1865." *American Quarterly* 17 (Winter 1965): 656–81.

Wooden, Howard E. "The Rectory of St. Paul's Parish, Baltimore: An Architectural History." *Maryland Historical Magazine* (September 1962), pp. 210–23.

INDEX

Abingdon, Maryland, 60, 61
Abolition Society of Baltimore, 56
Adams, John Quincy (U.S. president), 57
African Branch Bible Society, 103
African Colonization Society, 110
African Methodist Episcopal Church, 30, 32, 33, 50, 85
Alexander, Archibald, 39
Allen, Richard, 32
Allison, Patrick, 39, 63
American Bible Society, 103, 104
Anglican Church, 11, 29, 31, 52
Anne Arundel County, Maryland, 87
Anti-Masonic Party, 130
Arminianism, 86, 135
Asbury, Francis, 45, 60, 62, 86, 88, 119
Asbury Association Sunday School Society, 105–7
Asbury College, 61–62
Associated Methodist Church, 132
Associate Reformed Church: and controversy over creeds, 129–30; membership of, 22; polity of, 28–29; Sunday Schools of, 105–6; and use of music in worship, 68–69; mentioned, 73, 94
Atonement: Abelard's view of, 77; Anselm's view of, 77

Baltimore Annual Conference of the Methodist Episcopal Church, 45, 57, 62, 72, 88, 90, 104, 131
Baltimore Association for Publishing and Distributing Tracts on Moral and Religious Subjects, 110
Baltimore Baptist Association, 13, 45, 55, 123, 143
Baltimore Baptist Missionary Society, 102
Baltimore Benevolent Society, 101
Baltimore Bible Society, 102–3, 113
Baltimore Diocesan Synod of 1791, 30
Baltimore Female Humane Association, 59
Baltimore General Dispensary, 41
Baltimore Library Company, 41

Baltimore Methodist Episcopal Auxiliary Missionary Society, 102
Baltimore Sunday School Association, 106
Baltimore Temperance Society, 111
Baltimore Union Society, 131
Baltimore Unitarian Society for the Distribution of Books, 110
Baptists: and church discipline, 55, 56, 58; interchurch rivalries among, 123; membership profile of, 20, 23, 24; numbers of, 11, 137; polity of, 28; and use of music in worship, 66; mentioned, 45, 69, 91, 97, 100, 115, 118, 134, 142, 143
Beasley, Frederick, 78
Becker, C. L., 125
Bend, Joseph: controversies involving, 40; opposition of, to Methodism, 47, 92; sermons of, 63, 118; as spokesman of high-church party, 126–27; mentioned, 19, 41, 42, 57; quoted, 50, 66–67, 74–75, 84
Benevolent Empire, 112, 114
Bethel African Methodist Episcopal Church, 32, 33, 95
Black American churchgoers: involvement of, in anti-slavery movement, 101–2; involvement of, in colonization movement, 110–12; involvement of, in Sunday Schools, 107–8; leadership opportunities for, numbers of, 20–21, 25; mentioned, 12, 41, 85, 98, 103, 113, 138, 143–44
Boehm, Henry, 90
Bond, Thomas, 66, 132
Book of Common Prayer, 72, 74
Boston, Massachusetts, 42, 119, 120
Bourne, George, 30
Brancadoro, Archbishop, 124
Breckenridge, John, 44, 68, 73, 95
British and Foreign Bible Society, 102
Brosius, F. X., 125
Bruce, Dickson, Jr., 86
Burnap, George W., 72, 122

Calvinism, 76, 86, 128, 135

Camp meetings: described, 86–90; music at, 66, 94; mentioned, 93, 114, 134, 136, 139
Cane Ridge Meeting, 83
Carlisle, Pennsylvania, 86
Carr, Thomas, 68
Carroll, John: and controversy with F. C.
· Reuter, 49–50, 124–25; mentioned, 41, 60, 122; quoted, 64
Caucasian churchgoers, 13, 23, 143
Channing, William E., 120–21
Christmas Conference, 60
Christ Protestant Episcopal Church, 24, 40, 42, 54, 67–68, 72–73, 106, 126, 128
Church of England. *See* Anglican Church
Church of the Covenanters, 66
Church schools, 59–62. *See also* Sunday Schools
Claggett, Bishop, 49, 127
Clergymen of Baltimore: education of, 44–46; list of, 151–56; salaries of, 41–44; scandals involving, 47–50
Coate, Samuel, 88
Coke, Thomas, 45–46, 61–62
Coker, Daniel, 32, 50
Cokesbury College, 60–61
Cole, John, 68–69
Colonial era, religion in, 11
Colonization movement, 110–13
Columbia College, 39, 40
Committee on Indian Affairs, Society of Friends, 101
Congregationalism, 11, 134
Cooper, Ezekiel, 85
Cott, Nancy, 135, 138
Council of Nicaea, 119

Dashiell, George: controversies involving, 47–49, 126–28; Methodistic tendencies of, 40, 92; sermons of, 72; quoted, 55–56
Davis, John, 90
Deism, 117–18, 133–34
Denominations: membership profiles of, 21–24; polities of, 28–31; relative sizes of, 19–20; and status of lay officials, 34–36
Directory of Worship of 1644, 69
Disestablishment, effects of: 11, 39, 52, 100, 139
Dorsey, Dennis B., 131
Dorsey, William, 57
Dubourg, W. V., 122
Duke, William, 84
Duncan, John M., 69, 73, 129–30

Eastern Shore, Maryland, 87
Ebenezar Baptist Church, 23, 24, 43, 123
Emory, John, 45
Episcopalians: anti-Methodism of, 92, 99, 113, 137–38; clergy of, 40–41, 73–75; discipline of, 56–59; their houses of worship, 24–25, 92; lay leadership of, 33–34; low-church/high church differences among, 70, 126–29; membership profiles of, 21–23; numbers of, 19, 20; polity of, 29–31; sermons of, 71–76, 118; Sunday Schools of, 104–6; tract societies of, 109–10; use of music in worship among, 66–67; mentioned, 32, 42, 44, 47, 62, 63, 99, 101, 113, 115, 117, 142–43
Ethnicity: in Baltimore, 12; impact of, on church attendance, 20–21; Africans, 12, 25, 32, 35, 85, 103; English, 12; French, 12, 53, 103; Germans, 12, 23, 28, 30, 59, 92, 100, 103, 123–26; Scots, 12; Welsh, 12
Eutaw Street Methodist Episcopal Church, 61, 105
Evans, French, 89

Fasting, 90–91
Federal Hill School, 106
Federal Street Church, Boston, 120
Fells Point, 25, 91, 97, 100–101, 109
Fells Point Station Methodist Episcopal Church, 38, 90
Female Bible Society, 102
Female churchgoers: involvement of, in revivals, 88–89, 97, 135, 138–41; involvement of, in voluntary associations, 102–9; leadership opportunities for, 31–33, 35, 112; numbers of, 21, 25; mentioned, 119, 132
Female Mite Society for the Education of Heathen Children in India, 108
Female Society for the Dissemination of Religious Knowledge, 109
Female Union Society of Baltimore, 107
Female Union Society of New York, 106
Finlay, John, 43
Finney, Charles, 83, 97–98, 134, 136
First Baptist Church, 31, 43, 45, 54, 56, 92, 105–6
First Independent Unitarian Church, 24, 28, 31, 41–42, 45, 54, 68, 78, 110, 119–22
First Philosophical and Evangelical Association of Baltimore, 32
First Presbyterian Church, 22, 34, 39, 41–42, 46, 50, 54, 57, 68, 70–71, 76, 85, 94–96, 100, 105, 121
Fletcher, John, 63
Foster, Charles, 112–13
Fourth Presbyterian Church, 96
Frederick, Maryland, 86
Freeman, J. W., 119–20
Friends. *See* Society of Friends
Frye, Joseph, 38

Garretson, Freeborn, 92
Gasper River meeting, 83
General Assembly of the Presbyterian Church, 130
General Convention of Reformers, 132

General Synod of the Evangelical Lutheran Church, 13
General Theological Seminary, Protestant Episcopal Church, 128
Georgetown College, 60
German Lutheran Church, 19–20, 23, 29, 41, 59, 100. *See also* Lutherans
German Reformed Church: attitude of, toward the Lord's Supper, 70–71; membership profile of, 22–23; polity of, 28; size of, 19–20; and use of music in worship, 66–67; mentioned, 59, 85, 100, 123, 125
Glendy, John, 39, 42, 73, 95
Grellet, Stephen, 84–85
Griffen, Clifford, 112

Hagerstown, Maryland, 124
Hamilton, Alexander, 39
Hanley, Thomas O'Brien, 52
Hanson, James, 38
Hargrove, John, 43, 55–56, 78, 118–19
Harvard College, 42, 45, 120, 122
Healy, John, 43, 100, 123
Helfenstein, Albert, 126
Henshaw, John P. K.: as author of *The New Week's Preparation*, 71; as spokesman for the low-church party, 73, 92, 126, 128; mentioned, 30, 49; quoted, 104–5, 115
Hicks, Elias, 130–31
Hinkley, Edward, 119–20
Hollingsworth, Francis, 48
House of Bishops, Protestant Episcopal Church, 127

Indians, 55, 57, 101, 103, 113
Inglis, John: controversies involving, 39–40, 53; sermons of, 76–78; mentioned, 42, 50
Ireland, John, 40

Jackson, Andrew (U.S. president), 130
Jefferson, Thomas (U.S. president), 39
Jennings, Samuel K., 61
Johns, John: sermons of, 72–73; as spokesman of low-church party, 126, 128–29; quoted, 53
Johnson, Charles, 86
Johnson, Paul, 98, 135, 138
Jones, George, 130
Jones Falls, Baltimore, 100
Judgment Day, 50, 77, 139

Kemp, James: opposition of, to Methodism, 47, 92; as spokesman for high-church party, 126–28; mentioned, 30, 34, 41, 47, 74, 115, 118; quoted, 45, 46, 53, 54, 63, 75, 118–19
King's Chapel, Boston, 119
Krebs, Samuel, 93
Kurtz, Benjamin, 124
Kurtz, J. Daniel, 41, 45, 67, 115, 124

Ladies Branch Bible Society, 103–4
Lee, Jesse, 70
Leicester, England, 100
Levington, William, 33, 43
Lewis, Fanny, 88–89
Light Street Methodist Episcopal Church, 61, 100, 105
Lindenberger, Mrs. A., 48
Lord's Supper, 32, 65–66, 70–71
Luther, Martin, 63
Lutherans: attitudes of, toward the Lord's Supper, 70–71; and controversy over language, 123–24; membership profile of, 23; numbers of, 19–20; polity of, 29; sermons of, 72–73; and use of music in worship, 66–67; mentioned, 59, 63, 85, 91, 115, 131, 142–43
Lynchburg, Virginia, 86

McCaine, Alexander, 131–32
McKendree Sunday School Society, 105
Madison, James, 57
Marine Branch Bible Society, 103
Martin, Luther, 40
Maryland: Constitution of 1776, 31, 52; General Assembly, 56, 57, 101–2; mentioned, 12, 32, 86, 104
Maryland Auxiliary Bible Society, 103
Maryland Auxiliary Colonization Society, 110
Maryland Society for Abolition of Slavery, 101
Maryland Society for Promoting the Abolition of Slavery and Relief of Free Negroes, 41
Maryland State Colonization Society, 111
Mathews, Donald, 135
Mayer, Lewis, 126
Mertz, Father, 125
Merwin, Samuel, 93
Methodist *Discipline*, 32, 45, 91
Methodist Episcopal Church: Baltimore Annual Conference, 45, 57, 62, 72, 88, 90, 104; Baltimore City Station, 38, 58, 61–62, 72, 90–91, 98; General Conference, 43, 90, 131; mentioned, 13, 45, 85, 87
Methodist Protestant Church, 13, 30, 86, 88, 132
Methodists: abolitionism of, 55–57, 101–2; African, 32–33; anti-deism of, 118–19; class leaders among, 35–36; discipline of, 58; educational institutions of, 60–62; and itineracy, 38, 43–45; membership profiles of, 22–25; numbers of, 11, 19–20; polity of, 29–31; schisms of, 131–33; sermons of, 63–64, 71–74, 76; Sunday Schools of, 105–7, 113; and support of revivalism, 83–86, 89–95, 97–99, 110, 114–15, 134, 136–37, 139–40; and use of music in worship, 66, 68–69; mentioned, 54, 77, 101, 142
Miami Confederation, 101
Millennialism, 83, 96–97, 100, 114–17, 129–

30, 133, 140
Miller, Samuel, 110, 121, 129–30
Milton, John, 62
Missionary Mite Society of Baltimore, 94
More, Hannah, 62
Morrell, Thomas, 63–64
Morris, John, 73
Morrison, Pastor, 95
Mount Zion Baptist Church, 123
Musgrave, George W., 96
Music in worship services, 66–69, 92
Mutual Rights, 131–32

Nagot, F. C., 60
Neal, Abner, 102
Nettleton, Asahel, 94
Nevins, William: and acceptance of "new measures," 95–97; salary of, 42–43; sermons of, 76–77; mentioned, 41, 53, 57, 71, 73; quoted, 46–47, 50–51
New Jerusalem Swedenborgian Church; controversies involving, 55–56, 118–19; membership profile of, 24; numbers of, 20; polity of, 28; mentioned, 13, 43, 70, 72, 115
"New Measures," 83–84, 94, 96–97, 99, 105, 114, 136–38
New York City, 56, 97, 98, 103, 105, 128

Old Otterbein Church, 23
"Old School" Presbyterians, 96
Osage Indians, 55
Otterbein, Philip William, 41, 56, 92

Paine, Thomas, 118
Parks, Mayberry, 58
Patriotism: in sermons, 53, 63–64, 78–79, 116, 117
Patterson, Nicholas, 94
Peck, Nathaniel, 111
Pennsylvania Ministerium of the Lutheran Church, 29
Percy, William, 62
Philadelphia Baptist Association, 56
Philadelphia Bible Society, 102
Philadelphia, Pennsylvania, 12, 60, 97, 98, 105
Philadelphia Yearly Meeting, Society of Friends, 130
Polity: and varieties of church constitutions, 28–31
Powhatten Factory, 91
Presbyterians: in colonial times, 11; interchurch schisms of, 129–31; involvement of, in revivals, 94, 97–98; lay leadership of, 34–35; membership profile of, 22–23, 25; numbers of, 19–20; polity of, 28; sermons of, 63, 72–74, 76–78; mentioned, 41, 54, 59, 83, 85, 91, 101, 110, 111, 113, 134, 137, 140
Presbytery of Baltimore, 13, 130
Presbytery of Philadelphia, 94, 130

Princeton Theological Seminary, 121, 129
Protection Society of Maryland, 102
Protestant Episcopal Church: Diocese of Maryland, 13, 29, 48, 56–57, 126–29; Female Tract Society of Baltimore, 109; Society for Advancement of Christianity, 102. *See also* Episcopalians

Ralph, George, 40
Rattlesnake Springs meeting, 89
Rattoone, Elijah, 40
Red River, Kentucky, 83
Reiss, Edmund, 43, 45, 123
Religious Tract Society of Baltimore, 104
Reuter, Frederick Cesarius, 49, 50, 124–25
Richards, Lewis, 23, 43, 45, 123
Richmond, Virginia, 56
Roberts, George, 72
Rochester, New York: revival of, 98
Roman Catholic Cathedral, 54, 68
Roman Catholics: Baltimore Benevolent Society, 101; clergy of, 38, 41; eulogies of, on George Washington, 64; German language controversy among, 124–25; lay leadership of, 35; membership profile of, 22–23, 25; numbers of, 19–20; opposition to, 32, 53–54, 57, 115, 122; polity of, 30; schools of, 60; mentioned, 11, 56, 58, 66, 70, 72, 85, 91, 99, 121, 133, 137, 142–43
Roszel, Stephen, 93, 97
Rutgers College, 61
Ryan, Mary, 135

St. James African Protestant Episcopal Church, 33, 43
St. John's Evangelical Episcopal Church, 49, 128
St. John's Roman Catholic Church, 49–50, 54, 124–25
St. Mary's: Academy, 60; College, 122; Seminary, 38, 60
St. Patrick's Roman Catholic Church, 67, 100
St. Paul's Orphan Asylum, 41
St. Paul's Protestant Episcopal Church, 24–25, 34, 40–41, 44, 47, 54, 56–57, 59, 66–70, 73–74, 78, 100, 105–6, 118, 121, 126–28
St. Peter's Protestant Episcopal Church, 24–25, 40, 42–43, 47–48, 55–56, 59, 67, 70–73, 84, 92, 105–6, 126–28
St. Peter's Roman Catholic Church, 22, 67–68
Sales, François de, 62
Santo Domingo, 12, 59, 98, 113, 122
Schmucker, John George, 115
Scott, Donald, 38
Seamen's Union Society, 109, 113, 115
Second Baptist Church, 43, 54, 56, 71, 92, 106, 123–24
Second Presbyterian Church, 22, 34, 40, 42, 44, 54, 68, 94–96

Seminary of St. Sulpice, 60
Sharp Street Methodist Episcopal Church, 33
Shawnee Indians, 101
Shoemaker, Ignatus, 49–50
Simpson, David, 118
Slicer, Henry, 73
Smith, Henry, 89
Snethen, Nicholas, 88
Society for the Promotion of Ornamental Knowledge, 41
Society of Friends: antimaterialism of, 84–85; discipline of, 54, 56–58; divisions within, 129–31; female involvement in, 37; membership profile of, 19–20, 24; opposition of, to slavery, 101–2; polity of, 28; worship of, 64–66; mentioned, 32, 41, 62, 110, 143
Sparks, Jared, 42–43, 45, 50, 110, 120–22
Stone, William, 129
Summerfield, John, 72, 75, 95
Sunday Schools, 91, 94–96, 103, 105–8, 111, 112–13, 115, 136
Sunday School Union societies, 108
Swedenborg, Emanuel, 63
Swedenborgians: membership profile of, 24; numbers of, 20; opposition to, 117–18, 133; mentioned, 58, 63, 78, 99. *See also* New Jerusalem Swedenborgian Church

Taney, Roger, 130
Temperance movement, 111, 113
Third Baptist Church, 57
Third Presbyterian Church, 94–96
Tocqueville, Alexis de, 53
Townshend, Joseph, 56
Trinity Protestant Episcopal Church, 24–25, 34, 40, 42, 54, 56, 68, 106
Tyson, Elisha, 41, 56, 102

Union Board of Delegates of the Male Sunday School Society of Baltimore, 106
Unitarian Manifesto, 120
Unitarians: membership profile of, 24; num-
bers of, 20; opposition to, 117; polity of, 28; sermons of, 72–73, 119, 120–21, 133; support for colonization among, 110; and use of music in worship, 66, 68; mentioned, 13, 42, 58, 91, 99
United Brethren: attitude of, toward the Lord's Supper, 71; discipline of, 56–57; involvement of, in revivals, 92; membership profile of, 23–25; numbers of, 19–20; their opposition to instrumental music, 66; polity of, 30; mentioned, 13, 41, 59, 69, 123

Virginia Diocese of the Protestant Episcopal Church, 49

Walton, W. C., 94, 96
Washington, George (U.S. president): eulogies about, 62–64; Farewell Address of, 52–53; mentioned, 12
Washington, D. C., 60, 89
Waugh, Beverly, 38
Weems, Mason Locke, 62
Wesley, John, 60–61, 63, 69, 131
Wesleyanism, 23, 30, 38, 92
West, William, 41–42
Whitefield, George, 61
Wilmer, James John, 118
Wirt, William, 130
Worthington, Mr. and Mrs., 47–48
Wyandot Indians, 57
Wyatt, William: anti-trinitarism of, 121; his problems with vestry, 47; sermons of, 73–74; as spokesman for high-church party, 126, 128–29; quoted, 74

Yellow fever, 113, 121
Young Men's Bible Society of Baltimore, 103–4, 110, 113, 121

Zion Lutheran Church, 45, 67–68, 115, 123–24